EXTENDED OUTLOOKS

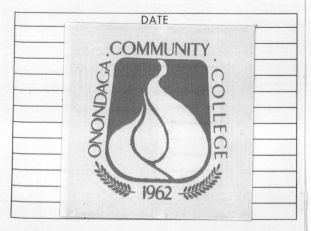

DATE

The Iowa Review Collection of
Contemporary Women Writers

EXTENDED
OUTLOOKS

EDITED AND WITH AN INTRODUCTION BY

Jane Cooper, Gwen Head,

Adalaide Morris, Marcia Southwick

COLLIER BOOKS
A Division of Macmillan Publishing Co., Inc.
New York

Introduction copyright © 1982 by Jane Cooper, Gwen Head,
Adalaide Morris, and Marcia Southwick

Copyright © 1981 by *The Iowa Review*

Macmillan Publishing Co., Inc.
866 Third Avenue, New York, N.Y. 10022
Collier Macmillan Canada, Inc.

All the selections in this book were originally published in the
1981 Spring/Summer issue of *The Iowa Review*.

Library of Congress Cataloging in Publication Data
Main entry under title:
Extended outlooks.
    "All the selections in this book were
originally published in the 1981 spring/summer
issue of The Iowa review"—Verso t.p.
    1. American literature—Women authors.
2. American literature—20th century.
3. Canadian literature—Women authors.
4. Canadian literature—20th century.
I. Cooper, Jane, (date)   II. Iowa review.
[PS508.W7E95 1982b] 810'.8'09287   82-12858
ISBN 0-02-049690-7 (pbk.)

First Collier Books Edition 1982

10   9   8   7   6   5   4   3   2   1

Printed in the United States of America

Extended Outlooks is also published in a
hardcover edition by Macmillan Publishing Co., Inc.

CONTENTS

Acknowledgments:

"Mornings remembering last nights" and "Epithalamion" by Olga Broumas will appear in a collection of her poems titled *Pastoral Jazz*, to be published in September, 1982, by Copper Canyon Press. Copyright © 1982 by Olga Broumas. Used by permission of the author.

"Poems for Maya," "Expatriate," "Endurance," "Because One Is Always Forgotten," "Message," and "Selective Service" by Carolyn Forché are from *The Country Between Us*, published by Harper & Row, Publishers, Inc., and are reprinted with the permission of the author. Copyright © 1982 by Carolyn Forché.

"Summer, An Elegy," by Ellen Gilchrist, is from her book *In the Land of Dreamy Dreams*, and is reprinted by permission of the University of Arkansas Press. Copyright © 1981 by Ellen Gilchrist.

"I Boudica" by Judy Grahn is from *The Queen of Wands*, published by The Crossing Press, and is reprinted by permission of the author. Copyright © 1981 by Judy Grahn.

"Helios and Athene" by H.D. is a previously unpublished work and is used by courtesy of the Beinecke Rare Book and Manuscript Library of Yale University. Copyright © 1928, 1980 by the Estate of Hilda Doolittle.

"Problems of Translation: Problems of Language" by June Jordan is used with the permission of the author. Copyright © 1980 by June Jordan.

"Leaving My Daughter's House" by Maxine Kumin is from her book *Our Ground Time Here Will Be Brief*, to be published in 1982 by Viking/Penguin. Copyright © 1982 by Maxine Kumin.

"Laocoön is the Name of the Figure" by Marge Piercy is from her book *Circles on the Water*, published by Alfred A. Knopf, Inc., and is reprinted with the permission of the publisher. Copyright © 1982 by Marge Piercy.

"For Ethel Rosenberg," "Mother-in-Law," and "Integrity" by Adrienne Rich are from her book *A Wild Patience Has Taken Me This Far: Poems 1978-1981*, published by W. W. Norton & Company, Inc., and are reprinted with the permission of the author and publisher. Copyright © 1982 by Adrienne Rich.

"Franz, the World is Abstract," and "Starkweather House" by P. Chase Twichell, are from her book *Northern Spy*, published by the University of Pittsburgh Press and used by permission of the author and publisher. Copyright © 1981 by P. Chase Twichell.

INTRODUCTION

—RESPECT FOR DIFFERENCE. *That's something we very much wanted to see in this anthology: representation of academic women, Black and Third World women, lesbian women, politically committed women, women committed to an aesthetic vision—all speaking in the same volume, and speaking to each other, across the pages.*

What brought the editors together was an accident of geography. During the academic year 1980-81, we were all living and working in Iowa City, and we welcomed the invitation to co-edit a Women's Issue for *The Iowa Review*. At our first meeting we were strangers; working together made us enduring friends. But though we are four white professional women, we span twenty-five years and both coastlines. We are: one single, one married, two divorced, one lesbian, three mothers, three poets, one scholar-critic, four feminists but of somewhat different allegiances. So when we wrote to potential contributors that we would like to do "justice to the rich variety of contemporary women's writing," we meant it.

Variety/consensus. We quickly agreed to accept poems, stories, tributes to undervalued women writers (rather than more conventional critical articles), and work that fell outside accepted forms provided it made sense to us as art and experience. We decided to print writers who, at this stage in the Women's Movement, ordinarily publish in different places, along with some who have hardly yet published at all.

We started by jotting down long lists of names—women across the country whose writing we had read and found vital and excellent. Then we contacted these women, relying on them to contact others or give us more names. By November, responses were pouring in. By spring, we had read literally thousands of manuscripts. Poets sent stories, story writers sent poems or experimental prose, a few sent near-books.

—*We saw our own lives fractured, recombined. When we laughed it was the kind of laughter that can attend a birth, a wedding, a reunion. Its sources were surprise, delight, and a hint of consternation.*

We agreed that all of us should read every manuscript. And we did, often more than once. We argued, groaned, shuffled pages, laughed, and reread, from January through May. Across meetings that lasted first three hours and finally seven hours every Saturday, we educated each other and the material educated us all. *Extended Outlooks* goes beyond any one person's taste—yet we all, essentially, chose everything.

—*One thing that kept us going was that we didn't just define the Issue; it kept defining us. Our outlooks kept getting extended.*

—*I think that was something we each learned to do: to allow ourselves to be changed by what someone else believed in or thought. It required a kind of submission of personality; you realized the power of women's commitments. I wrote a poem for the Issue that grew directly out of working on the Issue.*

—*The unapologetic nature of the material was important. It began to seem that you can say anything so long as it comes (and maybe this was one criterion for acceptance) from the heart of your experience.*

Extended Outlooks opens, in its alphabetical sequence, with a poem by Barbara Anderson about a child whose parents have split up, and it closes with a review of the first and only book by Sheila Zamora, a young poet murdered by her husband. Between these perimeters Margaret Atwood, Carolyn Forché, June Jordan, Maxine Hong Kingston, and others face the violence of living in a world torn by oppression and terror. Toi Derricotte and Audre Lorde speak of the violence to self that can result from a woman's decision to give, or not give, birth. Judy Grahn and Adrienne Rich seek to transform our visions of history; Grace Paley makes a comic fable for the future. The received myth of a woman's sexual coming-of-age is exposed by Sandra M. Gilbert, cheerfully replaced by Becky Birtha, and reconfirmed (or is it?) by Madeline DeFrees. Women are here in all the manifestations of their energy: tenderness and rage, jobs and love, exhaustion and exuberance.

—*Even those women who obviously are limited in personal circumstances seem to feel a strength of affirmation in their lives.*

—*Something is taken for granted now that wasn't there before. Women used to need to make clear that they'd been left out of society. But these women have gone past trying to address a world that doesn't listen; they simply assume society has been the loser.*

The contributors, aged twelve to ninety, are apprentices and adept, unknown and famous. Often it is the older writers who write more "openly," since that was their rebellion, while many younger ones are rediscovering traditional forms. Selections range from Ruth Stone's stubborn, infectious free verse to Judith Moffett's witty "Triple Ballade," from Ellen Gilchrist's elegant story structure to Kathleen Fraser's energy undergoing change. There is a lot of experiment, not all of it obvious, and some new names for new undertakings: "motableautins," "bio-mythography," "spaces," "sentences."

Who is the anthology for?

—*For one thing, it's for people who read literary journals and still find one or two women for every five men.*

—*For readers of feminist journals who want to cut across categories.*

—*For everybody who is tired of hearing only voices like her own all day.*

—*Yes, but there's something else, something crucial. There have been a lot of complaints lately that American poets speak only to other poets, etc. This anthology should reach beyond a purely literary audience, and that's what I see as its chief strength.*

—*The readers are the future, aren't they? the ultimate extension of outlook....*

—*They're going to read the stories and poems. Then what are they going to write?*

—*More important, what are they going to do? Do, be, write. Writing is only one form of action.*

—*Isn't there something political just in the fact of women who define themselves clearly and somewhat differently all speaking together in the same place? even if they disagree?*

—*The word "politics" comes from Greek polis, "city." You could say our anthology is really a city of this speaking of women's experience. And it's a very full city.*

—*A good feisty city.*

We wish to thank

David Hamilton, Editor of *The Iowa Review,* for his generosity and unfailing support as *Extended Outlooks* grew from a single to a double to a triple issue—the largest, to date, in *Review* history;

Norman Sage, Managing Editor of *The Iowa Review,* for wit, warmth, and technical mastery;

Judith Pendleton, our expert and patient typesetter;

all our contributors who suggested names of other women writers who in turn became our contributors; in particular, here, Michelle Cliff;

James Laughlin, who made available the hitherto unpublished work by H.D.;

Wendy Deutelbaum, friend and supporter, who in May 1981 arranged for our benefit reading for the Iowa City Domestic Violence Project and in March

1982 conducted the joint interview, passages of which are quoted in this Introduction;

Lisa Jones, who transcribed the interview tape;

Larry and Nick Levis, Ellen Morris, and Lee Schwartzman, with our love;

and finally, all the fine women writers whom we somehow missed but who have helped create the climate that made this collection possible.

Jane Cooper, New York City
Gwen Head, Seattle
Adalaide Morris, Iowa City
Marcia Southwick, Iowa City

EXTENDED OUTLOOKS

There and Here · *Barbara Anderson*

Someone's lost and someone turns on
the light. In the middle of the night

the boy rushes into his parents' room
but *they* are not there;

only the rustle
of his mother's nightdress as she packs

away his father's shirts, and books, binoculars.
The paperweight — faces of the old poets

magnified under glass: Coleridge,
Wordsworth, Tennyson, Whitman.

A gift from the woman they argued about
when his father returned from a trip.

"Thank you," the woman had written
on the note with the hotel letterhead.

His mother packs that away too, and what is hers
in another carton and the child's in a third,

and the words THERE and HERE in thick black print
on a lined tablet from the first year

he learned to read; his teacher
wanted him to know the difference,

the distance from school to home,
from this morning to afternoon

when he fell asleep for so long
he thought no one could find him.

Until his mother took him out
to feed the ducks in the park.

Really she wanted to tell him
that now he'd have two homes,

one here and the other there,
and her finger pointed away

towards the mountains on the other side
of town. "There in that direction."

Right here with the lemon trees
neither of them cried.

He didn't cry and his mother bought him
metal soldiers with cannons

that shot out if you pulled a lever,
soon they would be packed away

or broken. Isn't childhood
really a form of insanity, said his mother's new friend,

and the night to come when he would sit
with his father and look down through the binoculars

to the city lights—
a place that was neither here nor there.

from Book of My Hunger, Book of the Earth · *Sarah Appleton*

Knock, listen   The harsh fly shines   The beetle rubs
out of its casing   The brown butterfly with its fringe of
blue eyes in a halo of purple probing fluttering over the
fallen yellow maple leaves   The drip of dry leaves before
my eyes   The trees grown tall remembering the words of
the authors   The pine red hair falling like new catkins
on the leafless twigs   The human hand touching everywhere—
lifts and stirs   like slow wings

* * *

It is this way the work builds
as if someone had my hand, walked before me, gently drawing me

the effort, silence

these are the very lines of it

almost as if fleshless
blank

simple, as if old or very young; I follow simply
so caught, buoyed by fragility . . . so slight

I lie down in the sun, my back against the dry warm log bridging the stream
the sun in the stream   lights. Woodpecker, brittle like the paper leaves
spiralling down, brushing against tree bark

the late thrush fluffed   round

seen only by the life of his eye, then seen all

The balance of these words

falling again and again against and upon the sentence
barely breathing

* * *

The thrust of life within into the world, gathering the world

Why have the creatures come to our door hungering for bread? Why
does the amber light in the soul of the dog speak love, when
he has no words? They come to us

They wait endlessly for us, following our motions, but our
children run on ahead, or lag in their world, our voices are
filled with warnings, urgings

Being born   with the world

The tensions are here

* * *

Now I see myself making the stars. Within me I hold a vast
sky stars streaming out as if brushed by the wind from a star
and I see them more and more   and I can count them by their names
for as many names as I can name   to my content, to my
exhaustion of all my yearning. They do not fall and fall open
like flowers from a tree—shadows floating, catching light, spinning out—
or wings that carry seeds, or fluffs that whirl endlessly.   These
stars are the stars of all my desire   From their desire,
from their eyes looking forward to me. My face in theirs,
my voice, I meet them, here   here   here

* * *

Where is my body falling, quick, catch it! Shadow like
the others . . . run, catch it flying on the wind,
black smudges over snow . . . There, the glints, sun
motes against the blue . . . No higher, the butterfly beating
beating in a rare wind;   no, there . . . lights broken in the
face of a stream . . . here;   no there,   my small daughter
running to me

* * *

The teachers of my child have forgotten memory
have already hidden from my child her story

They didn't listen for it
she did not hear it leave her lips

Seeking, I asked her for it
She turned away, her mouth sealed

over her deepest desires
She seizes them with her hands, they work in her strong fingers

* * *

Who has lifted the pen!
Who has made the mark of the human face upon the page!
Who has seen here the invisible dictation!
I, just having taken it up, finding my life . . .

* * *

I stand here. I have arisen — into the dazzling, the different
as if jumping, each time feeling the hands won't be there

But I am so small. This . . . this calling, this searching, this
one come again and again to a place drawn here by this thread —

It is utterly difficult
utterly simple, like a new language

the wings of the old beating, beating
How can the journey be of words, sentences?

Is that how it is when the universe comes into us, accepting our smallness
using our eyes   looking at the autumn blue, autumn branch, thickening
    pond light

comes into our ears to our darkness

resists our fingers

is that how the universe is content, when we can no longer
think it

but return to our simple duties, of dishes, of picking up, of being the earth
as our children lean into us, of being worshipful to a dog who grows thin

from not running

of coming to you, my dearest, given silent understanding working in the
    terrors to come

working in a love that had no words before this

Bread · *Margaret Atwood*

IMAGINE A PIECE of bread. You don't have to imagine it, it's right here in the kitchen, on the breadboard, in its plastic bag, lying beside the bread knife. The bread knife is an old one you picked up at an auction; it has the word BREAD carved into the wooden handle. You open the bag, pull back the wrapper, cut yourself a slice. You put butter on it, then peanut butter, then honey, and you fold it over. Some of the honey runs out onto your fingers and you lick it off. It takes you about a minute to eat the bread. This bread happens to be brown, but there is also white bread, in the refrigerator, and a heel of the rye you got last week, round as a full stomach then, now going mouldy. Occasionally you make bread. You think of it as something relaxing to do with your hands.

Imagine a famine. Now imagine a piece of bread. Both of these things are real but you happen to be in the same room with only one of them. Put yourself into a different room, that's what the mind is for. You are now lying on a thin mattress in a hot room. The walls are made of dried earth, and your sister, who is younger than you, is in the room with you. She is starving, her belly is bloated, flies land on her eyes; you brush them off with your hand. You have a cloth too, filthy but damp, and you press it to her lips and forehead. The piece of bread is the bread you've been saving, for days it seems. You are as hungry as she is, but not yet as weak. How long does this take? When will someone come with more bread? You think of going out to see if you might find something that could be eaten, but outside the streets are infested with scavengers and the stink of corpses is everywhere.

Should you share the bread or give the whole piece to your sister? Should you eat the piece of bread yourself? After all, you have a better chance of living, you're stronger. How long does it take to decide?

Imagine a prison. There is something you know that you have not yet told. Those in control of the prison know that you know. So do those not in control. If you tell, thirty or forty or a hundred of your friends, your comrades, will be caught and will die. If you refuse to tell, tonight will be like last night. They always choose the night. You don't think about the night however, but about the piece of bread they offered you.

How long does it take? The piece of bread was brown and fresh and reminded you of sunlight falling across a wooden floor. It reminded you of a bowl, a yellow bowl that was once in your home. It held apples and pears; it stood on a table you can also remember. It's not the hunger or the pain that is killing you but the absence of the yellow bowl. If you could only hold the bowl in your hands, right here, you could withstand anything, you tell yourself. The bread they offered you is subversive, it's treacherous, it does not mean life.

There were once two sisters. One was rich and had no children, the other had five children and was a widow, so poor that she no longer had any food left. She went to her sister and asked her for a mouthful of bread. "My children are dying," she said. The rich sister said, "I do not have enough for myself," and drove her away from the door. Then the husband of the rich sister came home and wanted to cut himself a piece of bread; but when he made the first cut, out flowed red blood.

Everyone knew what that meant.

This is a traditional German fairy tale.

The loaf of bread I have conjured for you floats about a foot above your kitchen table. The table is normal, there are no trap doors in it. A blue tea towel floats beneath the bread, and there are no strings attaching the cloth to the bread or the bread to the ceiling or the table to the cloth, you've proved it by passing your hand above and below. You didn't touch the bread though. What stopped you? You don't want to know whether the bread is real or whether it's just a hallucination I've somehow duped you into seeing. There's no doubt that you can see the bread, you can even smell it, it smells like yeast, and it looks solid enough, solid as your own arm. But can you trust it? Can you eat it? You don't want to know, imagine that.

Letters from Three Women · *Wendy Battin*

We are moving from state to state,
as they say of excited electrons, or
of water when it freezes
and sublimes,
or of the mind when it enters a drug
like an airplane.

When the letters bloom out of their envelopes
I think it must be spring,
remembering winter and the mailbox empty.
The pages collect on my desk, interleaved
like hands in a public oath. What
are we swearing to?

One has married her solitude,
wants a divorce.

One imagines that she
has not been understood.

One imagines she has.

The snapshot
taken through a finger-printed lens
records identity and place: the smudge

floats on the landscape,
a halo whose saint has walked out.
One morning I watched from the beach
as a house rounded Long Point into the harbor.
Pennants, strung from the cupola
down to the barge, snaked in the wind and shot
the gulls through with panic.
The windows and doors had been boarded shut,
as if the house would founder if it woke.

You know me. I thought,
This is history: a house floating sullenly
over the ocean.
Just look at the baggage we carry.

It docked at Macara's wharf for months,
waiting for cranes from New Bedford to lift it
bodily, as we all wait

in our rented rooms, or when
there's money, in apartments.
Today I receive you all in my room,
which dangles over traffic. The last
huddled on the ground of a different
city, under the weight of those
families I heard in the night,
like Hansel in the oven, listening.

I hear, for example, that lessons learned
drunk are best remembered drunk,
that the mind
knows this on the ocean and something
else at the kitchen table over coffee;
and think
especially of the humpbacks, who pass
their songs from ocean to ocean
in intricate barter.
                    Some days
I read you between the mailbox and my door,
the way we've eaten whole meals cooking them.

The ocean is a mind with a tune running through it.

The sun here
travels into an ocean so monstrous we call it
peaceful, adrift on the land.

The Lives We Invite To Flower Among Us Flower Beyond Us · *Wendy Battin*

For just as a wild animal, if it shall have escaped and thus recovered its natural liberty, is no longer the property of its captor, so also the sea may recover its possession of the shore.
—Hugo Grotius

So just as that wild animal, the sea,
is never in our midst, is constantly
our border, so also
a leopard, even in a zoo
escapes us. He prowls
all our city's avenues by pacing
cage corner to corner, even
when we are most vigilant.

Set him free on a beach.
A body in a halo of senses,
he moves on the sand like water. The highest
wave casts down the shore like a spotted cat.
Nothing, our oldest lesson save one,
nothing is harder than water. The cat
on flat beach, the cat with no tree,
no ledge, as if caged,
cannot contain himself.

So also the thought containing the cat,
set in motion in a woman's
mind, a word
in a halo of sense. She makes
the leopard dark avenues
into the city of men, and then
she makes the seventh wave,
ending in foam still short
of the body poured out on the sand.
But even when she is

11

most circumspect, her mind
cannot contain itself, as a vase
may hold a flower but may not hold
itself. She loses the word
that strokes her into sense, that moving
cage and comfort.
The cat escapes
into the oldest lesson: no thing
is more yielding than water.

The woman rests
her mind in her body in
a halo of sense,
as if she were the sea,
and continent.

The woman in Buffalo
is given to waiting · *Becky Birtha*

She neglects her work.
English ivy rust on the sill.
The linen goes unwashed.
The poems do not get written.

The woman has no companion,
She has no man.
She neglects her friends—
If they were to come to her house
They would not find her
   waiting
   for them.

The waiting focuses:
The center of the morning
Pulls her taut,
Holds her still until she
Hears
   the iron lid drop
   against the iron box
Descends the stair to retrieve
   letters that will
   receive no reply—
   snapped into a rubber band.

   the one she awaited did not come
   if there were such a one.
She returns to her kitchen
Draws herself in to continue.

The woman in Buffalo
Will make an art of waiting
   in which she will achieve perfection
She will invest her strength in waiting
   dense as a massive brown mountain,
   go still and solid like a stone.
She will grow into waiting
Like an oak into an iron fence.

Johnnieruth · *Becky Birtha*

SUMMERTIME. NIGHTTIME. Talk about steam heat. This whole city get like the bathroom when somebody in there taking a shower with the door shut. Nights like that, can't nobody sleep. Everybody be outside, sitting on they steps or else dragging half they furniture out on the sidewalk—kitchen chairs, card tables—even bringing TV's outside.

Womenfolks, mostly. All the grown women around my way look just the same. They all big—stout. They got big bosoms and big hips and fat legs, and they always wearing runover house-shoes, and them shapeless, flowered numbers with the buttons down the front. Cept on Sunday. Sunday morning they all turn into glamour girls, in them big hats and long gloves, with they skinny high heels and they skinny selves in them tight girdles—wouldn't nobody ever know what they look like the rest of the time.

When I was a little kid I didn't wanna grow up, cause I never wanted to look like them ladies. I heard Miz Jenkins down the street one time say she don't mind being fat cause that way her husband don't get so jealous. She say it's more than one way to keep a man. Me, I don't have me no intentions of keeping no man. I never understood why they was in so much demand anyway, when it seem like all a woman can depend on em for is making sure she keep on having babies.

We got enough children in my neighborhood. In the summertime, even the little kids allowed to stay up till eleven or twelve o'clock at night— playing in the street and hollering and carrying on—don't never seem to get tired. Don't nobody care, long as they don't fight.

Me—I don't hang around no front steps no more. Hot nights like that, I get out my ten speed and I be gone.

That's what I like to do more than anything else in the whole world. Feel that wind in my face keeping me cool as a air conditioner, shooting along like a snowball. My bike light as a kite. I can really get up some speed.

All the guys around my way got ten speed bikes. Some of the girls got em too, but they don't ride em at night. They pedal around during the day, but at nighttime they just hang around out front, watching babies and running they mouth. I didn't get my Peugeot to be no conversation piece.

My mama don't like me to ride at night. I tried to point out to her that she ain't never said nothing to my brothers, and Vincent a year younger than me. (And Langston two years older, in case "old" is the problem.) She say, "That's different, Johnnieruth. You're a girl." Now I wanna know how is anybody gonna know that. I'm skinny as a knifeblade turned sideways, and all I ever wear is blue jeans and a Wrangler jacket. But if I bring that up, she liable to get started in on how come I can't be more of a young lady, and fourteen is old enough to start taking more pride in my appearance, and she gonna be ashamed to admit I'm her daughter.

I just tell her that my bike be moving so fast can't nobody hardly see me, and couldn't catch me if they did. Mama complain to her friends how I'm wild and she can't do nothing with me. She know I'm gonna do what I want no matter what she say. But she know I ain't getting in no trouble, neither.

Like some of the boys I know stole they bikes, but I didn't do nothing like that. I'd been saving my money ever since I can remember, every time I could get a nickel or a dime outta anybody.

When I was a little kid, it was hard to get money. Seem like the only time they ever give you any was on Sunday morning, and then you had to put it in the offering. I used to hate to do that. In fact, I used to hate everything about Sunday morning. I had to wear all them ruffly dresses— that shiny slippery stuff in the wintertime that got to make a noise every time you move your ass a inch on them hard old benches. And that scratchy starchy stuff in the summertime with all them scratchy crinolines. Had to carry a pocketbook and wear them shiny shoes. And the church we went to was all the way over on Summit Avenue, so the whole damn neighborhood could get a good look. At least all the other kids'd be dressed the same way. The boys think they slick cause they get to wear pants, but they still got to wear a white shirt and a tie; and them dumb hats they wear can't hide them baldheaded haircuts, cause they got to take the hats off in church.

There was one Sunday when I musta been around eight. I remember it was before my sister Corletta was born, cause right around then was when I put my foot down about that whole sanctimonious routine. Anyway, I was dragging my feet along Twenty-Fifth Street in back of Mama and Vincent and them, when I spied this lady. I only seen her that one time, but I still remember just how she look. She don't look like nobody

I ever seen before. I *know* she don't live around here. She real skinny. But she ain't no real young woman, neither. She could be old as my mama. She ain't nobody's mama—I'm sure. And she ain't wearing Sunday clothes. She got on blue jeans and a man's blue working shirt, with the tail hanging out. She got patches on her blue jeans, and she still got her chin stuck out like she some kinda African royalty. She ain't carrying no shiny pocketbook. It don't look like she care if she got any money or not, or who know it, if she don't. She ain't wearing no house-shoes, or stockings or high heels neither.

Mama always speak to everybody, but when she pass by this lady she make like she ain't even seen her. But I get me a real good look, and the lady stare right back at me. She got a funny look on her face, almost like she think she know me from some place. After she pass on by, I had to turn around to get another look, even though Mama say that ain't polite. And you know what? She was turning around, too, looking back at me. And she give me a great big smile.

I didn't know too much in them days, but that's when I first got to thinking about how it's got to be different ways to be, from the way people be around my way. It's got to be places where it don't matter to nobody if you all dressed up on Sunday morning or you ain't. That's how come I started saving money. So, when I got enough, I could go away to some place like that.

Afterwhile I begun to see there wasn't no point in waiting around for handouts, and I started thinking of ways to earn my own money. I used to be running errands all the time—mailing letters for old Grandma Whittaker and picking up cigarettes and newspapers up the corner for everybody. After I got bigger, I started washing cars in the summer, and shoveling people sidewalk in the wintertime. Now I got me a newspaper route. Ain't never been no girl around here with no paper route, but I guess everybody got it figured out by now that I ain't gonna be like nobody else.

The reason I got me my Peugeot was so I could start to explore. I figured I better start looking around right now, so when I'm grown, I'll know exactly where I wanna go. So I ride around every chance I get.

Last summer, I used to ride with the boys a lot. Sometime eight or ten of us'd just go cruising around the streets together. All of a sudden my mama decide she don't want me to do that no more. She say I'm too old to be spending so much time with boys. (That's what they tell you half the time, and the other half the time they worried cause you ain't interested in spending more time with boys.) Don't make much sense. She want me to have some girl friends, but I never seem to fit in with none of the things the girls doing. I used to think I fit in more with the boys.

But I seen how Mama might be right, for once. I didn't like the way the boys was starting to talk about girls sometimes. Talking about what some girl be like from the neck on down, and talking all up underneath somebody clothes and all. Even though I wasn't really friends with none of the girls, I still didn't like it. So now I mostly just ride around by myself. And Mama don't like that neither—you just can't please her.

This boy that live around the corner on North Street, Kenny Henderson, started asking me one time if I don't ever be lonely, cause he always see me by myself. He say don't I ever think I'd like to have me somebody special to go places with and stuff. Like I'd pick him if I did! Made me wanna laugh in his face.

I do be lonely, a lotta times, but I don't tell nobody. And I ain't met nobody yet that I'd really rather be with than be by myself. But I will someday. When I find that special place where everybody different, I'm gonna find somebody there I can be friends with. And it ain't gonna be no dumb boy.

I found me one place already, that I like to go to a whole lot. It ain't even really that far away—by bike—but it's on the other side of the Avenue. So I don't tell Mama and them I go there, cause they like to think I'm right around the neighborhood someplace. But this neighborhood too dull for me. All the houses look just the same—no porches, no yards, no trees—not even no parks around here. Every block look so much like every other block it hurt your eyes to look at, afterwhile. So I ride across Summit Avenue and go down that big steep hill there, and then make a sharp right at the bottom and cross the bridge over the train tracks. Then I head on out the boulevard—that's the nicest part, with all them big trees making a tunnel over the top, and lightning bugs shining in the bushes. At the end of the boulevard you get to this place call the Plaza.

It's something like a little park—the sidewalks is all bricks and they got flowers planted all over the place. The same kind my mama grow in that painted-up tire she got out front masquerading like a garden decoration—only seem like they smell sweeter here. It's a big high fountain right in the middle, and all the streetlights is the real old-fashion kind. That Plaza is about the prettiest place I ever been.

Sometimes something going on there. Like a orchestra playing music or some man or lady singing. One time they had a show with some girls doing some kinda foreign dances. They look like they were around my age. They all had on these fancy costumes, with different color ribbons all down they back. I wouldn't wear nothing like that, but it looked real pretty when they was dancing.

I got me a special bench in one corner where I like to sit, cause I can see just about everything, but wouldn't nobody know I was there. I like to sit still and think, and I like to watch people. A lotta people be coming there at night — to look at the shows and stuff, or just to hang out and cool off. All different kinda people.

This one night when I was sitting over in that corner where I always be at, there was this lady standing right near my bench. She mostly had her back turned to me and she didn't know I was there, but I could see her real good. She had on this shiny purple shirt and about a million silver bracelets. I kinda liked the way she look. Sorta exotic, like she maybe come from California or one of the islands. I mean she had class — standing there posing with her arms folded. She walk away a little bit. Then turn around and walk back again. Like she waiting for somebody.

Then I spotted this dude coming over. I spied him all the way cross the Plaza. Looking real fine. Got on a three piece suit. One of them little caps sitting on a angle. Look like leather. He coming straight over to this lady I'm watching and then she seen him too and she start to smile, but she don't move till he get right up next to her. And then I'm gonna look away, cause I can't stand to watch nobody hugging and kissing on each other, but all of a sudden I see it ain't no dude at all. It's another lady.

Now I can't stop looking. They smiling at each other like they ain't seen one another in ten years. Then the one in the purple shirt look around real quick — but she don't look just behind her — and sorta pull the other one right back into the corner where I'm sitting at, and then they put they arms around each other and kiss — for a whole long time. Now I really know I oughtta turn away, but I can't. And I know they gonna see me when they finally open they eyes. And they do.

They both kinda gasp and back up, like I'm the monster that just rose up outta the deep. And then I guess they can see I'm only a girl, and they look at one another—and start to laugh! Then they just turn around and start to walk away like it wasn't nothing at all. But right before they gone, they both look around again, and see I still ain't got my eye muscles and my jaw muscles working right again yet. And the one lady wink at me. And the other one say, "Catch you later."

I can't stop staring at they backs, all the way across the Plaza. And then, all of a sudden, I feel like I got to be doing something, got to be moving.

I wheel on outta the Plaza and I'm just concentrating on getting up my speed. Cause I can't figure out what to think. Them two women kissing and then, when they get caught, just laughing about it. And here I'm laughing too, for no reason at all. I'm sailing down the boulevard laughing like a lunatic, and then I'm singing at the top of my lungs. And climbing that big old hill up to Summit Avenue is just as easy as being on a escalator.

Summer, 1980
January, 1981

Family Script · *Anne Blackford*

*But not far away was the Big Swamp—the
"trembling earth," the American Indians called
it—and I was aware of the existence of this
swamp from my earliest years . . . I was told
that there was no solid foundation of rock under
its surface but only mysterious waters which
flowed ceaselessly from an unknown source . . .*
—Lillian Smith

I

I know the script
and what it calls for:

hushed voices, the thick green
baize of the forest floor,

an inability to walk far
without tripping

The roots have all grown here
much larger than real life

I could say "like a dream"

I could say—interrupting the script—
that this is not real

This is the scene where the family
is called for

to plead for absolute loyalty

the myth where the eldest daughter
sacrifices herself

Iphigenia reciting her speech
before her father's troops

younger than me at fourteen

imploring the gods
to stop the murderous anger

between mother and father

And these are the younger children:
my dark-eyed little brother

my younger sister who would avenge me
padding softly over the forest floor

They've slept with me
all their lives in this tangled overgrowth

In the mosquito-damp night
I gradually count away

the terrors of their dreams

II

Cut off from each other —
from ourselves — we move steadily

toward the heightened climax
No one's called this murder

but it is
This bay at Aulis soaks up

my voice like rain
None of them have questioned

what we are doing here
Blood sacrifice — even of one girl —

seems the only necessary sign

Now I pace over the stages
of this hallucination — rain forests

alive with buzzing insects,
moist green leaves, dazzling birds

I have to invent my lines
as the script keeps veering

I have to keep imagining
when to throw myself between my parents

to implore for peace

III

This script is a weapon:
a way out as well as a death sentence

Being a victim
of human sacrifice,

I have to choose my real identity
to survive the last act

My little brother
comes up to kiss me goodbye

His child's arms
encircle my neck tightly

Sunlight slants
from the roof of twisted vines;

leaves swarming with gnats
gleam emerald-green

I've had to plead with my father
for the right to grow up

I've had to fight all this time
for my own body

This is the script
I've come back to act

to rehearse the familiar cycles
of retribution and anger

Whatever traps I have to face
leaving this script

I can't go back to claim
my sister and brother

I've come back here
only to really leave

to scrutinize the variant texts
under the handwriting

This ground is treacherous

sunken with quicksand
and rope-thick roots—I walk carefully

over the moss-grown floor
I can't afford to trip this time

Nobody speaks
for my voice except me

thousands of years after I
took back my life

I'm still just inventing
what needs to be said

after I throw the script away

Falling South · *Martha Boethel*

Gunshot, or a pin oak falling; I still
can't tell. I know only
a few things: the river rises, swilling
sand from old roots; mosquitoes
and crawfish breed in the bar ditches.
Tin cans on the fence
spook jackrabbits, crows, but not
hunters. My cousin from the highway
department puts up our mailbox—but who
pulls it down, snaps the flag, upturns it
on the road like a dead armadillo?

"You two don't belong," my mother
declares. "Women only come here
on family day." (In a dream,
someone strings barbwire
between me and the tank. When the snake
circles back, I hang my feet
on the wire, for safety.)

Thanksgiving: surrounded. We see deer
flee the pasture, turn, turn again. Ribbons
of geese in the sky; gunshot. We eat
mutton, turkey, deploring the slaughter.
At dusk owls call; geese
squawk, roll in formation like DNA.
One white crane on the rideaway.

The truth is, I can't live here. The stars,
geese, press down; their wings . . .

The truth is, I always lived here.
Caretaker; axe; crane
in the bar ditch, gulping crawfish. Drank
from both mugs, "Pop" and "Mom."
Now the ghosts of family days, old
hunters, move the constellations
too near. I can't look at the night;
it's all so close, and falling.

Mornings remembering last nights ·
Olga Broumas

Stairs arise out of a village
The olive thickets couch the bare
Rock veins
Anticipating a season
A jagged uphill terraced for the goat
Their bearded kneecaps
Yes their bells
Fiction these thickets
As if a flight of birds were always restless
To feel the cold that calls the sands of Egypt
Home and the pungent fruit
Loll in its brine beneath some ship's
Cold and nostalgic course

Bring me a tangerine
Next to a pack of camels
Draw back the curtain answer me
What curled around your all-night lip
No not the light
The light light roll call up your thigh
Your empty sheet

My absent one my sweet
Was she sweet?
Now did you argue?
The dark and the milky let me lick
High-pitched and fertile without interruption
A human flight of birds
Change is your whim

Hand over water waving
They come with knives now in the dreams
If we don't spend
A morning soon adrift
In promise of music and physical
Like Arabs that were born in Crete
I won't you will I won't you will
Animal skin-flick torture
I let the mornings pass
Footwork of reels jigs and strathspeys
Light of the moon I read a *cathodic* embodiment
The mornings cold maybe very cold
Full of misunderstanding
Eyes startled dice in the crook of sleep

Epithalamion · *Olga Broumas*

Our mound of earth dug up
        for a new sidewalk
is as graceful as the dunes we drive to see
        The seen
dwarfs our scale   we feel it
        tugging at our brow

and bow
        like guests in it yet we
for bending are allowed to
        sing
some blond dune's surface
        We believe what we see

through the image is the song
        at its source
and so assume the world
        love   shares our intelligence
of heart the natural
        hug   the quick kiss overturned   The smug

like their smiles more than what makes them
        smile
white cows in November meadows
        in the galactic ravines
Venus enters the Bull at birth and again at will
        A door shuts twice

The twelve rings of the night   outposts
        reefs pockets of great abandon what
we expected poetry to be
        as children   yield   As women
we are beautiful for remembering
        how to relax all force

in an unmeasured field
        The moment heals
Out past where the shale you think is
        going to hold and doesn't
silverfish leap from the water
        Tears are worlds not seen

Two, Remembered · *Constance Carrier*

They stand in the sun by the pool,
beautiful, warmed by a light
like some god's benison lying
golden upon them.
        What god,
what god would devise their dying? —

one of them beaten and knifed
in a casual holdup, left
to die on the sill of the year;
one shaven-headed and blind,
the tumor thrusting to flower
in bone its rage would devour,
the flesh transparent, the mind
to the last moment clear.

Was a reckoning fixed from the first,
had Nemesis marked them out
to punish excess with excess?
Could they, from fear of the night,
have summoned their own nightmare,
met the reprisal they forced?
I remember the shadows there,
beyond the circle of sun
where they stood like two who invite
the bolt of the flung spear.

Their sun has been quenched, has set.
Horror does not grow less;
it carves on the mind, like stone,
the scenes we fight to forget.
We can do nothing now
to pay them a final grace
but keep their image alive,
held like an amulet
to show us one side of the coin
whose other face is despair.

Travel Notes · *Michelle Cliff*

I wanted to be the lone figure on the landscape.
The cat burglar passing silent in the night.
The fast driver—unaffiliated—unnoticed.
This is not how it is.

Sometimes I see a small house—sometimes shacks attract me. I wonder how it would be to live hidden.

I am standing in the doorway of the dining room at Haworth Parsonage. *My sister Emily loved the moors. . . . Out of a sullen hollow in a livid hill-side, her mind could make an Eden.* —I stare at the horsehair sofa where Emily Brontë died.

Outside are the thousands of graves. Wind and rain obscuring the vision. Mosses cross the outer walls.

While inside glass cases display the tiny notebooks filled with stories. The needlework of the sisters.

Downstairs is the souvenir kiosk. The portraits of Keeper, Grasper, the hawk Hero. Views of the moors—heather—gorse. Top Withens. Kitchen. Churchyard. *She found in the bleak solitude many and dear delights; and not the least and best-loved was—liberty. Liberty was the breath of Emily's nostrils.*

Across from this kiosk is a bulletin board advising women of the existence of the Yorkshire Ripper and the necessity that we remain indoors.

The North Wind demolished their already weakened lungs—Anne and Emily. Charlotte died of pregnancy. Branwell of opium and drink. The old man of old age. Much earlier a mother and two other sisters: cancer, consumption, typhoid.

Back home—I find a suspect has been caught. He kept to himself. He was a shy man. He and his wife had no children. The police have his wife under guard. There are threats on her life.

"But we already know that women are oppressed," the student said to me. "I had hoped this course would deal with something else."

How do we keep their attention?
Our own.

***

As a child I saved maps. Haunted airports. Begged for travel brochures and posters of bazaars and castles. I wanted to go overseas. Always looked forward.

Traveling through my own time I often look back.

I am in Brighton where England's Neo-Nazis have headquarters. Where Fanny Imlay—Wollstonecraft's daughter—killed herself, wearing her mother's watch and undergarment. (Godwin did not claim her body, ashamed at her method of death.)

Brighton is an hour from Lewes—where Virginia Woolf walked into the River Ouse. I think about a memoir written by Woolf's cook—Louie Mayer—how she described the last afternoon: as Virginia wandered through the garden, bumping into branches. And Leonard suggested Virginia dust—but she lost interest.

These details crowd me.

What is left of Wollstonecraft's grave is a plaque by King's Cross Station.

In King's Cross once I saw a woman in the ladies' room—a large naked white woman accompanied by her belongings. She was standing in a corner against a wall, calmly washing herself. Wetting and soaping and drying herself with brown paper.

Other women came and went.

***

As a child I pressed my fingers against my closed eyes—watched the stars, planets, comets, and meteorites move against them. As if I could contain the universe behind my eyelids.

It is the anniversary of the first imprisonment of suffragists —
Annie Kenney and Cristabel Pankhurst.
Someone has left a bouquet of irises — purple
tied with ribbon — green:
the colors of the movement.

These lie in front of Emmeline Pankhurst's statue which stands to the
side of the Houses of Parliament. The note attached to the bouquet is in
a strong and older hand — perhaps of a woman who actually remembers
1905. The ink runs in the drizzle.

Now the meaning of green ribbon has shifted. They are killing black
children in Atlanta — also elsewhere. Georgia Dean, a retired factory
worker, suggests wearing an inverted V of green — the color of growing
things.

Each newspaper report seems more clouded than before: today they claimed
the children died at the hands of a "gentle" killer: does this translate as
female? homosexual?

What are they getting at?

The Mark of the Beast — a special issue on the Klan. On the cover a member clasps a child; his eyes seem hollowed — the child's, I mean — the
member is a woman.

* * *

I meet two women in Texas — they live on a farm in a small town north
of Austin. Outside their kitchen is a pile of rocks where their cat stares
down a diamondback.

They prepare a noose of cord — slide one rock back. The diamondback
raises her head to strike. They slide the noose around her neck.

She stretches to her length. "Four feet of solid muscle" — one woman explains.

They place the snake in a garbage can — secure its lid by rope.

There is another snake in the rockpile — then another.

"We're lucky we had seven cans," says one woman—and a pickup to drive the diamondbacks twenty-five miles away and let them go: one by one.

A solid day's work.

The Children's Ward · *Jane Cooper*

NANNY WAS IRISH, I told my mother, *born* in Scotland. Her sister was Head of Ladies' Ready To Wear at the biggest shop in Greenoch. Her oldest sister that was, there were nine in the family. The youngest of all was Our Joseph, not much older than me, and when the little princesses visited Greenoch, Nanny went to see them, along with all the other people lining the streets, but they couldn't hold a candle to Our Joseph. Nanny took care of me because once before she had taken care of a little boy who was sick the same way I was. So she understood my diet. "Poor wee thing," she would say and tell how one day somebody brought her a box of chocolates and the boy took some, which of course he wasn't supposed to do, and when he heard her coming he sat down on the box and squashed the chocolates flat. But when she caught me lifting icing off my sister's birthday cake, I was spanked. "This hurts me more than it does you," Nanny would say, her wrists like steel, while I screamed. Yet she looked back on that boy with tenderness. "Poor wee lamb"—and she explained how with the disease we had you were supposed to die before you were seven. "And did he die, Nanny; Is he dead now?" But I never found out.

Curds without whey—four times a day Nanny put the junket through the ricer and squeezed it dry—bananas, the lean of bacon, protein milk that tasted like chalk. I was standing holding up my glass and crying. I cried all the time now, every morning playing with the other children I would start to cry. My grandmother's stylish heels clicked across the floor. "Here Junebug, it's not as bad as all that, I'll show you." She took a gulp, puckered up her lips and rushed out into the hall. Nanny handed the glass back to me. "Drink up," she said, out of patience. "If you don't drink your milk like a good girl, we'll be planting daisies on your grave by August."

There was a woman in their town who lost all five sons in the War, and when the Armistice came and they had the big parade, she closed her window shades and refused to watch. I imagined how that house looked, small, between two taller houses, with black shades. I liked the stories about Our Joseph better. And how they all slept together in the one big bed. I used to wake up early and see Nanny lying in the other half of our bed, her nose pointing to the ceiling, her firm chest rising and falling under the saint's medal and small gold cross. "When Father says *turn*," she would command, "we all turn."

God knew Nanny would have saved my life if she could, but since there was apparently no saving it, she did her duty. Her duty was to see I didn't die any sooner than I had to and make sure I got to Heaven when I did die. So I had *A Child's Tales from the Bible*, in red and gold, every night and "The Catholic Hour" over the radio on Sundays. All day I looked forward to bedtime. My favorite was Moses in the Bulrushes. Fancy finding a live baby floating in a nest down our river, the way Pharoah's Daughter had! But I hated Abraham. In the picture he held the knife over Isaac's head and Isaac looked terrified; the ram bleated in the bushes. When I had been really sick, lying on my back in bed with a swollen stomach, someone brought Harriet to visit me. Harriet was three, a year younger than me. Over the curve of my huge stomach, I could just see her wedged between the foot of the bed and the wall. She was carrying a present for me but was too scared to budge. After she had gone Nanny said, "Harriet's a Jew." "What's a Jew?" I said. "They're God's chosen people." A few days later I announced, "I'm going to be a Jew." "You can't"—Nanny stopped folding—"you have to be born one." "Can't I ever?" I thought about Harriet's curls and dark, reproachful eyes. She was the most beautiful child I had ever seen. I wanted to be chosen more than anything.

"You have to learn to read now you're five because I learned to read when I was five," said Isabel importantly. I was squeezed into the old highchair because I liked looking down on things; no one used it any more. "No, I don't," I said, "nobody has to learn to read till they're six." At eight, Pen was still learning. Besides, I didn't want to keep growing older this way. The other children raced up and down the room. Nanny burst in, her hands still red from the soapsuds. "There," she declared, plucking me out of the highchair, "can't you see you've gone and made Jane cry again?" "I didn't, I didn't," protested Isabel, "you're unfair." "Don't be impertinent," said Nanny—she pronounced it im*pair*tinent. In her arms I was crying harder, leaning my head into her white, starched shoulder. Pen and Isabel must hate me. Even when the circus came to town, on its way north from winter quarters, they might not get to go for fear they'd bring home another germ.

But the first night I got sick Pen had been excited. We were in our small summer house then, where I used to stand up in my crib to watch the mountains and the long black freight train hooted out of its tunnel in the clear evening light. I was perched on the toilet; a bare light bulb burned against the wall. Pen danced across the bathroom, shrieking and laughing. "There goes the King!" he shrieked. "There goes the Queen!" That was an old game we had, whenever a bad thunderstorm hit. Pen played chess, and he liked to pretend the thunder was giant chessmen falling off the board of Heaven and rolling around on the ground. But tonight the thunder was my farts. Bent over on the toilet seat, queasy and trembling, I hurt with laughter because of Pen. My brother's wiry body flashed by. A shadow jerked up the wall. "There goes the Queen!" I shouted wildly. "There goes a pawn!"

Then I was lying in bed with my stomach puffed so high I couldn't bear to sit up even against pillows. I hurt all the time. My mother read *The Water Babies*. Every time she got to the last page and shut the book I would demand to hear it over again, right from the beginning. Poor Tom, dirty and miserable, sank underneath the river and the whole husk of his body was washed away, and soon he was clean and shining, no bigger than Daddy's thumb. My father blocked the light in the bedroom door. We stared at each other. Then the doorway was empty, he had left without saying anything. "He can't stand to see anybody sick," said my mother to my aunt, in a voice I wasn't supposed to catch. My aunt began to sing to me so my mother could go lie down. Far away the black freight train hooted. "She'll be comin' round the mountain when she comes," sang my aunt.

When we finally traveled north it was on a long black train. We had a drawing room on the Southern Railway. The trip took two nights and a day. I sat with my legs straight out in front of me and looked out the window. Every once in a while I would push the green plush of the train seat the wrong way — dark-light, dark-light; then I would peer around at my mother. What should I talk to her about? For months I had been with almost no one but Nanny.

Every Sunday the two of us would dress to go to Mass. Under the tent of her white cotton nightgown Nanny would mysteriously draw on first her underclothes, then her long, best silk stockings. Then over the top went her best striped silk dress, and the nightgown fell down in a little puddle at her feet. She fastened the neck of the dress with a cameo brooch, slipping the medal and gold cross inside. Then she would dress me. Daddy would drop us off on his way to his own church, where he was a vestryman. By this time I had a medal of my own—St. Teresa, carrying a sheaf of lilies. The Little Flower was Nanny's special saint. That was her middle name, Teresa, after Bessie. Nanny had said I could have St. Teresa for my special saint, too.

Out of respect for St. Paul, Nanny always wore a dark, short-brimmed felt hat which she pulled down almost to the tops of her fiercely blue eyes. I had to wear a bonnet with a snap under the chin that scratched. At the door of the church she would dip her fingers in the scalloped shell over my head and cross my forehead with holy water. The water dropping into the stone shell made a pleasant tinkling sound.

I loved the inside of that church. It was large and dark, like a cave, and you couldn't say anything, but still it was always warm with the rustle of skirts and prayer-book pages and the low groans of old men getting up off their knees. As Nanny leaned forward to pray, I would look up at the reds and blues of the stained-glass windows or try to find through the rows of bodies the pink dress of the plaster saint stretching out her hand from the side aisle. Then the priest would start to chant, little bells would ring, and the church would fill up with the smells of all the different people and the stuffy, interesting smell of incense shaken out by a boy. Above me Nanny's profile was stern but not angry, and I knew she was praying for her brothers and sisters at home, for her father who never made more than two pounds ten a week, and also for the young man she had come over to this country to meet. He had paid her way out, but as soon as she saw him standing on the dock she knew they could never marry. So she went back to being a nanny. The priest in his gold or green or purple cape lifted his hands to the sky. Before him on the altar was a large gold cross. At home we had a black cross with a twisted Jesus hanging over the bed where we slept; there were nails through His feet and the blood ran down, and on His head was the crown of thorns.

One day the side aisle was crowded with children. Their mothers were trying to line them up two by two and making shushing noises. The boys had on dark blue suits, some even wore long pants, but I couldn't take my eyes off the girls. They were dressed in white, like little brides, and on their heads were white veils fastened with wreaths of daisies or wax orange blossoms. Each one carried a bouquet in a white paper ruffle just like a real bride. Nanny had a friend in Greenoch who became a nun—bride of Christ, she called her. Were these the brides of Christ? "Wouldn't you like to make your first Communion?" whispered Nanny. "But you have to be seven. The age of reason," she added practically.

Nanny took the hairbrush to me. "This hurts me more than it does you," she was almost crying. I had been standing by the ironing board. "Go to the bathroom, Jane," she said. But I wouldn't go. And then I couldn't hold it in any longer, shameful and brown it poured down my legs. The hairbrush hissed through the air. I got down off the bed again stiffly.

I hated Abraham. "*Dis*obedient!" proclaimed Nanny. But was it Abraham's fault or God's? How could God ask Abraham to kill his only son if He loved him? And how could God let His own Son die? I stared and stared at the twisted Jesus hanging over Nanny's side of the bed. There were nails through His hands, too.

In Isabel's room hung the picture of Paradise. Little boys and girls in yellow and red and blue dresses were standing holding flowers, while lambs and rabbits and sparrows played about their feet. "He prayeth best who loveth best," Isabel read to me from the borders, "All things both great and small." On Pen's wall was the face of a tiger, coming out from among reeds at a water hole in Africa. I never went into Pen's room now if I could help it.

My sins were crying, lying and not wanting to go to the bathroom. "Don't touch yourself, Jane," Nanny pursed up her lips in disgust. One day she said to me, "If you don't stop touching yourself, we'll have to take you to the hospital and get it cut off." I screamed with terror. For a long time I wouldn't stop screaming. Nanny still had all her own teeth. And she had a right to feel proud of them, they were so white. "Soot and salt," she declared—who could afford toothpaste? Their father had taught them all to reach right up the chimney. I watched her smile in fascination. How could anything so white come from anything as dirty as the fireplace? Was this what the priest meant when he said our sins would be washed whiter than snow?

Nanny went up to Communion. She always did that, leaving me alone in the dark wooden pew. But today I felt tired. The people shuffling back down the aisles seemed farther away than usual; the murmur of their prayers was like the sound of the river out our dark bedroom windows on a still winter's night. Nanny was bending over me. My face was cold with sweat. "You fainted," she said with concern. I was surprised to find myself lying in the pew as if it was our bed; a man's jacket lay across my knees. "Poor wee lamb." Daddy came to fetch us, looking worried. Tenderly she carried me out to the car. But after that I couldn't go to church any more, I could only have the Bible stories at bedtime.

"Jane, Jane, Go to Spain, And never come home again!" they chanted at a birthday party. But would I go to Heaven or Hell? I felt very tired. I was standing beside the table where the others were already eating their ice cream and angel food cake. At my place was a bowl of curds.

It was the Depression. But fortunately Nanny's mother had always been a good manager. When nobody else ate liver, she got it off the butcher for dog scraps and they all made a good meal. Not one of them had ever missed a day at school or on the job because of illness. With relish Nanny told how her older sister lost her first post in the hat department in Glasgow. "What you need, madam," Agnes talked back to the customer, "is not a new hat, it's a new face."

Even though it was the Depression, we could still have our new Easter dresses. Mine was to be yellow, with baskets of flowers on a white path down the front. But to wear it, I had to get through the Crucifixion. "Away in a manger, No crib for His bed," we had sung at Christmastime. Now Jesus was the Lamb of God caught by His horns in the bushes. He was betrayed and whipped and they mocked Him and hung Him on the cross saying, "This is the King of the Jews." And they gave Him vinegar to drink. And after He was dead one of the soldiers pierced His side with a spear, and blood and water ran out. And doubting St. Thomas had to thrust his hand into Our Lord's side to make sure He was risen. How could he do that?

All during Lent we read these stories about Jesus. Nanny had no use for people who gave up things for Lent, like my grandmother. When you were really poor, she said, what was left to give up? It was better to show devotion.

I woke up crying. Nanny fussed a bit but brought the water. Then she climbed back into bed and turned her shoulder on me, so as to get back to sleep. I watched the white mound of her body in the thin crack of light from the bathroom door and listened to the slap-slap of the river against the pilings below the house. How could God let His only Son die? And how could Jesus, if He loved me, possibly let me die and go to Hell? After all I was only a child. I tried not to think of the face of the tiger gleaming through the dark from Pen's wall. At any moment he might bare his fangs. Other little animals came down to the water hole, Pen said, and the tiger lay in wait for them.

But suppose there was no Hell? How could God send anybody to Hell if He loved them? Jesus even loved the thief on the next cross. I was almost asleep now. I decided God couldn't have created Hell, there was no room for it.

On Easter morning the sun shone beautifully. Isabel and Pen and I put on our new clothes and were driven through the white streets to our grandparents' house for the big Easter dinner. "Liked a picked chicken," one of the uncles said, seeing me in my yellow dress. But Nanny told me I looked a picture. Seated on the high cushion facing my glass of protein milk, I felt high and far away above the rest of the table. The sun shone in on the colors of their new dresses and newly washed hair. Jesus loved me. But today it hardly mattered. For if everybody bad and good went to Heaven, what was the point of being good? There was no Heaven. You died, and that was that.

III

"Take her north to a doctor you can trust. She's dying, and you're dying watching her." That's the way my mother told the story to my aunt, after my father brought home the first real cash he'd been paid in over a year and laid it on the dresser. Never had he worked so hard, complained my mother, but it was because everybody was going bankrupt. We were in Schwartz's toy store. I couldn't make up my mind between a doll with a whole trunk full of clothes and a cardboard village that had a church, a town hall with a star over the front door, a castle, and a lot of horses, sheep and pigs. Finally my mother said I could keep them both. I couldn't believe it. At home we almost never had new toys. Back in the hotel bedroom she helped me pile up the pillows to make snow-capped mountains. On the top peak stood the castle, down below was the church, and on the green blankets over my knees I arranged the little cardboard houses where people really lived, which I liked best of all. But I still couldn't think what to talk to her about. There were three men and three women in that village. One of the women had no hair and a very red face. She looked bossy, and I decided she had no children of her own. She could take care of the pigs.

The nurse in the waiting room called me "she," though I was standing right there. "But she didn't cry," the nurse kept saying stubbornly to my mother, turning the white-rimmed barium glass round and round in her fingers. "Are you sure you didn't just pour it out? They always cry."

He was not stooping or kneeling down to be at my level. Instead he had put his large square hands under my naked armpits and lifted me up to stand on the examining table. From where I stood I could look directly into his blue eyes. He had white curls all over his head, and I thought that was why he was called Dr. Kerley. Naked, I regarded him with trust. "You know," he said at once, "you're going to be all right." How could he understand all that I had felt? He told me before he told my mother.

IV

My mother didn't want to leave me alone on the ward but I was delighted. Every day while we shared the small room at the hospital I would creep down to the end of the hall and peer in at the ward door and wonder about the children who lived there. Those children were old campaigners. They could tell the names of the various diseases and how they affected you. Frances, for instance, was an epileptic. That meant you fell down in fits. Frances was very pretty, and I used to love to lie and watch her still profile through the thin cheesecloth curtain that at rest hour divided our two cots. She had long, pale braids, and when she sat up they slid silkily down her back. Frances was almost nine and rarely smiled. After a while I decided she would not get better. You could usually tell.

For over a year I had weighed 42 pounds. Because of the diet my second teeth might not come in with enamel. But I didn't have celiac disease, all I had to do was stay in the hospital and learn how to eat again. Dr. Kerley stood at the foot of my cot, my mother was perched on the side. But I wouldn't look. I held the brimming spoonful up so that it sparkled under the bedside bulb. It was my first real supper—cornflakes, with sweet, thin cow's milk.

The nurses on our ward never felt sorry for anyone. That was what was grand about them, they treated us just like ordinary children. Every morning at 6:30 they would wake us by switching on the harsh overhead lights and wiping our faces with grainy washcloths soaked in cold water. Then we had to wait a long time before they brought up breakfast. "Happy birthday, Jane!" announced the chief nurse, setting down across my knees with a thump a tray that had a green cardboard cake on it. Out of the cake came a sunburst of yellow ribbons, and at the end of each ribbon was a small green box. At last I was six. I turned my shoulder on the rest of the ward. Secretly I opened the first box. Inside was a tiny wooden tea set with red trim. As I balanced the long line of cups and plates down the longer line of my sheeted leg, I pretended they were overflowing with chocolate ice cream, cornflakes and angel food. That night I asked the nurse please to tie up all my presents again, so I could have the same birthday tomorrow morning.

The baby with tubes lay on one side of the hall door and Billy was on the other. They were the youngest children on the ward. Billy was only two and a half. The baby slept most of the time, and the tubes curled out from under his white knitted crib blanket and fell in a red garland to the floor. It was rumored he had kidney trouble. My cot was in the far corner, safe between Frances and the wall.

Once a week we were taken up on the roof to listen to stories. There we would be joined by groups of children from other wards, and crippled children would be wheeled in by their nurses in special chairs or carried on portable beds. It was sunny and crisp on the roof, and as you stepped out of the elevator you could see a great sweep of sky, blocks of apartment buildings with a few trees down below, and in the distance the glittering river that was still not as wide as our own river at home in Jacksonville. The storyteller wore a long, flowing robe and had an unusually sweet voice, and we would all sit or lie or stand listening while she recited fairy tales and sometimes sea gulls or a pigeon flew by overhead. My favorite was Boots and His Brothers, where the third child that everyone thinks is stupid grows up to win the princess by kindness or good luck.

One day when we came down off the roof and were crowding through the ward door, we discovered the baby had been taken away. His crib looked flat and white, and the bunch of red tubing was gone from underneath. "Gone for an operation," said the brisk young nurse who was folding his crib blanket. But he never came back. We all knew he must have died, though someone argued he could just have been put in a private room because he was so sick. Soon his place was taken by a cheerful girl with one leg in traction. They had run out of bed space in the bone and joint pavilion downstairs.

"Nurse-ah. Nurse-ah. Nurse-ah." The whole place smelt like a zoo. There was the smell of fear, the warm animal smell of sleeping bodies, and the sharp stink of hospital disinfectant coming up from the floor and the sheets. Billy had started it. He had waked up wanting the nurse and no one was on duty. She must just have stepped down the hall. By the time I woke up, everybody was shouting or crying. The ward was almost dark, and it took me a few moments to make out Billy clinging to the bars of his crib and beating on the top rail with his fist. Billy couldn't talk clearly yet and he was shrieking in panic. Nobody could get over the bars of their own beds to help him. I sat up, then I stood and leaned over the high end of my bed and kicked at the bottom railing with my bare foot. We all began to pound the rails with our hands. The smell grew heavier. Gradually a rhythm was pounded out, and together we began to shout as loud as we could for Billy: "*Nurse*-ah! *Nurse*-ah! *Nurse*-ah!" At last we could see flashlights coming down the hall, sending slanted shadows toward the ceiling as they got closer. Then the overhead lights glared on, and three nurses started fussing through the ward, telling the children to lie down and tucking us in with strict tightness. One of them picked up Billy, who was soaked through. Almost at once he fell asleep with his head on her shoulder. But I couldn't sleep for a long time, thinkof how we had all called together to save Billy.

I fell in love with George. George was a tall, well-built boy of seven, with a fleshy jaw and brown hair that started straight up from his forehead. All that was wrong with him was that he was waiting for another operation on his harelip. We were two of the well ones now, and every day we spent a lot of time together on the sun porch, building towers out of blocks, eating jello at a low table, or chasing each other around the room. "Be quiet, Jane. Now do be quiet, George," the nurses had to say, as we laughed and scuffled. Once they even had to separate us while we were wrestling, pulling George off from on top of me by the back of his blue shirt collar. Another day George was sitting in the big red fire engine pedaling hard and I was sitting on the back and he drove straight through the ward where our cots were and out the door to the hall and ran into the legs of Dr. Kerley. We ricocheted off the wall then, and both of us fell out laughing. When my mother came to visit, she was shocked to find I had learned to talk just like George. That was harelip language. There were hardly any consonants, only animal noises, and the lilt of true sentences running up and down. George and I always talked that way. It was our secret code to fool the nurses.

It was getting cold. Soon it would be time to go home. My mother came to visit, bringing with her a pair of brown leather leggings outgrown by my northern cousins. She got permission to take me for a walk outside the hospital, and together we set off down the strange city streets. At home I was used to grass and trees, so I stared at the gray, flashing pavements. Then I was leaning against an iron railing, looking down on ranks of boys in gray uniforms who marched and gestured rapidly with their hands. My mother kneeled down next to me and took my body in her arms. "They're deaf and dumb boys, darling," she said. "It's the deaf and dumb school. Those poor boys can't hear anything, and so they have to learn to talk with their fingers." I examined her face in surprise. Her eyes had blurred with tears. Then I pulled away a little and slipped one hand out of its glove, experimentally. It certainly was a cold day not to be able to wear gloves. Over the curve of my mother's shoulder, I looked down at the boys again where they wheeled and beckoned without a sound from across their paved field. But didn't she know we all had something?

Hanging the Pictures · *Madeline DeFrees*

Every day I hang a different picture. They are
mostly the same—Vermeer's girl
in blue turban—a woman, clothed or not,
looks from the matte into distance, the first time
knowing her name.

                What holds together or binds,
syllables roll on the tongue. No matter
how late, how ordinary or not, the given
covers the rapt body, wine-colored dress—Dolce—
lowered into light.

              Figures assume a shape she has
always practised, cat and cricket shut out
where sleep cannot touch them. The other night,
good luck in the house, I killed a cricket, the second
one got away.

            The left-handed woman whose thought
is awash on my wall, and the tree that is always a woman
held in the storm's wake, a sky
not her own and larger: they are the same white
body of the charcoal nude who brings back the strait

and the water's precision, gradually louder, lapping
ashore. I drive two nails into wood to hang her.
On the floor Modigliani's red-haired woman
falls forward into the room's frame and a black
leap I recognize but cannot stop from singing.

Extended Outlook · *Madeline DeFrees*

November days, and the vague shape of a wing,
of a claw at the sill, at the drawn
shade of the bedroom,
signals the oncoming freeze. Setting
the scent-baited trap for the shadow mouse
back of the dark pine cabinet,
the tenant hears the cat downstairs
whining to be let in.

                      The tree is a violin bow
scraping the sound box of the house
all day. Close to the ribbed
breath, the scrolled end of wind under the eaves
turns back on the fine-tuned neck,
answers the shrill
jay in the caterwaul of blue
and falling light.

                   Trying to score this weather
for strings, no hurricane, but a planned
diminuendo, I pretend that the house is my own;
the cat, my pet. That Canada
wishes me well. That the blue shriek and the wail
are a cradlesong and the gulf
repeating this gale in my ear, is an old friend
or no friend of mine.

Agave Americana · *Madeline DeFrees*

THE DAY AFTER the deflowering, which she thought of as a late flowering, the rains came down from the Olympics. The time had been exactly two days less than five years more than half the age presumed necessary to bloom the century plant, and, as always, very few onlookers had survived the watch.

Sunday seemed to demand this complicated reckoning. Sky and sea, collusive in their mirage of union, had exchanged positions, and land was an absence, not to be relied on. Her sign, water. His, air. She smiled down at that benign divinity, remembering that his name, also, started with a *J*.

Presumption was the first error. That storied amaryllis blooms in twenty years or thirty, but the law of supply and demand enhances the legend. Her slow gain stands out among the willing perennials, out-blooms the annuals that flash across a season and disappear while the wife who tends them between snacktime and siesta, vacations with her husband.

Meanwhile, the human need to exaggerate grows wild. The heart recognizes a rare event. The head confirms it. The hand, if it be steady or in luck, helps it happen, and the eye preserves the vintage underground.

She knew a record was required — some means of validating what had come to be, and she hoped that the letters would provide that. With the journals, they constituted an account more trustworthy than the motel register she had not seen or the bloodstained mattress cover she had.

Vermillion road-markers blocked the left-turn lane she had already entered on her way to the afternoon Mass, and it was too late to go back. With her blinkers on right, she eased into the first lane across the intersection and headed towards the airport turnoff. His plane, the one he hadn't missed, had been four hours late, and she had spent three of them in the terminal because the telephone lines were jammed and she didn't want to risk misunderstanding.

"Dear J," she wrote, her eye on the mounting speedometer as she retraced the highway, "this delay reminds me of another absurdist favorite, the assignation twice postponed."

After his body's refusal to drive on through her pain, they had read her notebooks together, propped against the headboard, her naked shoulder resting against his white undershirt. He had looked at everything: the log book of her personal mail—old notes signed with love; acceptances and rejections couched in the same admiring rhetoric. Work sheets, unfinished poems, odd lines cherished, anxieties laid bare. Compulsive verbalizing of routines like dreams and visits to the doctor.

Later in the laundromat, the woman in charge had fallen into a gossipy undertone with another Saturday regular, and this morning, one of the Austins had slipped under the inside door a crumpled piece of newspaper torn from its context. She had expected it to be the *Times* reprint of a campus PR man's flat-footed interview—"Beyond the Convent"—that had already invaded what was left of her privacy. "She enjoys expressing herself as a woman," he had written, then when she had objected, "She likes to be regarded as a woman." Instead, the Austins' newspaper extract was a marvel of obscure communication. On one side, somebody was still seeking a " 'Big' Man." A Female Writer was "Back on Shelf," and one-half of a Mutual headline had been torn away. On the reverse, the front page, judging from the type, a man who could have been J's brother smiled conspiratorially, his black glasses inscrutable under "He Has Friends, Masters." She remembered very clearly using the plural *friends* in accounting for her absence—an explanation she could not omit in view of certain rituals involving lights, garage doors and routines hallowed by repetition. It had taken her several minutes to realize that innuendo was unintentional. Mr. Austin had merely presumed her professional interest in this account of a 57-year-old blind man who had earned the master's degree, serving two, Biology and Business.

The painful probing had been as urgent as the pleasure, abrupt and physical, the cries that signaled both undifferentiated; the words, when words came, foolish.

The notebooks had given her time to erase the sense of failure, and the four hours she lay beside him while he slept had given her courage. Women could fake orgasm, he had told her, but they could not simulate the nipples erect or the faint blush along the pectoral arch. Deception implied the faker's ability to tell the false from the true, the wish from its fulfillment. Surely when he wakened from that place where experience is fused, their indiscriminate needs might come together in a way their bodies witnessed, love pitching its mansion in the place of excrement.

It was 3:45 when she turned right, off the highway, but instead of going directly to the church, she stopped to post her letters. Dr. G would be amused, his touch of anticipatory anxiety released, she thought, merging smoothly with the westbound traffic. Then, instead of going to the church, she reversed direction again and headed for the motel restroom. Too much coffee. Why should anyone suffer through Father Carringham's monotonous homily like a child waiting to be relieved? Surely her physical needs were more important than getting to the church on time. She could forget about the Sunday ritual, count the will for the accomplished fact, avoid the further necessary choice and return to Landsend and the beginning of landladies. She liked the turn of phrase if not the interference it signified. Mrs. Austin was a good woman, no doubt, but much too curious and in the wrong directions. She had been purposely vague about the length of her absence, not knowing J's travel plans, which had already shifted several times.

She bought a newspaper from the desk clerk, who appeared not to recognize her, although he called after her back to ask whether she had picked up *The Traveler* or *The Victorian*. "Yes," she said, "I have," and darted into the anteroom marked LADIES. From behind the inner door, a voice warned, "There's somebody in here." She would wait in the corridor, her watch unreliable. Another postponement. At last both doors opened. Blue jeans, then a younger woman's self-possessed smile. "It's dark in there," the girl said, "john's on the right."

She tried to remember the room-plan, already vague. Tried the light switch knowing it wouldn't work. The girl would have discovered that. One thing she did remember—the lock worked, intruders could be barred, no words required. She let the newspaper fall, turned the knob and pushed in, groped along the wall. Nearly every week she stopped here on her way to or from the church. It was clear the management felt no interest in a comfort station for country residents who roamed the Sabbath streets or the tourists without reservations. She remembered the towel, lolling like an obscene tongue ("Call 202-5557 for Service") to announce that no calls had been placed. Whatever maid service the motel budget allowed was obviously attached to the overpriced rooms with their private baths and sanitized glasses, the towels she had forgotten to use just when they would have been most helpful.

J had made the reservations, had canceled and re-made them twice. He had whisked her through a back door, transparent in her dark glasses, while he took care of whatever it was you did at the desk. She wanted to see what he had written there (his first act after presenting his cheek to be kissed at the airport had been to memorize the license of her green Nova) but when she asked him, he answered with his own street address and a guarded jest about blackmail. She thought of the out-of-state license, out-of-his-state too, and wondered how he'd gotten around that. She had remembered to remove the luggage tags, but anyone whose curiosity was serious could check the car registration. Victorians were not receptive to the *Ms.* Most were tenacious about the either-or. J said you simply signed—he did not say how—and gave the number in your party. That should have closed the matter. Instead, it conjured up an orgy. Group sex. Unthinkable positions.

At a local art show she had bought, on impulse, a charcoal study of a female nude. She might have ignored the invitation to the exhibit if the landlady, who read everything that did not require a letter opener, had not urged attendance. She had even been rash enough to tell Mrs. Austin about buying the piece. Afterwards, repenting the indiscretion, she had left the drawing in the studio for a month, finally mailing her check and agreeing to have the drawing delivered. She had paced the road for twenty minutes, waiting for the artist's husband, and as soon as he was out of sight, had hidden the Nude in the coat closet. Meanwhile, the near-naked Indian brave's appeal to the Great Spirit continued to dominate her fireplace beside the badly painted seascape, the maps and joyful hounds. The hours she spent in these cold quarters faced always towards the window and the changing channel, although the foreground suffered the occasional domestic intrusions of the owners.

In the motel she had invented wild explanations for the two-to-three-a.m. knocking at the room next door, repeated calls for Mr. Plummer, official as the sound of keys that didn't fit, then coarsely familiar in an unstaged whisper calculated to arouse. Then, intervals of silence before the knocking started over. Through most of this, J slept, rising once to listen at their own door and try to make sense of the whole incident, as she had tried to piece together the truth of the motel register. At last he had come back to their bed while she resumed her vigil.

In the dark water closet she imagined the towel with its scarlet lip wounds and violet shadows, a mask removed adroitly as bra and bikini, the tired traveler's welcome of the sullied touch. Precisely when delay was least acceptable she found herself losing balance. One hand had discovered the tissue—enough left there—but the other roving hand could not surprise the feel of sweating porcelain.

All direction lost, she disengaged her right hand from the roll and moved it, like a white cane, across the nap of carpet. It found the angle where the walls joined and she rose from her knees to grope, spreadeagle, along the steaming tile, until she found the door again. The hard knob, a widening crevice, she located her goal and straddled the waiting john.

Already fifteen minutes late, she went back to pick up the newspaper, thought again of the dry house, decision moving towards her on the red second hand at her wrist. The need to confess had been sophisticated into analysis. The search for absolutes outlives the putting by of lifetime habits, and the new theology invites familiar choices. What used to be called mortal sin—and fornication was surely that—had been redefined as the will to separate oneself finally from God.

She had never wanted that. Had, in fact, thought less of separation than of union, needing to believe that it was not too late to join the human race. She had hoped to find him in places less remote, shorn of his forbidding capital, his too-proper name. Still, she knew when she had agreed to sleep with j that the second question would be whether to sleep through the sermon. And if she decided to keep on attending Mass, the next would be whether a defiled virgin (the phrase wore an odd, archaic ring) a defiled virgin—willingly defiled—could presume to share the Eucharist. She felt certain she would not risk telling Father Carringham: his labels were unreliable. The century plant again. Sex divinized or turned demonic, it came to the same lie at the last. Besides, she was not sorry, so it would be a mockery of Penance. Whatever confession she made would have to be of the more enlightened kind, and her doctor had programmed her to open like a passion flower. That was a triumph in itself, considering the brevity of his letter in response to her longer, more ambivalent one. He had said he felt very positive about the encounter, that she shouldn't get spooked. And his letter had arrived in the same mail with one from j, who had suggested that they must not expect too much. Orgasms are nice, he had written, but love can climax in so many other ways. Then, quite improbably, the purse in her closet had yielded up the keys lost earlier, and she had read that as a favorable omen.

The double assurance of sage and lover had put her conscience to bed long before she joined it. Authority can be liberative, too, a way to ease the burden of responsible decision, though she no longer required a guarantee of salvation, only the thin promise of a lifeline, a momentary freedom from the single night. She remembered a dry time, now far behind her, when carnal knowledge—and she had always valued knowledge—could be imagined only as rape, experience without responsibility. Her move towards liberation was out of step in a world of rising feminism, but she pardoned herself and resisted current forms of compromise.

She had even been afraid that they would find a necessary part missing or atrophied with disuse. That the ruptured disc in her spine would collapse in instant punishment or the ache in her arm subside into paralysis. It was learning to drive all over again: accidents and natural disasters, the imminence of catastrophe. She had checked off all the reasons that would make him turn away from her. The call she had made against her better judgment, his cold voice at the end of the line, her timing off in some unforgivable way. That had seemed like a DEW signal, and for a while she had considered returning his letters with no explanation. Instead, she had resumed the customary waiting. The next morning he had telephoned with a simple story about a visit from his son. She wanted to believe him, regretted her inconstant faith. And yet she could not help the scenes that came uncalled from some extended sex tour of the North American continent, a sacrilegious fantasy she had admitted, waiting for him to begin, in the first flush of their nakedness. And she had followed that confession with reassuring words, her reiterated promise to file no claims, her conviction that she was lucky to be included on the tour. He had said, "I doubt if there are that many stops left in the old boy."

She had been more cautious this time even though it was the need to forsake caution that impelled her. She must remain cool, one part of her detached, not overpowered by that stormy, irrational need that had first sent her to Dr. G three years earlier. Her choice of a younger, interested and interesting sex partner had gone well so long as they merely talked of pot and poems, and he had driven five hundred miles to tell her that the homage was appreciated but the execution was untimely. One month later he had returned to tell her how she had changed his life, directed him to the Scriptures. By summer's end he was on his way to South Dakota to be ordained assistant pastor in a Gay Liberation church.

Two weeks before j's visit, when she discovered athlete's foot, she had fallen into mild panic, had written a frantic letter to her R.N. friend begging for an instant cure. She had forgotten accusing herself to the notebook of this parasitic growth, had really written it down only because of the way it had sharpened her sense of aging. She hated the very words *athlete's foot,* the way she had once hated *masturbation.* The names betrayed some carelessness, promiscuity even, not unlike the specter of VD, less fearsome as *social disease,* a milder disorder from which she had always suffered. In the lopsided instruction received along the way, VD was a modern version of the Egyptian plagues. It stood for efficient retribution.

She had, at least, avoided the tempting indirection: *When the kids used to get a fungus infection. . . .* and had asked the pharmacist to suggest a nonprescription remedy for athlete's foot. There was, she remembered, a painful, though highly effective purple mixture for a footbath. He had laughed at her, said *that* treatment dated back twenty-five years; that today most doctors recommend Tinactin.

j had read the anecdote, leafing through. She waited for him to turn fastidious, to make excuses. Instead, after one of his trips to the bathroom, he had showed her his own prescribed tube of the patent remedy she had purchased. It made her think of the way Dr. G stretched out his hand to take her tear-soaked kleenex instead of passing the wastebasket. After that, she stopped asking j, "Is this my drink?" when he offered either of the bourbon glasses from the bedside table—on *his* side of the bed—between them and the one waiting empty.

She passed the crude sign advertising winter pears, the world still for her an unripe metaphor. What kind of mansion is it, thrown up like a tent? It could be a house of the zodiac, one reading that appeared believable. The superstitious mix of lust and ignorance, the crude, addictive reliance on unknown heavenly bodies. A pseudo-science or quasi-science, in which we read our fears and wishes before we act them out.

Teresa of Avila had written of the Interior Castle in a long tradition merging the sacred and the secular. Her own attempted poem had begun, "All the signs say *Merge.*" From that diamond-shaped opener it had hurtled rapidly into wrecks and rude investigations, and she had decided to give it up. Teresa's ecstasy, religious as it was, was human too, persuasive as the frying pan she gripped with both hands while levitating in the kitchen. Old as the Canticle of Canticles, this kind of synthesis enjoyed a current revival among writers who fused the mystical and the obscene in ways more convincing than the opposites she had been brought up on.

Agape, the love feast, the Eucharist, was the opposite of *Eros,* that dark and dangerous love. *Eros Turranos,* a poet had called it. An earthly and a tyrannical love, she presumed. Another bondage just when she was moving towards what looked like freedom. And *agápe* was nearly *agáve,* although the stresses were different: that once-in-a-lifetime flower, the slow rich opening that prefigures death. A difference of one letter, and she had almost overlooked the distinction.

j had arrived tired, and after the first awkward explorations had pulled away for a nap. In a few minutes, aided no doubt by the bourbon, he was snoring. The intimacy of that unromantic regular sound made her unaccountably tender. She let her hand graze his body, and the breathing altered, then resumed its former pattern. After a while she tried reading, but the light was too dim and she did not want to risk disturbing him. She rose, moved closer to the lamp, put on her glasses. The story could not engage her. As quietly as she could, she rummaged through her suitcase until she found the nightdress chosen with such care. More useless baggage. Yet she put it on, tried again to read and failed.

She was beginning to feel hungry. She had eaten nothing since breakfast at seven, afraid of missing a single instant of j's arrival. She peeled and ate the banana stashed away in her briefcase with the notebooks, a leftover from last night's contingency plan for meeting j's plane. The loaf of sourdough bread j had brought rested on the table. He had asked about buying wine for their unceremonious meal, but he had already overslept the hour when the liquor stores closed. It was uncivilized to prohibit the sale of wine in grocery stores, but in this region, one confronted these historic restrictions everywhere, the restaurants flashing neon invitations: *Licensed Premises.* Still hungry, she mourned the absence of the wine, waiting for him to awaken.

At last he came to, looked at his watch, yawned, asked about restaurants. They avoided the motel coffee shop, went finally to the Peacock, where she declined a drink, refused wine even, because they would share that tomorrow.

The Peacock, no gourmet's paradise by any standard, displayed a bird bleached common as the sea gull that should have been repainted. The best thing about the place was the general seediness of its patrons. She had looked about quickly, hoping not to identify a fellow-parishioner or a campus colleague, though it mattered less here than in the motel. The shrimp chow mein she ordered was an ungodly mixture, and j's pork was not on her low-fat diet. j served their plates family-style before an improvised grace. The Chinese waiter hovered.

Attentive in an undiscerning way, the waiter had forced them to express satisfaction with the entree they had scarcely touched. He accomplished this at the same time he managed to ignore the cups repeatedly waiting to be filled, and he pressed them to try exotic desserts—mandarin oranges and lichee fruit—that, when he brought them, were clearly straight from the can.

She looked cheerfully towards the next day's lunchtime. Bread and wine—maybe cheese—the simple, honest sharing. But they had found the liquor store closed—it was Election Day—the processed cheese tasted like plastic, and the bread was stale. They had gouged it from the loaf passed back and forth like a common roll, using their teeth because its age and general conformation, as well as the absence of cutlery, resisted more genteel handling.

No rest from words, specious reasons. And yet . . . if *agape* was linked to Penance, its whole reality confined to that single distinctive *p*, it had not always been so. For the primitive Christians, it had been a meal, a sharing, whatever threats of unworthiness had accumulated after. *Agave*, not Biblical but Latin, took its special character from the V. Virtue. Strength, the Romans called it. *Virility:* what it means to be a man in the general sense. Virginity could as readily be the interpolation, as some feminist theologians had been at pains to document.

That was what she had written Dr. G; that she felt she couldn't skip any of the stages of growth. She had borrowed words from him to build a wall against the guilty flood, the gates of Eden closed.

Claudel had made his hero, intent upon adultery, invoke the Virgin's aid in pursuit of a woman. She had thought that marvelously ironic at the time; had even pitied the blindness of that fictive fellow-Catholic. But the link between giver and gift, strengthened by well-oiled joints, had moved her towards a similar petition. She had found it necessary to remind herself that one does not pray for violation, and she had ended her letter to Dr. G with, "Hoping to stay on the highway until I hear from you."

The customs official had tiresomely insisted on the failure of her temporary driving permit to cover any driver except herself. That was why they had agreed on the most obvious motel. It equalized the risks. She drove badly under tension. His unfamiliarity with the car and the island might steer them both head-on into the law. They took their chances, taking turns.

He had been driving on the morning of the second day when they decided to tour the peninsula. She had told him exactly where to turn to get to Landsend—they would stay well away from the house—but just as they had passed it they ran directly into the landlady's husband returning from an unscheduled walk on the road. Wiser now, she had asked j to slow down, waved to Mr. Austin in an eager, obvious way behind the dark glasses. In any case, he would have recognized the car, and he had smiled in a faintly insolent fashion when she told him not to leave the garage lights on for her. After she had returned from j's departing plane she had been ready for Mrs. Austin's questions: "How long did you say you were in the convent? . . . How do you manage to adjust so well? . . . Why don't you come to town with Dad and me?" She heard the landlady's husband rev the motor as she tried to bring the conversation to a stop. "Well, *enniway*," the landlady said, moving into second gear, "every time you go out of here to go out you look like one of those—what's that New York place?—Powers! like one of those Powers models! The sisters at the hospital weren't like that *a-tall*, but I always knew they liked the men. They were always talking to them in the corridors."

And when the landlady had returned from town, she had brought flowers—chrysanthemums, golden and bronze, those sturdy fall flowers that survive the frost. In the cold basement room they had turned frowzy as acrylic wigs while the single tea rose j had bought her after she had learned enough control to let him in, opened wide, lingered like a blessing.

During those three hours of hanging on the flight bulletins she had noted that the only customs inspector she knew, the one from the ferry terminal, had been transferred to the airport. Between dodging him and evading the female professor en route to Mexico with her husband, some of the other anxieties had been dispersed.

She was nearer to the church now on this zigzag revisit to the scenes of the crime, this pilgrimage of veneration or atonement. Both words broke down in satisfying ways, rooted as they were in contradiction. She reviewed the stations: the airport vision, the motel shrine, the restroom abandoned, the mansion conjured out of deprivation. The good names were not right either.

In the church lot as she bypassed the scant room next to the Austin to park the car in the only remaining space—a tight fit between an old Dodge and an Alfa Romeo—she felt quite certain she would not see j again, would not be offered that alternative. It would be beautiful, she thought, to have a god you could count on for both wisdom and love. She was already making up the next letter to Dr. G as she stood with the latecomers in the vestibule for the last of Father Carringham's too literal exegesis of today's end-of-the-world extravaganza. When he had run out of rhetoric, she tried to slip quietly into the end of a pew, but the faithful women would not be budged from dead center, forced her to negotiate a tangle of legs and rosaries in embarrassing confusion. She settled, after much shuffling, beside a young man who surprised her by offering to share his missal. At the offertory collection, she resisted the impulse to substitute a five for her usual two-dollar bill. Then she joined the singing.

> Now thank we all our God
> With heart and hands and voices,
> Who wondrous things has done
> In whom his world rejoices. . . .
>
> * * *
>
> Preserve us in his grace
> And guide us when perplexed
> And free us from all ills
> In this world and the next.

A few minutes later, while a fortyish couple in her row hung back, she climbed over their feet, seeing them nailed to the pew by French-

Canadian guilt as she had been chained to the dark decades that told the cult of the Virgin. The flowers on the altar, looking slightly used—they must be left over from the potluck—veered towards the candles. In the narrow aisle, hands folded, she joined those other innocents, their faces lost in no expression, steadily propelled towards the new communion.

Madeleine's Dreads · *Alexis DeVeaux*

Madeleine's dreads
are fertile like the lips
of good friends
intoxicate quick
like an expensive brandy

Madeleine's dreads
are weaved on a loom
of balsam flowers
are planted roots/ exposed
a forest in a fog
unfathomable

are full/ of peppermint oil
olive oil or
vaseline
when everything else
just plain runs out

Madeleine's dreads
are extensions of shake
shake
shekeres
are hand dipped
in mythology & double
dutch tournaments

When Madeleine plays the calabash
she carries OPEC in her hair
she carries the PLO in her hair
she carries the Peoples Republic of Nicaragua
in her hair
on her shoulders

Madeleine's dreads
are full of uprisings in Haiti
and Mississippi
and Brooklyn.

from Natural Birth · *Toi Derricotte*

The following sections are from a booklength narrative poem, *Natural Birth,* which related my reactions to an unwanted pregnancy and the birth of my son in a home for unwed mothers.

When I arrived in Kalamazoo, with two months to go until the birth, there was no room in the maternity home. I was placed with a family who had generously offered their home until space was available.

> *With all the things working against it, things that could go wrong, things that must be perfectly timed—it seems amazing that even one child is conceived. . . .*
> —Dr. Roland Dean in conversation

II NOVEMBER

nun meets me at the station. first month with carol and dick waskowitz. set the table. clean the kitchen. vacuum. thank god she didn't ask me to take care of the children.

i dry dishes in the afternoon. watch her can apples from the backyard, put them in the cellar to save for winter.

*why is everything so quiet? why does the man come home
from school everyday at 3:30 and read the paper? why a
different casserole on the table every night and everyone
eats one portion and one portion only? why is there always
enough, but never too much . . .*

try to understand this quiet, busy woman. is she content? what are her reasons to can, to cook, to have three children and a pregnant girl in her house? try to be close, lie next to their quiet ticking bedroom, and hear no sound, night after night, except soft conversation. in the morning, before light, i hear the baby's first cry. i picture her in there with her bra unhooked and her heavy white breast like cream on the cheek of that baby.

inside i wonder what she thinks, feels, who she is. and every night it gets dark earlier, stays dark later. i don't want to wake up smiling at cereal. dark overshadows snow, and a fear comes into my cold heart: *i am alone.*

one afternoon, drying dishes, her cutting apples by the sink, i ask her about college. i picture her so easily in penny loafers, peck and peck collar, socks, and a plaid skirt on her skinny still unchilded body. here she is today with hips and breasts, a woman thirty who had taught school—she must have some thought about her life, some arguments and passions hidden in this kitchen.

finally, she tells me her favorite book is *the stranger.* we go and find it on the living room shelf. i wonder, though she never says, what she understands about being a stranger . . .

i meet her mother—all the same—they treat me all the same: human. i am accepted, never question who i am or why. never make me feel unwanted or afraid. but always human love and never passion, never clutching need, lopsided devouring want, never, not one minute, extending those boundaries to enclose me . . .

oh soul,

i feel

cold and unused to such space as breath and eternity around me . . .

so much room in silence . . .

how will *my* house ever run on silence, when in me there is such noise, such hatred for peeling apples, canning, and waking to feed baby, and alarm clocks in the soul, and in the skin of baby, in the rind of oranges, apples, peels in the garbage, and paper saved because it is cheaper to save and wrap and wash and use everything again. and clean, no screaming in that house, no tears, one helping at dinner, and no lovemaking noises like broken squeaky beds. where is that part i cannot touch no matter where or how i turn, that part that wants to cry: *SISTER,* and make us touch . . .

she is kind. though i never understand such kindness. cannot understand the inner heart of how and why she loves: *i am the stranger.*

somewhere in the back of my mind, they are either fools or the holy family, the way we all should be if we lived in a perfect world and didn't have to strive to be loved, but went about our quiet business, never raising our voices above the rest, never questioning if we are loved, or whether what we do is what we want to do, or worth it . . .

and if they are fools who don't have hearts or brains or chords in their necks to speak, then why have they asked for me? why am i in their house? why are they doing this?

i never dare to ask because it is too simple, too direct a question. i am afraid of their answer.

one night in my round black coat and leotards, i dress up warm against the constellations, go down the snowy block alone in time. i am only going to the drugstore, but for some reason, the way i feel, pregnantly beautiful walking into the bright fluorescent drugstore, it is the most vivid night in my mind in the whole darkening november . . .

IV MATERNITY

when they checked me in, i was thinking: *this is going to be a snap!* but at the same time, everything looked so different! this was another world, ordered and white. the night moving by on wheels.

suddenly the newness of the bed, the room, the quiet, the hospital gown they put me in, the sheets rolled up hard and starched and white and everything white except the clock on the wall in red and black and the nurse's back as she moved out of the room without explanation, everything conspired to make me feel afraid.

how long, how much will i suffer?

the night looked in from bottomless windows.

VI TRANSITION

the meat rolls up and moans on the damp table.
my body is a piece of cotton over another woman's body.
some other woman, all muscle and nerve, is tearing apart
and opening under me.

i move with her like skin, not able to do anything else,
i am just watching her, not able to believe what her
body can do, what it *will* do, to get this thing accomplished.

this muscle of a lady, this crazy ocean in my teacup.
she moves the pillars of the sky. i am stretched into
fragments, tissue paper thin, a nazi lampshade. the blood-
thick light shines through to her goatness, her muscle-thick
heart that thuds like one drum in the universe empty
of stars.

she is
stuffed
inside
me
like sausage
like wide sky
black
night bird
pecking
at the bloody
ligament

trying
to get
in, get
out
i am

holding out with
everything i
have
holding out
the evil thing

when i see there is
no answer
to the screamed
word
GOD
nothing i can do,
no use,

i have to let her in,
open the door,
put down the mat
as if she
might be the
called-for death,
the final
abstraction.

she comes
like a tunnel
fast
coming into
blackness
with my headlights
off

you can push . . .

i hung here. still hurting, not knowing what to do.   if you push too early, it hurts more. i called the doctor back again. *are you sure i can push? are you sure?*

i couldn't believe that pain was over, that the punishment was enough, that the wave, the huge blue mind i was living inside, was receding. i had forgotten there ever was a life without pain, a moment when pain wasn't absolute as air.

why weren't the nurses and doctors rushing toward me? why weren't they wrapping me in white? white for respect, white for triumph, white for the white light i was being accepted into after death. why was it so simple as saying you can push? why were they walking away from me into other rooms as if this were not the end the beginning of something which the world should watch?

i felt something pulling me inside, a soft call, but i could feel her power. something inside me i could go with, wide and deep and wonderful. the more i gave to her, the more she answered me. i held this conversation in myself like a love that never stops. i pushed toward her, she came toward me, gently, softly, sucking like a wave. i pushed deeper and she swelled wider, darker when she saw i wasn't afraid. then i saw the darker glory of her under me.

why wasn't the room bursting with lilies? why was everything the same with them moving so slowly as if they were drugged? why were they acting the same when, suddenly, everything had changed?

we were through with pain, would never suffer in our lives again. put pain down like a rag, unzipper skin, step out of our dead bodies, and leave them on the floor. glorious spirits were rising, blanched with light, like thirsty women shining with their thirst.

i felt myself rise up with all the dead, climb out of the tomb like christ, holy and wise, transfigured with the knowledge of the tomb inside my brain, holding the gold key to the dark stamped inside my genes, never to be forgotten . . .

it was time. it was really time. this baby would be born. it would really happen. this wasn't just a trick to leave me in hell forever. like all the other babies, babies of women lined up in rooms along the halls, semiconscious, moaning, breathing, alone with or without husbands, there was a natural end to it that i was going to live to see! soon i would believe in something larger than pain, a purpose and an end. i had lived through to another mind, a total revolution of the stars, and had come out on the other side!

one can only imagine the shifting of the universe, the layers of shale and rock and sky torturing against each other, the tension, the sudden letting go. the pivot of one woman stuck in the socket, flesh and bones giving way, the v-groin locked, vise thigh, and the sudden release when everything comes to rest on new pillars.

Formal Garden Series · *Shirley Eliason*

Note: Motableautin—*combining the French* mot *and* tableautin *(small painting)—is an invention of mine to identify certain of my visual works, singly or in a series, which include a text. The text may appear directly within the image, on the same surface as the image, or separately as an accompanying text. Works reproduced here are of the latter kind.* —S.E.

Motableautin II

In general, it was a pretty fine day although on the way back to Limoges we witnessed a fatal car accident.

Acrylic on paper.   1979

Motableautin III

Later we made inquiries and no one could explain
it. One individual did remark that he had never
heard of such a thing.

Watercolor.   1979

Motableautin IV

Apparently many visitors noted it and some even
thought it may have belonged to the stranger's
child. The approaching storm was violent. For
days the child grieved.

Watercolor.   1979

The Sleeping · *Lynn Emanuel*

I have imagined all this:
in 1940 my parents were in love
and living in the loft on West 10th
above Mark Rothko who painted cabbage roses
on their bedroom walls the night they got married.

I can guess why he did it.
My mother's hair was the color of yellow apples
and she wore a black velvet hat with her pajamas.

I was not born yet. I was remote as starlight.
It is hard for me to imagine that
my parents made love in a roomful of roses
and I wasn't there.

But now I am. My mother is blushing.
This is the wonderful thing about art.
It can bring back the dead. It can wake the sleeping
as it might have late that night
when my father and mother made love above Rothko
who lay in the dark thinking *Roses, Roses, Roses.*

Silence. She Is Six Years Old ·
Lynn Emanuel

She sleeps on a cot in the living room.
This is her father's mother's house.
And in the kitchen the men run their knife blades
across the oilcloth with roses on the table
and grandmother cooks them steak and eggs.
She is pretending to be asleep but she is listening
to the men talking about their friends
and grandmother in her white dress
walks back and forth past the door
and a hand reaches for salt and water.
Her father talks about divorce.
Now it is quiet.
Grandmother has left, her tight stockings
showed rainbows
and someone's upstairs undressing,
his dog tags making faint noise.
Her father walks into the room.
He is naked and there are certain
parts of him that are shadows.
And he pulls the blankets to the floor
and then the sheet — as if not to wake her —
and he lifts her up and whispers his wife's name —
Rachel, Rachel
and he takes her hand, small with its clean nails,
and he puts it to the dark:
Oh Rae, Oh Rachel he says
and over his shoulder she can see
the long hall mirror framed in black wood
and she smells lavender in her father's hair
when he gets up, first onto his hands
and knees like someone playing horse,
and puts her on the chair
and she sits and rocks like a deaf woman.

In My Father's Cabin · *Kathy Engel*

Today we walked into the forest
to a place where the pines have parted
in a circle to let the light in,
where under thick green moss
is damp mulch, the sweet home.
It was so soft and moist underfoot,
you'd think anything could grow,
you'd think there was only growing
and warm. The knobs on the maples,
like chestnuts, those extra toes
on horses' legs, grow in the dark
the way things always grow and die
in the dark and you miss them.
That's why tonight I'll sit here
while everyone sleeps, and look out
at the cuts and dives on Camel's Hump
and listen to Turk's curving bark
at the foot of the hill, so nothing
no one will leave while I'm asleep.

Tonight Northern Lights streak
across a dark sky and my father
walks out of this cabin he built,
anytime, to pee anywhere he chooses,
the tap of Vermont air waking him,
waking him. Up here,
between woods and meadow,
the wind turns you like age.

Up here,
my father doesn't care what time it is,
snowshoeing up the hill in winter,
pulling his food on a sled,
or at the table writing on a yellow lined pad
the film he has always wanted to write.

Soon it will be morning
and my father will be standing at the door
asking, "Anyone feel like a little breakfast?"
and the coffee will be going
and I remember
all the mornings as a child
when I walked in my socks
straight to the telephone before breakfast
before anything
to place a collect call
just to hear his voice —
"Kath, how are you Kath?" —
just to hear the pause.

And I remember
how sometimes the only safe place
was on his shoulders, above any home.
And nights I couldn't sleep,
so tired from walking the bridge
back and forth in the dark
from mother to father.

This night
I choose to stay awake
while shadows of the old trees
are taken up as young ones get tall,
and the blight nearly over,
maple leaves point everywhere,
flushed, about to flame out.
This night
there is no bridge — footless, obsolete.
The walls have not shot up.

This late September night in my 22nd year
my father and his wife lie sleeping in the other room,
my love sleeps here on the floor in his sleeping bag
and I see again
soon it will be light out.

Letter to Sandra McPherson ·
Abbie Huston Evans

400 N. Walnut Street
West Chester, Pa. 19380

March 18, 1972

Dear Sandra McPherson,

        I appreciate deeply your letter of February 26th which has just now been forwarded by the University of Pittsburgh Press.

It is no exaggeration to say it has really warmed the cockles of my heart to find I've been able to communicate to you a little of the unfailing excitement I've always felt over *being alive in this incredible universe.* As I've often exclaimed to my younger brother, *"I'm glad I didn't miss it!"*

If your Young Poets' Anthology should ever develop and you should still want me included, I'd be glad. (After all, the final test of poetry is *"Does it wear?"*)

Sincerely yours,

Abbie Huston Evans

P.S.
You know perhaps that I'm 90??

Poem for Maya · *Carolyn Forché*

Dipping our bread in oil tins
we talked of morning peeling
open our rooms to a moment
of almonds, olives and wind
when we did not yet know what we were.
The days in Mallorca were alike:
footprints down goat-paths
from the beds we had left,
at night the stars locked to darkness.
At that time we were learning
to dance, take our clothes
in our fingers and open
ourselves to their hands.
The *veranera* was with us.
For a month the almond trees bloomed,
their droppings the delicate silks
we removed when each time a touch
took us closer to the window where
we whispered *yes,* there on the intricate
balconies of breath, overlooking
the rest of our lives.

Expatriate · *Carolyn Forché*

American life, you said, is not possible.
Winter in Syracuse, Trotsky pinned
to your kitchen wall, windows facing
a street, boxes of imported cigarettes.
In The Realm Of The Senses, you said,
and piles of shit burning and the risk
of having your throat slit. Twenty-year-old poet.
To be in love with some woman who cannot speak
English, to have her soften your back with oil
and beat on your mattress with grief and pleasure
as you take her from behind, moving beneath you
like the beginning of the world.
The black smell of death as blood and glass
is hosed from the street and the beggar holds
his diminishing hand to your face.
It would be good if you could wind up
in prison and so write your prison poems.
Good if you could marry the veiled face
and jewelled belly of a girl who could
cook Turkish meat, baste your body
with a wet and worshipful tongue.
Istanbul, you said, or *Serbia,* mauve
light and mystery and passing for other
than American, a *Kalishnikov* over
your shoulder, spraying your politics
into the flesh of an enemy become real.
You have been in Turkey a year now.
What have you found? Your letters
describe the boring ritual of tea,
the pittance you are paid to teach
English, the bribery required for so much
as a postage stamp. Twenty-year-old poet,
Hikmet did not choose to be Hikmet.

Endurance · *Carolyn Forché*

In Belgrade, the windows of the tourist
hotel opened over seven storeys of lilacs,
rain clearing sidewalk tables of linens
and liquor, the silk flags of the non-
aligned nations like colorful underthings
pinned to the wind. Tito was living.
I bought English, was mistaken for Czech,
walked to the fountains, the market
of garlic and tents, where I saw
my dead Anna again and again,
hard yellow beans in her lap,
her babushka of white summer cotton,
her eyes the hard pits of her past.
She was gossiping among her friends,
saying the rosary or trying to sell me
something. Anna. Peeling her hands
with a paring knife, saying *in your country*
you have nothing. Each word was the tusk
of a vegetable tossed to the street
or a mountain rounded by trains
with cargoes of sheep-dung and grief.
I searched in Belgrade for some holy
face painted *without hands* as when
an ikon painter goes to sleep and awakens
with an image come from the dead.
On each corner Anna dropped
her work in her lap and looked up.
I am a childless poet, I said.
I have not painted an egg, made prayers
or finished my Easter duty in years.
I left Belgrade for Frankfurt last
summer, Frankfurt for New York,
New York for the Roanoke valley

where mountains hold the breath
of the dead between them and to each
morning a fresh bandage of mist.
New York, Roanoke, the valley —
to this Cape where in the dunes
the wind takes a body of its own
and a fir tree comes to the window
at night, tapping on the glass like
a woman who has lived too much.
Piskata, hold your tongue, she says.
I am trying to tell you something.

Because One Is Always
Forgotten · *Carolyn Forché*

When Viera was buried we knew it had come to an end,
his coffin rocking into the ground like a boat or a cradle.

I could take my heart, he said, and give it to a *campesino*
and he would cut it up and give it back:

you can't eat heart in those four dark
chambers where a man can be kept years.

A boy soldier in the bone-hot sun works his knife
to peel the face from a dead man

and hang it from the branch of a tree
flowering with such faces.

The heart is the toughest part of the body.
Tenderness is in the hands.

in memoriam, José Rudolfo Viera, 1939-1981, El Salvador

Message · *Carolyn Forché*

Your voices sprayed over the walls
dry to the touch by morning.
Your women walk among *champas*
with baskets of live hens, grenades and fruit.
Tonight you begin to fight
for the most hopeless of revolutions.
Pedro, you place a host on each
man's chant of *Body of Christ Amen.*
Margarita, you slip from your house
with plastiques wrapped in newsprint,
eyes broken into blindfolds,
the dossier of your dearest friend
whose hair grew to the floor of her cell.
Leonel, you load your bare few guns
with an idea for a water pump and
co-operative farm.
     You will fight
and fighting, you will die. I will live
and living cry out until my voice is gone
to its hollow of earth, where with our
hands and by the lives we have chosen,
we will dig deep into our deaths.
I have done all that I could do.
Link hands, link arms with me
in the next of lives everafter,
where we will not know each other
or ourselves, where we will be a various
darkness among ideas that amounted
to nothing, among men who amounted
to nothing, with a belief that became
but small light
in the breadth of time where we began
among each other, where we lived
in the hour farthest from God.
       1980-1981

Selective Service · *Carolyn Forché*

We rise from the snow where we've
lain on our backs and flown like children,
from the imprint of perfect wings and cold gowns,
and we stagger together, wine-breathed into town
where our people are building
their armies again, short years after
body bags, after burnings. There is a man
I've come to love after thirty, and we have
our rituals of coffee, of airports, regret.
After love we smoke and sleep
with magazines, two shot glasses
and the black and white collapse of hours.
In what time do we live that it is too late
to have children? In what place
that we consider the various ways to leave?
There is no list long enough
for a selective service card shrivelling
under a match, the prison that comes of it,
a flag in the wind eaten from its pole
and boys sent back in trash bags.
We'll tell you. You were at that time
learning fractions. We'll tell you
about fractions. Half of us are dead or quiet
or lost. Let them speak for themselves.
We lie down in the fields and leave behind
the corpses of angels.

Energy Unavailable for Useful Work in a System Undergoing Change · *Kathleen Fraser*

from *Leda. & Swan.*, a work-in-progress

SHE PUSHES a silver pin into the fourth corner of the ink-on-paper drawing. The fourth corner has been unanchored for days.

She has noticed it again, as she sits down and becomes calm, in focus. She has noticed the loose corner of the drawing before and has instructed herself to go get another pin.

Pin it down.

But as soon as she leaves this room, there is the back porch with its large old windows to look out of towards the valley, the bridge, Mt. Diablo's pale Oriental cone on a clear.day. Or she opens the door into the kitchen where, noticing the bowl of fruit, she forgets the loose corner.

She savors the sugar-mottled surface of the tangerine, its bright rind nuzzling against the navel orange, paler and thin-skinned but true to its umbilical folds. Its entrance to the body's thousand liquid parachutes.

The bananas have disappeared. There were four. David ate two in a row, breaking them from the bunch the instant after she had arranged their curving tubular forms at an angle to the brown Bosc pear. Winter Nellis pears. Anjou.

* * *

Once, she brought four kinds of plums to her friend's house as a contribution to the dinner. She found a small space in the conversation in which to say: *Damson, Greengage, Sugarplums, Kelsey.*

* * *

I dropped the words into the air, heavy and dark. I arranged the names so that her friends could taste the suggestion of more than those round green and purple fruits. She wanted that particular season on their tongues, a certain history of soil and gardeners carrying roots wrapped in cotton handkerchiefs from Genoa and Malaga. (I am inventing this part; what I wanted, then, was a kind of instant pleasure of distinctions tasted only in language.)

This is a demonstration of how I lose sight of the fourth corner, which I had initially pinned in place when displaying Karl's dense and troubled drawing in the bathroom, above the light switch and next to the Creeley poem:

> *There is a world*
> *underneath, or*
> *on top of*
> *this one—and*
> *it's here now.*

It was the first poem David ever responded to with excitement. I won't forget how he came out of the bathroom one afternoon, when he was nine. His eyes were shining when he told me. Someone had said it. This thing he knew and had been carrying alone, inside himself, at night, in his room.

***

When she notices the fourth pin missing and the feeling, again, of something unfinished, she also catches a faint odor of expensive cigar smoke lingering. It belongs to Karl who has arrived earlier, with long-stemmed Japanese iris, he whom she can now name, who has the attractive quality of attending to loose corners at the time he notices them. She is more than often preoccupied with the interior, so she borrows his eyes in this peculiar way. She thinks of how he would pin down this loose corner, soon after seeing it. Then she goes to find a pin, unless there is something out the window which distracts her—tonight's almost full moon with its unusually deep, bisque-bright aureole.

***

She is unfinished. She is structurally out-of-breath. When she comes close to something achieved, she enters a low and constant warning buzz. On Sunday, in the middle of her exercises, she begins to cry quite unexpectedly. The fourth corner loose, unanchored, unattended. She can't seem to stop.

***

The dream begins this way:
He is sitting with this younger, dark-haired, smart-mouthed woman who, when I come up to them, is utterly indifferent to me and will not acknowledge me with any eye-contact. David and I have been in the concert hall where Karl has brought us, listening faithfully to a complicated and somewhat chaotic concert of "new music." The concert takes place in a large tent, filled with people. Karl has grown restless and has disappeared. When the performance is over, we go to look for him and find him laughing and talking with the other woman. They are sitting on metal fold-up chairs, completely apart from any of the other people in the audience. It is cold. I notice that he has done exactly what he wants, while I have remained where he brought me. I slide up to him playfully, as if to third base after making a hit. "You are sitting with someone beautiful," I say in a playful mood of acknowledgement. He is neutral. She avoids me.

Dark purple iris, long green curving leaves and stem. Tangerine.

Then, a cruelty. He is calling her on the phone, with me standing right there. He is being his most charming, flirtatious self. He is saying, "I was really knocked-out, just now, by everything you've been telling me. How about letting me knock *you* out with *my* irristible version of life."

* * *

This text is using the pronoun "I." This text often makes the "I" central.

("Too personal," "too self-referential" . . . the pig critic grunts and roots.)

* * *

She wakes up in historic time. Low-grade hysteria. Abandoned feelings from the dream, as real as if this had really been happening just now — *"There is a world / underneath,* or */ on top of"* . . . she likes the way the comma makes a pause before the lurch of *or.*

And it's here now.

* * *

She lies awake but feels unable to move. The passion of their early morning love has been washed from her by the dream's refusal to leave. Its teeth still graze her neck. He comes back into bed. He holds her. With intention. He holds her head, her face. He kisses her face. He looks. He gazes her to him. She tries to re-learn his face with her numb fingers. She tries to leave the blindness. He kisses her face again and again with a pause after each tenderness. She hears his love coming in, though he doesn't say a word.

* * *

I am mute and he covers me with his gaze. He pulls me into belief. He pours me into myself. I remember. I begin to remember what it is like, who he is for me now. He is not the person in the dream. Yet he is, in some way that grazes my dream, in which I split myself into two selves who do not know if it is safe to acknowledge each other's existence. Difficult music. Seeing it through to the end. These two women threaten each other. He likes them both.

* * *

After months of starting and stopping, not liking what I write, not finishing, I have, meanwhile, been building the difficult structure of belief, of trust.

* * *

Entropy: energy unavailable for useful work in a system undergoing change.

* * *

A thought arrives to derail her. *Water the plants.* A distraction to inhibit this dread, this struggle to claim oneself by inventing it out of thin air, in each push against gravity. The pull of the given. Abandoning herself forever, to it. Turning her back. Shutting the door on the known.

* * *

He has given her a new pen. The point is fine. It makes a line that gives her pleasure. It invites her writing, she thinks, as if in some way there were a bird harnessed to it. Taking off. A *swan*, she thinks. She has harbored in her mind a duckling who honks awkwardly and swims in circles, who forgets the long stretch of the imagined neck, the rising into air, leaving the earth's insistence. The pull down pulls. It doesn't want her feathery ascension. Oh Mother, oh Father, do not do me in.

* * *

The unwillingness to take one's own most. To work for it. To work is to push against the mud, to push against inertia. Fear of not staying aloft. Falling. Falling. Fear of maintaining altitude, of not maintaining altitude. The will, to go up.

Catching the up-draft—the way gulls do, out at the beach, a pure attention to air currents as they glide by at a tilt.

* * *

Inertia, ennui, losing momentum, lights dimming, broken generator. Letting someone erase you. Not wanting you there. Saying the sky is private property. Ours.

Ours = not yours.

But generating for another? One good way to accelerate the imagination. Because another takes notice, has an eye which delights in the insect's shining carapace. Worries about a spot of spilled chocolate. Pulls the table's unsteady supports into place. Facing him, has she lost her place?

He finds it. A divining rod at the whiff of water, just underground.

* * *

"I don't know why I'm crying. I can't seem to stop. There's nothing wrong I can think of."
"Maybe it's because you're so happy."
"Isn't that ridiculous?"

* * *

She has put her trust in him. Put her trust.

She reads Fannie Farmer with a certain vividness:

About Plums: Height of Season: July and August. What to look for.
Plump fruit with good color, slightly soft but with smooth, unshriveled
skins—purple, red, blue, yellow, green—and may be round or oval in
shape. *About Persimmons:* Availability: October through December.
What to look for. Deep orange or red color with green cap intact and no
signs of damage.

Saying those sentences aloud gives pleasure. She locates something found
in the world's structure.

* * *

Back at her place, she notices a tear in the lining of the lamp. She wonders if it has always been there. She notices a large piece of cracked paint
peeling back from the perfect Desert White of the ceiling. The light fix-
tures are naked, dusty Sylvania bulbs bulging asymmetrically for years
from their sockets. Exposed. One could spend a life fixing, arranging,
mending, covering, improving, touching-up. She'd rather touch. Yet
there did remain this yearning for completion, symmetry, a formal ascen-
dancy to the next level. Her attempts were full of falterings and lurchings
They were insufficient, awkward, premature, repetitive. They were
loose threads, a button missing. A pin falls. The drawing is unanchored.

* * *

Trying to become perfect, a way of pulling against this displacement.

She has chosen this distinction to hover over, to use as a certain axis for
mobility. Wing flutter. Warming up. Finding her wingspan. Wanting the other's witness. *See me!* This insatiable woman, this hooded
young girl. She needs this, oh she needs. And not just anyone's.

* * *

Not to lean. *Do not lean.* Not to ask for a little prize. A little Hershey's
kiss, with a message for you tucked inside the foil wrap. She is breaking
the code. She is a system undergoing change.

* * *

There are mirrors. They are mirrors. She is not enough, alone, in that silvery image returning herself to itself. She wants to push off, to transcend what she knows. The lover's invitation is her sinew. So, now:

A little essay in the middle, or a little more traveling circuitously to locate a thought's progress, as she's begun to track it down.

When, for years, she had to push hard against adversity, when outside the tent she had to stand in the presence of his life with others' crossed legs, dark hair, folding metal, face turned away, then she knew herself daily in each wish and motion. Adrenalin packed itself into every cell and sent her information. On the alert, productive, she learned not to gag on the truth, which gave her substance. And form. She felt new strength in each bit of flesh grown wily with feathers. Her power was in eiderdown. her power was in a sudden rush from the mud, into bright air hovering. A shaking-out of golden light. A phoenix in her with a different sort of song. A reclassification of duck into swan. Sunday into Monday. Dross into slippers that fit. Her desire was on a grand scale and she empowered it as vision. Slowly, belief. Then a seizure of voice. Asking for, saying *this*. This is what I want. And it's here, now.

Now, he one day wanted. Now, she did have. Now he had suggested a life. She'd heard it dimly at first through the glass pane she'd nailed across her brow. Now had stretched into a year. It was here. Is near. And holds her inside his belief in her, holds tightly and won't let go. She knows this. She says: *It is so. It is. So.*

* * *

To lift off, to remain in her strength in the air. Gets circling but gets lost but loves this Sunday papers/French Roast; this Fred Astaire/Art Tatum lemon-in-the-dressing; this fifth-floor, high-windowed view of waving flags above rooftops of grand hotels; this tasting of the white wine and the red; this making the bed from both sides, loving in the middle on both sides, this burnished black and burnt orange. Pomegranate. Tangerine.

We talk of what we think and what we see. With him I see more. I sniff and I listen. Then I tell him what I understand. My sentences begin to gain confidence. I am storing up belief. It has been a lifetime, waiting for now. *There is a world / underneath, or / on top of / this one — and / it's here.* How to be in it? Absolutely. Without penury of soul. To give but not to lose, that self who risked everything and felt the swan's neck stretching in her own.

* * *

She had been writing a poem in her dream. It was exactly the one she'd been waiting for. It showed her how her writing wanted to go. She was saying the lines over and over so as not to forget them on waking. But she could only hold onto the last line which said: "All I wanted was to feed the white swans."

* * *

The dream:
All I wanted was to feed the white swans. They did not glide on water but traveled in packs on flat dirt beneath trees which were green, large of leaf and effulgent. We were walking near them. The white pebbles were their food and lay glistening on raised wooden trays. Rick beckoned to me and approached the swans; he understood their food, how it should be scattered, and his clothes were soft and dark from living in the woods. His hand beckoned, he was my guide, there was a gravity in his walk, a separateness. The swans moved in large formations which shifted. Their wings did not shine but were slightly dusty. They grouped and scattered, grouped and scattered, keeping a gliding pattern. I wanted to feed them their white food. I wasn't afraid. I was moving towards the shining pebbles and I was concentrated in my task.

* * *

"What do you make of the white stones?" I asked my friend Daidie. She said that white stones were magic objects, to be held in high regard. She said in many ancient stories this sort of pebble was an object of power, the sustaining food of the soul. "Manna from heaven," Karl had suggested. I remembered, then, the dish of shiny white buttons in another dream, earlier in the summer. I remembered my blindness in this dream, how I had tried to explain to someone from a past life that I'd changed, that I was no longer the person he'd known. "I am not who you think I am. There is nothing to eat but a dish of white buttons."

* * *

Now the swan food arrives on its wooden trays. The words unloose in me. The earth is tipping into dawn after twelve hours of darkness. I want to be in the company of swans, catching my own currents. My dream has provided the peculiar glistening food. My mouth waters. Something outside is pulling.

Each Bird Walking · *Tess Gallagher*

Not while, but long after he had told me,
I thought of him, washing his mother, his
bending over the bed and taking back
the covers. There was a basin of water
and he dipped a washrag in and
out of the basin, the rag
dripping a little onto the sheet as he
turned from the bedside to the nightstand
and back, there being no place

on her body he shouldn't touch because
he had to and she helped him, moving
the little she could, lifting so he could
wipe under her arms, a dipping motion
in the hollow. Then working up from
the feet, around the ankles, over the
knees. And this last, opening
her thighs and running the rag firmly
and with the cleaning thought
up through her crotch, between the lips,
over the V of thin hairs—

as though he were a mother
who had the excuse of cleaning to touch
with love and indifference,
the secret parts of her child, to graze
the sleepy sexlessness in its waiting
to find out what to do for the sake
of the body, for the sake of what only
the body can do for itself.

So his hand, softly at the place
of his birth-light. And she, eyes deepened
and closed in the dim room.
And because he told me her death as
important to his being with her,
I could love him another way. Not
of the body alone, or of its making,
but carried in the white spires of trembling
until what spirit, what breath we were
was shaken from us. Small then,
the word *holy.*

He turned her on her stomach
and washed the blades of her shoulders, the
small of the back. "That's good," she said,
"that's enough."

On our lips that morning, the tart juice
of the mothers, so strong in remembrance, no
asking, no giving, and what you said, this
being the end of our loving, so as not to hurt
the closer one to you, made me look to see
what was left of us with our sex
taken away. "Tell me," I said,
"something I can't forget." Then the story
of your mother, and when you finished
I said, "That's good, that's enough."

Internal Geography — Part One ·
Joan Gibbs

This then
    be for real:
    a blank sheet of white paper
    the world,
    filling up with black dots,
    words,
    that stay put,
    come back to haunt
    and never change.

How does one talk about change?
like going from day to night
you notice the difference
but not the second
the blueness replaced
by a growing darkness —
in summer the blue stays longer
and the darkness is cooler.

How does one feel change?
the sensation of swimming
on shore
watching turtles
as a child
I am afraid of water
but
the turtles' backs
glistened in the sunshine.

sex bores me
like showers
you know the results
in advance
and I like
long hot baths
gentle hugs
and stolen kisses.

How does one know about change?
like feeling pain
it needs to be identified
the cure is in recognition.

yesterday my sister died
in a dream 4 years later
the memory frightens me still—
in cars
I sometimes travel to the graveyard
tears on the way to a friend's house.
In my mind
the day going further away
returns.

How does one talk about change?

This morning
I did my laundry
the clothes smell sweeter
and the dirt
disappeared
in the water.

The Love Sequence · *Sandra M. Gilbert*

You Fall

You were the proud one, the kid in the secret room
lit by organdy curtains white as milk,
the one who had a special destiny
inscribed on her forehead with invisible ink.

April evenings sparrows lined up on your fire escape
to tell you their tales of old verandahs,
palm trees, Florida afternoons:
you were going to walk on warm sands, marry

the master of the plantation, command
the fountain that gushed cream.
Love would rain on you like geranium balm, love
would fortify your heart against everyone

except the one who was just, the one who loved you
more than his own bones, the one
whose beard shone in the wind
like the wild grass behind the schoolyard.

What happened? Who took you to the door of the grimy
oven? Who walked you into the cooking pot? Who
introduced you to the vizier of silence with his
wand of ice, his cape of dead leaves?

You knew he'd enlisted under the blank banner, knew
he was missing crucial fingers, knew
he was the agent for somebody else.
But it didn't matter, you stayed put,

you baked in the cave of change,
your hair dampened, your
secret organs hummed with love.
When you came out,

he turned toward you, his pale gaze fell on you
like the headlights of a dark car
rounding a bend in an empty road at midnight.

He told you how little you mattered.

Behind him you heard the sea
falling and falling onto terrible rocks.

You were sticky and thick with love
like the broken windowpane the witch painted over with sugar.

You Meet the Real Dream Mother-in-Law

In the anteroom of silence you waited to meet
the dream mother-in-law,
fingering old magazines, their exhausted edges, the places
where recipes were torn away. . . .

You sat straight as a washboard in your
naugahyde chair, holding your breath,
never complaining: you knew
she was in there and how it would be —

the long still room with blood-colored rugs,
the tables on eighteenth-century stilts, the hair
Atlantic gray, the bone china cups
with blue frost, the silver-tipped cane, the misty

voice of Ethel Barrymore, saying
I've waited so long, *he's* waited so long,
but how glad we are, my dear,
that you're the one!

And then the talk would unfold like fine lace,
the talk of women who'd take a lifetime
to trace this intricate design.
Silk the color of tea leaves, fingers keen as crystal,

she'd love your sonnets, give you
sherry that had slept in the cabinet
since her impudent sister ran off with that
bad metaphysician: she'd

want you to have her grandmother's sapphire,
tell you legends of somber attics,
clasp your hand between ivory gloves
and make you hers, hers. . . .

When they opened the double doors and led you in,
you were surprised to find a naked waitress
sulking on a shell-shaped sofa.

Her son winked and blew poison darts at you
like the bad kid next door, the one
who was always stoned on something rotten.

She accused you of doing awful things in the dark,
told you to hurry up and start sorting grain, said
you should remember there was a mountain you'd have to climb.

You stared like a fool at her granite breasts, her great
snowy belly, her whole
ferocious body.

       Smoke
curled from between her thighs
like the terrible breath of factories.

You Discover You're in Love with the Dead Prince

You thought, He must be pale, he must be silent,
he must sit by the river all morning gazing at nothing.
And when he sat on the bank, his eyes focused on nothing,
you thought, It's me he sees in the middle distance,
he's watching my dance, he's in love
with the dance of my invisible bones.

For him you turned your skin to cream.
He'll lick it away, you thought, he'll sip my body
like a spirit potion, and come to the secret
place of my heart—for he's the one
who loves my eyelids, he's the one
who bathes his wrist in the cold stream
because he dreams of the blue vein behind my ankle.

And all the time he was dead, he was the boy king
in the coffin of ice, the one with the mirror splinter
caught in his left eye, the royal child
attended by women and mourners,
whose long trance was demanded, they said, by mystic
signs from the stars.

        In his dead cellar,
among the jewels and mirrors,
the sacred nurses feed him cream through tubes,
they bathe his silence in sweet wine.
All night a fire of thorny twigs
flickers cold, cold. . . .

You looked into the pale flames. You watched
the ceremonies of shadow. You wept.
You said you couldn't believe it.
You said, O prince, O friend, O lover,
climb out of that snowdrift
and come to this meadow where the blackberries ripen
and the bees hum like summer.

And he smiled in his trance, and said,
What snowdrift? What meadow? What summer?

The One He Loves

She's the figure skater you've always hated,
the princess of the spelling bee, the ice queen
in velvet and fur
with muscles tough as tusks
and hair the color of charm bracelets.

Next to her you're flabby and noisy, something
made of jelly instead of sinew,
something that shivers and whimpers
and passes out in the dark, a princess of pain
with weak ankles and a head full of misspelled sentences.

Once you asked her the secret: how do you
always keep your skates on, how do you memorize
the whole dictionary? She smiled and talked too slowly,
a native telling a foreigner
the way through an inexplicable city.

In the palace of his mind
they reign forever on twin frost thrones.
Suave servants in black and white
circle them like gulls, offering trays
on which odd canapes swarm thick as wishes.

She nibbles, royal, muscular, silent.
He watches, a furtive cat on the edge of shadow:
he wants her to burn his skin, wants her
to crack his bones, wants the fine spray from her skates
to baptize his wrists like radioactive sleet.

Around them expensive dancers loop and spin.
She and he yawn, hum, play chess, play Scrabble.
A cold flame flickers between them
on polished granite: only they
know what it means, only they

know there's never the slightest need
to touch or talk or spell things out for strangers.

The Love Sickness

You lie on the sofa all day, washed in fog,
your heart twittering like a thrush among prickly branches.
You think you're that last black tree before the beach, the one
that trembles so close to the cliff edge it seems to have
one toe in the abyss.

Your toes are dissolving like that, your whole body
melting and thinning, becoming transparent, becoming
the room, the sofa, the fog, the twittering inside.

It's the love sickness! It's the damned old nausea
of desire, the ague that shakes the last right angle
of reason from your bones
and turns the world to terrible
metaphors for passion.

You peer through the fog like a nearsighted hiker
on a stony seaside path.
Your toes and knees are gone, the rest of you
dissolving fast:· soon you'll be nothing
but the buzz of love, the ache, the fever.

And now, out there, where a window once was,
you think you see the face of the one you love!
It shines toward you like a tiny moon
on a misty night, or a lucky penny,
or a pale expensive sugar candy.

The Cure

I

Hate is the cure. Dislike. Contempt. Rage. Hate.
You go to see the lover, the kind physician, you say
I'm sick of love.
          He says
you're a fool, a nuisance, a joke.

You swoon with desire, you beg him to stroke your forehead
with his chill fingers, you offer him your knuckles, your wrists,
your ankles, and all your fingernails.

He declines.
Polite but cold. Explains he's allergic to your skin.
Implies you have a noxious odor.

His icy instruments flash, the chains he fastens to your ribs
are colder than the waters of Lapland, they're made of black iron
dug from the trenches of death.

But even as you cringe from them,
you smile, you toss your curls like a cheerleader in Houston,
show him your eyelids, invite him
to a picnic in the honey-colored meadow
you found last summer.

He says never, he says
forget it, he looks at your bones the way a logger
looks at redwoods: he wants to chop you down, only
he wonders which way you'll fall.

2

So you fall for him, thinking
what a beautiful axe he has, what a shame
to dull that shimmering blade with blood.

Now you're very far down, among stumps and tufts: now
the cure begins, here where the granite banks
cut off the sun and the nettles teach your skin to hate.

A fine dust of dislike rubs in through your pores,
your nostrils inhale contempt like swamp gas,
you thrash and grunt in the furious ditch

until the acid takes hold, your blood floods
with the dark brew that collects under stones, rots logs,
lops trees into witchy shapes.

You get on your feet slowly, you're as strong as anyone now,
at last you can stand up for yourself:
you've become a natural marvel, a beautiful pink nettle.

Even your mother would scream
if she touched you.

Summer, an Elegy · *Ellen Gilchrist*

HIS NAME WAS SHELBY after the town where his mother was born, and he was eight years old and all that summer he had to wear a little black sling around the index finger of his right hand. He had to wear the sling because his great-granddaddy had been a famous portrait painter and had paintings hanging in the White House.

Shelby was so high-strung his mother was certain he was destined to be an artist like his famous ancestor. So, when he broke his finger and it grew back crooked, of course they took him to a specialist. They weren't taking any chances on a deformity standing in his way.

All summer long he was supposed to wear the sling to limber up the finger, and in the fall the doctor was going to operate and straighten it. While he waited for his operation Shelby was brought to Bear Garden Plantation to spend the summer with his grandmother and as soon as he got up every morning he rode over to Esperanza to look for Matille.

He would come riding up in the yard and tie his saddle pony to the fence and start talking before he even got on the porch. He was a beautiful boy, five months younger than Matille and a head shorter, and he was the biggest liar she had ever met in her life.

Matille was a lonely little girl, the only child in a house full of widows. She was glad of this noisy companion fate had delivered to Issaquena County right in the middle of a World War.

Shelby would wait for her while she ate breakfast, helping himself to pinch-cake, or toast, or cold cornbread, or muffins, walking around the kitchen touching everything and talking a mile a minute to anyone who would listen, talking and eating at the same time.

"My daddy's a personal friend of General MacArthur's," he would be saying. "They were buddies at Auburn. General MacArthur wants him to come work in Washington but he can't go because what he does is too important." Shelby was standing in the pantry door making a pyramid out of the Campbell's Soup cans. "Every time my daddy talks about going to Washington my momma starts crying her head off and goes to bed with a backache." He topped off the pyramid with a can of tomato paste and returned to the present. "I don't know how anyone can sleep this late," he said. "I'm the first one up at Bear Garden every single morning."

Matille would eat breakfast as fast as she could and they would start out for the bayou that ran in front of the house at the end of a wide lawn.

"Did I tell you I'm engaged to be married," Shelby would begin, sitting next to Matille in the swing that went out over the water, pumping as hard as he could with his thin legs, staring off into the sky.

"Her daddy's a colonel in the Air Corps. They're real rich." A dark secret look crossed his face. "I already gave her a diamond ring. That's why I've got to find the pearl. So I can get enough money to get married. But don't tell anyone because my momma and daddy don't know about it yet."

"There aren't any pearls in mussels," Matille said. "Guy said so. He said we were wasting our time chopping open all those mussels."

"They do too have pearls," Shelby said coldly. "Better ones than oysters. My father told me all about it. Everyone in New Orleans knows about it."

"Well," Matille said, "I'm not looking for any pearls today. I'm going to the store and play the slot machine."

"You haven't got any nickels."

"I can get one. Guy'll give me one." Guy was Matille's uncle. He was 4-F. He had lost an eye in a crop-dusting accident and was having to miss the whole war because of it. He couldn't get into the Army, Navy, Marines or Air Corps. Even the Coast Guard had turned him down. He tried to keep up a cheerful face, running around Esperanza doing the work of three men, being extra nice to everyone, even the German war prisoners who were brought over from the Greenville Air Force Base to work in the fields.

He was always good for a nickel, sometimes two or three if Matille waited until after he had his evening toddies.

"If you help me with the mussels I'll give you two nickels," Shelby said.

"Let me see," Matille said, dragging her feet to slow the swing. It was nice in the swing with the sun beating down on the water below and the pecan trees casting a cool shade.

Shelby pulled a handkerchief from his pocket and untied a corner. Sure enough, there they were, three nickels and a quarter and a dime. Shelby always had money. He was the richest boy Matille had ever known. She stared down at the nickels, imagining the cold thrill of the slot machine handle throbbing beneath her touch.

"How long?" she said.

"Until I have to go home," Shelby said.

"All right," Matille said. "Let's get started."

They went out to the shed and found two rakes and a small hoe and picked their way through the weeds to the bayou bank. The mud along the bank was black and hard-packed and broken all along the water line by thick tree roots, cypress and willow and catalpa and water oak. They walked past the cleared-off place with its pier and rope swings and on down to where the banks of mussels began.

The mussels lay in the shallow water as far as the rake could reach, an endless supply, as plentiful as oak leaves, as plentiful as the fireflies that covered the lawn at evening, as plentiful as the minnows casting their tiny shadows all along the water's edge, or the gnats that buzzed around Matille's face as she worked, raking and digging and chopping, earning her nickels.

She would throw the rake down into the water and pull it back full of the dark-shelled, inedible, mud-covered creatures. Moments later, reaching into the same place, dozens more would have appeared to take their place.

They would rake in a pile of mussels, then set to work breaking them open with the hoe and screwdriver. When they had opened twenty or thirty, they would sit on the bank searching the soft flesh for the pearl. Behind them and all around them were piles of rotting shells left behind in the past weeks.

"I had my fortune told by a voodoo queen last Mardi Gras," Shelby said. "Did I ever tell you about that? She gave me a charm made out of a dead baby's bone. You want to see it?"

"I been to Ditty's house and had my fortune told," Matille said. "Ditty's real old. She's the oldest person in Issaquena County. She's older than Nannie-Mother. She's probably the oldest person in the whole state of Mississippi." Matille picked up a mussel and examined it, running her finger inside, then tossed it into the water. Where it landed a dragonfly hovered for a moment, then rose in the humid air, its electric-blue tail flashing.

"You want to see the charm or not?" Shelby said, pulling it out of his pocket.

"Sure," she said. "Give it here."

He opened his hand and held it out to her. It looked like the wishbone from a tiny chicken. "It's voodoo," Shelby said. He held it up in the air, turning it to catch the sunlight. "You can touch it but you can't hold it. No one can hold it but the master of it. Here, go on and touch it if you want to."

Matille reached out and stroked the little bone. "What's it good for?" she said.

"To make whatever you want to happen. It's white magic. Momma Ulaline is real famous. She's got a place on Royal Street right next to an antique store. My Aunt Katherine took me there when she was baby-sitting me last Mardi Gras."

Matille touched it again. She gave a little shudder.

"Well, let's get back to work," Shelby said, putting the charm into his pocket, wiping his hands on his playsuit. His little black sling was covered with mud. "I think we're getting someplace today. I think we're getting warm."

They went back to work. Shelby was quiet, dreaming of treasure, of the pearl that lay in wait for him, of riches beyond his wildest dreams, of mansions and fine automobiles and chauffeurs and butlers and maids and money, stacks and stacks of crisp five-dollar bills and ten-dollar bills and twenty-dollar bills. Somewhere in Steele's Bayou the pearl waited. It loomed in his dreams. It lay in wait for him beneath the roots of a cypress or water oak or willow.

Every morning when he woke he could see it, all morning as he dug and raked and chopped and Matille complained and the hot sun beat down on the sweating mud and the stagnant pools of minnows and the fast-moving, evil-looking gars swimming by like gunboats, all day the pearl shone in his mind, smooth and mysterious, cold to the touch.

They worked in silence for awhile, moving downstream until they were almost to the bridge.

"Looks like we could get something for all these shells," Matille said, examining the inside of one. It was all swirls of pink and white, like polished marble. "Looks like they ought to be worth something!"

"We could make dogfood out of the insides," Shelby said. "Mr. Green Bagett had a dog that ate mussels. My grandmother told me all about it. He would carry them up to the road in his mouth and when the sun made them open he would suck out the insides." Shelby leaned on his hoe, making a loud sucking noise. "He was a dog named Harry after Mr. Bagett's dentist and he would eat mussels all day long if nobody stopped him."

"Why don't we carry these mussels up to the road and let the sun open them?" Matille said.

"Because it takes too long that way," Shelby said. "This is quicker."

"We could make ashtrays out of the shells," Matille said.

"Yeah," Shelby said. "We could sell them in New Orleans. You can sell anything in the French Quarter."

"We could paint them and decorate them with flowers," Matille said, falling into a dream of her own, picturing herself wearing a long flowered dress, pushing a cart through the crowded streets of a city, selling ashtrays to satisfied customers.

Now they were almost underneath the bridge. Here the trees were thicker and festooned with vines that dropped into the water like swings. It was darker here, and secret.

The bridge was a fine one for such a small bayou. It was a drawbridge with high steel girders that gleamed like silver in the flat Delta countryside. The bridge had been built to connect the two parts of the county and anyone going from Grace to Baleshed or Esperanza or Panther Brake or Greenfields had to pass that way. Some mornings as many as seven cars and trucks passed over it. All day small black children played on the bridge and fished from it and leaned over its railings looking down into the brown water, chunking rocks at the mud turtles or trying to hit the mean-looking gars and catfish that swam by in twos or threes with their teeth showing.

This morning there were half a dozen little black boys on the bridge and one little black girl wearing a clean apron. Her hair was in neat cornrows with yellow yarn plaited into the braids. Her head looked like the wing of a butterfly, all yellow and black and brown and round as it could be.

"What y'all doing?" the girl called down when they got close enough to hear. "What y'all doing to them mussels?"

"We're doing an experiment," Shelby called back.

"Let's get Teentsy and Kale to help us," Matille said. "Hey, Teentsy," she called out, but Shelby grabbed her arm.

"Don't get them down here," he said. "I don't want everyone in the Delta in on this."

"They all know about it anyway," Matille said. "Guy told Granddaddy everyone at the store was laughing about us the other day. He said Baby Doll was busting a gut laughing at us for chopping all these mussels."

"I don't care," Shelby said, putting his hands on his hips and looking out across the water with the grim resignation of the born artist. "They don't know what we're doing it for."

"Well, I'm about worn out," Matille said. "Let's go up to the store and get Mavis to give us a drink."

"Let's open a few more first. Then we'll get a drink and go over to the other side. I think it's better over there anyway. There's sand over there. You got to have sand to make pearls."

"We can't go over there," Matille said. "That's not our property. That's Mr. Donleavy's place."

"He don't care if we dig some mussels on his bayou bank, does he?"

"I don't know. We got to ask him first. He's got a real bad temper."

"Let's try under this tree," Shelby said. "This looks like a good place. There's sand in this mud." He was bending down trying the mud between his fingers, rubbing it back and forth to test the consistency. "Yeah, let's try here. This feels good."

"What y'all tearing up all those mussels for," Kale called down from his perch on the bridge. "They ain't good for nothing. You can't even use them for bait."

"We're gonna make ashtrays out of them," Shelby said. "We're starting us an ashtray factory."

"Where about?" Kale said, getting interested, looking like he would come down and take a look for himself.

"Next to the store," Shelby said. "We're gonna decorate them and sell them in New Orleans. Rich folks will pay a lot for real mussel ashtrays."

"That ought to hold them for awhile," he said to Matille. "Let them talk about that at the store. Come on, let's open a few more. Then we'll get us a drink."

"All right," Matille said. "Let's try under this tree." She waded out into the water until it was up to her ankles, feeling the cold mud ooze up between her toes. She reached out with the rake. It caught, and she began pulling it up the shore, backing as she pulled, tearing the bark off the edges of the tree roots. The rake caught in the roots and she reached down to free it.

"Matille!" Shelby yelled. "Matille! Look out!" She heard his voice and saw the snake at the same moment, saw the snake and Shelby lifting the hoe and her hand outlined against the water, frozen and dappled with sunlight and the snake struggling to free itself and the hoe falling toward her hand, and she dropped the rake and turned and was running up the bank, stumbling and running, with Shelby yelling his head off behind her, and Teentsy and Kale and the other children rose up from the bridge like a flock of little blackbirds and came running down the hill to see what the excitement was.

"I got him," Shelby yelled. "I cut him in two. I cut him in two with the hoe. I got him."

Matille sank down on the edge of the road and put her head on her knees.

"She's fainting," Kale called out, running up to her. "Matille's fainting."

"No, she ain't." Teentsy said. "She's all right." Teentsy sat down by Matille and put a hand on her arm, patting her.

"It was a moccasin," Shelby yelled. "He was big around as my arm. After I killed him the top half was still alive. He struck at me four times. I don't know if I'm bit or not."

"Where's he gone to now?" Kale said.

"I don't know," Shelby said, pulling off his shirt. "Come look and see if he bit me." The children gathered around searching Shelby's skin for bite marks. His little chest was heaving with excitement and his face was shining. With his shirt off he looked about as big around as a blue jay. His little black sling was flopping around his wrist and his rib cage rose and fell beneath the straps of his seersucker playsuit.

"Here's one!" Teentsy screamed, touching a spot on Shelby's back, but it turned out to be an old mosquito bite.

"Lay down on the ground," Kale yelled, "where we can look at you better."

"Where do you *think* he bit you?" Teentsy said.

But Shelby was too excited to lay down on the ground. All he wanted to do was jump up and down and tell his story over and over.

Then the grown people heard the commotion and came out from the store. Mavis Findley and Mr. Beaumont and Baby Doll and R.C. and Overflow came hurrying down the road and grabbed hold of Shelby so they could see where the snake bit him.

"Didn't nothing bite him, Mr. Mavis," Kale said. "He kilt it. He kilt it with the hoe."

"He almost chopped my hand off," Matille said, but no one was listening.

Then Mavis and Baby Doll and Overflow escorted Matille and Shelby back to the big house with the black children skipping along beside and in front of them like a disorderly marching band.

By the time the procession reached the house the porch was full of ladies. Matille's mother and grandmother and great-grandmother and several widowed aunts had materialized from their rooms and were standing in a circle. From a distance they looked like a great flowering shrub. The screen door was open and a wasp buzzed around their heads threatening to be caught in their hairnets.

The ladies all began talking at once, their voices rising above and riding over and falling into each other in a long chorus of mothering.

"Thank goodness you're all in one piece," Miss Babbie said, swooping up Matille and enfolding her in a cool fragrance of dotted Swiss and soft yielding bosom and the smell of sandalwood and the smell of coffee and the smell of powder.

Miss Nannie-Mother, who was 96, kissed her on the forehead and called her Eloise, after a long-dead cousin. Miss Nannie-Mother had lived so long and grown so wise that everyone in the world had started to look alike to her.

The rest of the ladies swirled around Shelby. Matille struggled from her grandmother's embrace and watched disgustedly from the doorframe as Shelby told his story for the tenth time.

"I didn't care what happened to me," Shelby was saying. "No rattlesnake was biting a lady while I was in the neighborhood. After I chopped it in two the mouth part came at me like a chicken with its head cut off."

"He almost chopped my hand off," Matille said again, but the only ones listening to her were Teentsy and Kale, who stood by the steps picking petals off Miss Teddy's prize pansies and covering their mouths with their hands when they giggled to show what nice manners they had.

"This is what comes of letting children run loose like wild Indians," Miss Teddy was saying, brandishing a bottle of Windsor nail polish.

"Whatever will Rhoda Hotchkiss think when she hears of this?" Miss Nell Grace said.

"She'll be terrified," Miss Babbie answered. "Then go straight to her knees to thank the Lord for the narrow escape."

"I knew something was going to happen," Miss Hannie Clay said, her hands still full of rickrack for the smock she was making for her daughter in Shreveport. "I knew something was coming. It was too quiet around here all morning if you ask my opinion."

Matille leaned into the door frame with her hands on her hips watching her chances of ever going near the bayou again as long as she lived growing slimmer and slimmer.

Sure enough, when Matille's grandfather came in from the fields for the noon meal he made his pronouncement before he even washed his hands or hung up his hat.

"Well, then," he said, looking down from his six feet four inches and furrowing his brow. "I want everyone in this house to stay away from the bayou until I can spare some men to clear the brush. Shelby, I'm counting on you to keep Matille away from there, you hear me?"

"Yes sir," Shelby said. He stood up very straight, stuck out his hand and shook on it.

Now he's done it, Matille thought. Now our luck's all gone. Now nothing will be the same.

Now the summer wore on into August, and Shelby and Matille made a laboratory in an old chicken house, and collected a lot of butterflies and chloroformed them with fingernail polish remover, and they taught a fox terrier puppy how to dance on his hind legs, and spent some time spying on the German prisoners, and read all the old love letters in the trunks under the house, and built a broad jump pit in the pasture, but it was not the same. Somehow the heart had gone out of the summer.

Then one morning the grown people decided it was time for typhoid shots, and no matter how Matille cried and beat her head against the floor she was bathed and dressed and sent off in the back seat of Miss Rhoda's Buick to Doctor Findley's little brick office overlooking Lake Washington.

As a reward Matille was to be allowed to stay over at Bear Garden until the pain and fever subsided.

In those days vaccinations were much stronger than they are now, and well cared-for children were kept in bed for twenty-four hours nursing their sore arms, taking aspirin dissolved in sugar water and being treated as though they were victims of the disease itself.

Miss Rhoda made up the twin beds in Shelby's mother's old room, made them up with her finest Belgian linens and decorated the headboards with Hero medals cut from cardboard and hand-painted with watercolors.

The bedroom was painted ivory and the chairs were covered with blue and white chintz imported from Paris. It was the finest room Matille had ever slept in. She snuggled down in the pillows admiring the tall bookcases filled with old dolls and mementos of Carrie Hotchkiss's brilliant career as a Rolling Fork cheerleader.

Miss Rhoda bathed their faces with lemon water, drew the Austrian blinds and went off for her nap.

"Does yours hurt yet?" Shelby said, rubbing his shot as hard as he could to get the pain going. "Mine's killing me already."

"It hurts some," Matille said, touching the swollen area. "Not too much." She was looking at Shelby's legs, remembering something Guy had shown her, something that had happened a long time ago, something hot and exciting, something that felt like fever, and like fever, made everything seem present, always present, so that she could not remember where or how it had happened or how long a time had passed since she had forgotten it.

"Just wait till tonight," Shelby rattled on. "You'll think your arm's fixing to fall off. I almost died from mine last year. One year a boy in

New Orleans did die. They cut off his arm and did everything they could to save him but he died anyway. Think about that, being in a grave with only one arm." Shelby was talking faster than ever, to hide his embarrassment at the way Matille was looking at him.

"I can't stand to think about being buried, can you?" he continued, "all shut up in the ground with the worms eating you. I'm getting buried in a mausoleum if I die. They're these little houses up off the ground made out of concrete. Everyone in New Orleans that can afford it gets buried in mausoleums. That's one good thing about living there."

"You want to get in bed with me?" Matille said, surprised at the sound of her own voice, so clear and orderly in the still room.

"Sure," Shelby said, "if you're scared. It scares me to death to think about being buried and stuff like that. Are you scared?"

"I don't know," Matille said. "I just feel funny. I feel like doing something bad."

"Well, scoot over then," Shelby said, crawling in beside her.

"You're burning up," she said, putting a hand on his forehead to see if he had a fever. Then she put her hand on his chest as if to feel his heartbeat, and then, as if she had been doing it every day of her life, she reached down inside his pajamas for the strange hard secret of boys.

"I want to see it, Shelby," she said, and he lay back with his hands stiff by his sides while she touched and looked to her heart's content.

"Now you do it to me," she said, and she guided his fingers up and down, up and down, up and down the thick tight opening between her legs.

The afternoon was going on for a long time and the small bed was surrounded by yellow light and the room filled with the smell of mussels.

Long afterwards, as she lay in a cool bed in Acapulco, waiting for her third husband to claim her as his bride, Matille would remember that light and how, later that afternoon, the wind picked up and could be heard for miles away, moving toward Issaquena County with its lines of distant thunder, and how the cottonwood leaves outside the window had beat upon the house all night with their exotic crackling.

"You better not tell anyone about this ever, Shelby," Matille said, when she woke in the morning. "You can't tell anyone about it, not even in New Orleans."

"The moon's still up," Shelby said, as if he hadn't heard her. "I can see it out the window."

"How can the moon be up," Matille said. "It's daylight."

"It stays up when it wants to," Shelby said, "haven't you ever seen that before?"

It was Matille who made up the game now. They cleaned out an old playhouse that had belonged to Matille's mother and made a bed from a cot mattress. Matille would lie down on the mattress with her hand on her head pretending to have a sick headache.

"Come sit by me, Honey," she would say. "Pour me a glass of sherry and come lie down till I feel better."

"God can see in this playhouse," Shelby said, pulling his hand away.

"No, he can't, Shelby," Matille said, sitting up and looking him hard in the eye. "God can't see through tin. This is a tin roof and God can't see through it."

"He can see everywhere," Shelby said. "Father Godchaux said so."

"Well, he can't see through tin," Matille said. "He can't be everywhere at once. He's got enough to do helping out the Allies without watching little boys and girls every minute of the night and day." Matille was unbuttoning Shelby's playsuit. "Doesn't that feel good, Shelby?" she said. "Doesn't that make you feel better?"

"God can see everywhere," Shelby insisted. "He can see every single thing in the whole world."

"I don't care," Matille said. "I don't like God anyway. If God's so good why did he let Uncle Robert die. And why did he make alligators and snakes and send my daddy off to fight the Japs. If God's so good why'd he let the Jews kill his own little boy."

"You better not talk like that," Shelby said, buttoning his suit back together. "And we better get back before Baby Doll comes looking for us again."

"Just a little bit more," Matille said. "Just till we get to the part where the baby comes out."

August went by as if it had only lasted a moment. Then one afternoon Miss Rhoda drove Shelby over in the Buick to say goodbye. He was wearing long pants and had a clean sling on the finger and he had brought Matille the voodoo bone wrapped in tissue paper to keep for him.

"You might need this," he said, holding it out to her. He looked very grown up standing by the stairs in his city clothes and Matille thought that maybe she would marry Shelby when she grew up and be a fine married lady in New Orleans.

Then it was September and the cotton went to the gin and Matille was in the third grade and rode to school on the bus.

One afternoon she was standing by the driver while the bus clattered across the bridge and came to a halt by the store. It was a cool day. A breeze was blowing from the northeast and the cypress trees were turning a dusty red and the wild persimmons and muscadines were making.

Matille felt the trouble before she even got off the bus. The trouble reached out and touched her before she even saw the ladies standing on the porch in their dark dresses. It fell across her shoulders like a cloak. It was as if she had touched a single strand of a web and felt the whole thing tremble and knew herself to be caught forever in its trembling.

They found out, she thought. Shelby told them. I knew he couldn't keep a secret, she said to herself. Now they'll kill me. Now they'll beat me like they did Guy.

She looked down the gravel road to the house, down the long line of pecan and elm trees and knew that she should turn and go back the other way, should run from this trouble, but something made her keep on moving toward the house. I'll say he lied, she thought. I'll say I didn't do it. I'll say he made it up, she said to herself. Everyone knows what a liar Shelby is.

Then her mother and grandmother and Miss Babbie came down off the porch and took her into the parlor and sat beside her on the sofa. And Miss Hannie and Miss Nell Grace and Overflow and Baby Doll stood around her in a circle and told her the terrible news.

"Shelby is dead, Matille," her grandmother said. The words slid over her like water poured on stones.

Shelby had gone to the hospital to have his finger fixed and he had lain down on the table and put the gas mask over his face and the man who ran the gas machine made a mistake and Shelby had gone to sleep, and nothing could wake him up, not all the doctors or nurses or shots or slaps on the face or screams or prayers or remorse in the world could wake him. And that was the Lord's will, blessed be the name of the Lord, Amen.

Later the ladies went into the kitchen to make a cold supper for anyone who felt like eating and Matille walked down to the bayou and stood for a long time staring down into the water, feeling strangely elated, as though this were some wonderful joke Shelby·dreamed up.

She stared down into the tree roots, deep down into the muddy water, down to the place where Shelby's pearl waited, grew and moved inside the soft watery flesh of its mother, luminous and perfect and alive, as cold as the moon in the winter sky.

Clanking to Byzantium · *Ellen Gilchrist*

for Gwen

This is no country for old women,
the young in one another's lyrics
guitar picks all over the place,
joints for breakfast, joints for dinner,
more joints. His young shoulders,
sweeter than wisdom. So much
for theories, so much for understanding,
so much for knowing better.

A full moon, that old betrayer,
covers me in silver armor, soft
as pale blue Cannon sheets, softer
than bad poems, some armor.

Joy, that old pimp, shuffles away
while this boy moves,
as I foretold,
across my balcony,
across the room
and opens and closes
the inevitable door.

Oh, my quick clever compadres,
my candid friends, see what I've learned
from Ingrid Bergman, how I stand, coiled
and still, balancing on one foot. So much
for fame and its rewards, so much
for tenure, so much for star billing.

Oh, well, as Anne says, I'll save myself,
plant both feet on this balcony I would
never dream of diving from, turn back
to the work, to the heart's stone. So much
for being a pussy, so much for being
a sparrow, so much for going soft around
the edges.

Here is how I pray. Bill Miller Jim
Boogie Otto Ginny Merlee Fu
Drew Pierre Rita Roy Brenna Tree
Jeannie Rose Gwen Patsy Forche
James Genn Jordan, the names of my friends
fall from my lips like music.
Oh, compadres, if I could resolve this poem
the mountains would call on me for wisdom.

To a Friend Going Blind · *Jorie Graham*

Today, because I couldn't find the shortcut through,
I had to walk this town's entire inner
perimeter to find
where the medieval walls break open
in an eighteenth century
arch. The yellow valley flickered on and off
through cracks and the gaps
for guns. Bruna is teaching me
to cut a pattern.
Saturdays we buy the cloth.
She takes it in her hands
like a good idea, feeling
for texture, grain, the built-in
limits. It's only as an afterthought she asks
and do you think it's beautiful?
Her measuring tapes hang down, corn-blond and endless,
from her neck.
When I look at her
I think *Rapunzel,*
how one could climb that measuring,
that love. But I was saying,
I wandered all along the street that hugs the walls,
a needle floating
on its cloth. Once
I shut my eyes and felt my way
along the stone. Outside
is the cash crop, sunflowers, as far as one can see. Listen,
the wind rattles in them,
a loose worship
seeking an object
an interruption. Sara,
the walls are beautiful. They block the view.
And it feels rich to be
inside their grasp.

When Bruna finishes her dress
it is the shape of what has come
to rescue her. She puts it on.

I, Boudica · *Judy Grahn*

During the reign of Nero, Roman colonizers occupied what is now southern Britain, having forced the Celtic tribes who lived there to render up one half of their produce and goods. Red-haired Boudica was Queen of the tribe Iceni, but the Romans negotiated with her husband, Prasutagus. Following his death in 61 A.D., the Romans drastically increased their oppression, land-grabbing and massacre of refugees fleeing their rule. When the Queen protested they publicly flogged her and raped her two daughters, to undermine her authority. Consequently she united a large number of tribes for a massive, broad-based, woman-led rebellion that shook Nero's emperorship and left London burned to the ground. The Romans won a last decisive battle/massacre, using war-machine methods against the Celts, and then venting their fear and rage on the civilian country-side, particularly concentrating on Boudica's own tribe.

Because she rocked the Roman world, and because of her place in the Celtic tradition of female warriors, and because of the native Celtic institutions of homosexual love for women and men, which shocked the Roman military, the conquerors attempted to obliterate Queen Boudica's name and memory. Their harshness only drove the Queen's name and reputation underground. There it has stayed for nineteen centuries, passed through lowerclass slang as the word "bulldike" or "bulldagger," describing a serious, tough-appearing, warriorlike lesbian. For personal as well as historical reasons, rediscovering this meaning of Queen Boudica's story has been one of the most thrilling acts of my life.

I, Boudica

A queen am I,
a warrior and a shaman.
Shameless is my goddess and ferocious;
my god's foot cloven.

I am protectress of my horsebound clansmen.
A red-haired, full-robed, bronze-belted swordswoman,
I am a queen of sacred groves and other old realms
where astronomers divine from droves of animals
or flocks of birds, and study the signs in palms;
a queen of times when men are lovers to the men
and the women to the women,
as is our honored pagan custom.
Ever and ever did we think to reign
in such an independent fashion,
until the day the foe came.

He came to my temple.
In ships he came to me.
Our possessions upon the prow of his ship he put.
He with hired soldiers came
to our self-ruled regions.
The foe, he with legions, entered my court.
He put his hands upon me, he filled me with fear.
My garments he tore away, and sent them to his wife.
The foe stripped off my jewels and put them on his son.
He seized my people's lands and gave them to his men.

He put his hands upon me, he filled me with rage.
I spoke to him in anger.
I told him of his danger.
So for me myself did he seek in the shrines.
In front of my folks he had me beat;
and this was not the worst I had to meet:
he seized my young daughters and had them raped.

> He seized my daughters
> and had them raped,
> Oh queen of heaven, queen
> who shatters the mountains;
> how long before you must my
> face be cast in hate?

A queen am I, my cities have betrayed me.
A queen, Boudica am I, my cities have betrayed me.
In that rebellious year
of sixty-one A.D. I rose up
I, Boudica, over the countryside
from clan to clan and ear to ear,
I drove round in a chariot,
my daughters with me.

To every woman and every man
I spoke:
    "Now is the battle drawn
    which must be victory or death.
    For today I am more than your queen,
    and more than your mother deeply wronged,
    I am all the power of women brought down;
    one who will fight to reclaim her place.
    This is my resolve. Resolve is what I own.
    We women shall fight. The men can live,
    if they like, and be slaves."

And so we went to war.
Our men went with us.
And for centuries since, the foe has
searched for us in all our havens,
secret circles, rings and covens;
almost always we elude him,
we who remember who we are;
we who are never not at war.

    On that day
    didn't I, Boudica
    Didn't I up rise
    didn't I slay,
    didn't I hold fast
    the ancient ways.

    Wasn't I like a wall
    wasn't I a great dike
    against a giant spill,
    that iron sea
    of Roman pikes
    that came to conquer Gaul.

Even if for one day
didn't the foe almost fall,
didn't his teeth gnash,
wasn't his bladder galled,
didn't the foe, even he,
know fear;
he feared me.

He feared me, then
in his being
unable to fully win
unable to fully kill
the rebel things
my name means,
he fears still.

He fears me still,
for my shameless guise
and lesbian ways;
for undefeated eyes,
a warrior's spine
and all my memories
of women's time.

A queen am I, my city
needs to find me.
Meantime the foe arrives
unceasingly
from every steel-grey sea,
by every mountain road on earth
he enters   all my cities
and for me myself he seeks
in my varied shrines,
in my temples he pursues me,
in my halls he terrifies me,
saying, "Cause her to go forth."
He goads. He burns, he murders.
He erodes.

A queen am I,
a warrior and a shaman.
Shameless is my goddess and ferocious;
my god's foot cloven.

A queen am I, a living memory
who knows her own worth
and who remembers that the future
is the past rehearsed,

> and *not should I go forth*
> unless it be for battle girthed.
> Unless it be for battle girthed,
> and belted, *not should I go forth*

until the foe is driven from the earth.

March 29, 1980

Well Enough Alone · *Debora Greger*

Blood red, blood purple, jet and jade
—hands dripping slippery stones,
she clambered back a dry-rocked shore
that should have told her not about
foothold or balance but that when,

in rows on her bureau, the prized ones
dried, they too would dull. She glowered
toward the feigned or real uninterest
of two men outside, desultorily sweeping
leaves from the square's broken tree.

In dream's ceaseless present, I'm benched
at that window, my mother's reflection
glassily rising. This time when I turn
around, I'm wearing a mask of a man's face.
My hand swaggers to her temple—

under her powdered skin, the warm stone
of her small skull. I kiss her surprise-
rounded mouth—words into wakefulness,
resolving nothing. Again the square's pigeon
cries, "Who cooks, who cooks for you?"

There was no question in it when my mother
would ask, "Why can't you leave
well enough alone?" as if the present
were already being told in another person,
first in the simple past tense, as now,
and soon in the perfect.

The Shallows · *Debora Greger*

Rolling pants' legs, bundling skirts,
they have come down the shore with gunnysacks,

birdcages, dresses knotted together —
tonight not the moon but a run of smelt

silvers the shallows, night water's deep opacity.
Gray gone black, the wet sand chills, floor-hard

as long as, like those boys, I don't stand still.
Coaching and taunting, a chorus of spring frogs,

they leap the fish. Even the woman I've seen
walking daily in the village is here, the one

with her arm in a sling and a three-legged dog.
Her slowed passage rippling the crowd,

she's the domestic tamely obscured
by the raucous dark. Down from this inlet,

a basket of lights lists where the family living
on the grounded freighter finishes another

tilted day. Finally, I think, that canted home
would seem no longer maddening or novel

but cramped like any other. Out in its vast
and watery front yard, below the level of all this,

a cold current tunnels unremittingly north.

De Arte Honeste Amandi · Linda Gregerson

I What Love Is

Fred Kessler, of the East and West of Castro Street
Improvement Club, is willing to roll with the times. For the drought,
he's added Tips to his flyer: Catch the water
that's still too cold, your garden will be green on it.

You want to recycle? For next week's flyer, leave
this rubber band here on your doorknob.
On alternate Sundays for seven years, he's picked up dog shit
from Noe to Church and back again. Don't talk about heart.

You can see what becomes of a neighborhood:
kids half the time, and nobody visibly
off to a job. Curtains like his mother had, the lace
with the squares, for a joke he doesn't quite get.

His mother went to garage sales too. *Save water.*
Shower with a friend.
I'm no prude, Fred Kessler says. What kind of people
would put up the sign and the curtains too?

II Between What Persons Love May Exist

I don't want feelings, his wife said more
than once, especially where family's concerned.
So he didn't say boo when Agnes took the old man's watch.
I'll stick to my own back yard, he thought,

the breeze isn't bad, it's a wonder it gets around.
If he sits with the bottlebrush tree on his right, and the Murphys
aren't back from church, he can look in turn at the full four sides
of wooden stairs, and can nurse an idea he's had. It's the breeze.

I could harness this thing for a job or two, if once
I got the patterns down. And has started to save small pieces of paper,
the blues in a bag, the reds in a bag, for the purpose of experiments
to be devised. Later he'll ask the different tenants to open

or shut their windows in teams. Sunday,
safest to have the Murphys shut. *Back to Ireland,* he roars
while she cooks, the notion that starts with communion wine
and moves through a lonelier bottle to be slept off. The young ones

swing from the fire escape, pretending to be lost.

III How Love, When It Has Been Acquired, May Be Kept

That was when the war was on, the one we felt good
to hate, so of course I thought he'd come from there.
It was June. The light grown long again.
She'd roll his chair to the window

and back. But no, you said, it was love.
They were getting it wrong.
A leg. A leg. An arm to the elbow.
Like the man who burned his daughter to get

good winds. The sea for days had been flat
as the sky. He'd walk while the light went down
and could only tell the water from the air by the drag
below his knees. So this is what it's like

to have no body. A perfect benevolent temperature.
The wheels of the chariots grind
in the hulls of the ships. He lay so still he honeycombed,
may he be safe, may we be sound. The time

they bargained for came piece by piece.

IV The Love of Nuns

This one I won't tell you about, since you ought not to know
how it's done. Instead I'll tell you about a way my grandmother had
of closing her mouth, conspicuously, while we displayed the gaps
in our bringing up. Fresh milk made me sick,

for example, and hay made me wheeze. I liked the landscape best
shut down, the white that made a field and a road one thing.
You can't get there from here, but the windows are good
for writing on. Good frost. Good steam. We'd sleep in a bed

that was theirs before, when both of them could make the stairs.
The light had a string that was tied to a post
above my head. If I reached for the light, the cold
came in. You must cover up the children to their chins.

v Indications That One's Love Has Returned

There's an illness, of the sort that's named for a man
who first imagines that disparate threads might be threads
on a loom, that is called his syndrome, and frightens
the weaver, who cannot unravel by night

what she sees in the day. Their table had the sun for hours.
The piazza was white. They talked
about physicians at home, whose stories were longer, if less
in accord. And about the morning, months ago,

when the color first spread beneath her eyes.
From cheekbone to cheekbone, the smallest vessels had burst
in a pattern called *butterfly,* they'd named that too,
as tour guides name rocks till you can't see the sandstone plain

anymore, but Witch's Cauldron and Hornet's Nest.
The wings went away. The course of the river that carved the rock
is air now, and baffles intent. She'd been used to a different notion
of course, the kind you might follow for love of the thing,

or of knowledge, the wings in the glass.

Places · *Lois Elaine Griffith*

THE GIRLS FROM the alternative annex hung out in the dining area after school. The boys from vocational engineering would already be there since they got out at 2:00. Everything was plastic and chrome-lit under fluorescent light. Orange bang and coconut frost. While the boys sat around sipping sodas, the Challenger and Honey Bun girls had their afternoon fight. There were a few drops of nose blood and part of a sleeve from a floral printed blouse on the floor when security came. The best punches had already been thrown. Maintenance was quick to follow and clean up the wet spots. Someone might slip and fall and sue.

Marsha watched the whole scene over Gussie's shoulder. They took their coffee break time to make out in the stairwell of the emergency exit.

"Give it to me, baby. Spread out."

Marsha obeyed and opened her legs a little wider.

"Come on, let me make you feel good. Let me give you some tongue."

"Augustina, are you crazy. Not here."

"Come on, baby, I need you."

Marsha's pants were already around her knees. Why not she thought. She watched the girls get the fight on in the plastic eating area. Everybody's got to get their rocks off somehow.

When Gussie finally made her come, she adjusted her clothes and the two women started making their way back to work along the indoor avenues of the shopping mall.

"Relax next time. Then I won't have to work so hard," Gussie said.

"Someone's going to catch us one of these days, you know."

"Admit it. That black beefeating dick you go out with doesn't turn you on half as much as I do."

"Tony's O.K. You're just jealous. He has his good points."

"So do I," Gussie reminded her, "otherwise you wouldn't be out there in the emergency exit." She laughed.

"You want some ice cream. My treat." Marsha stopped at the slush stand between Wendy's and Italian Blimpy's.

"I wish that Tech HiFi would get it together with their system."

Gussie watched the workmen in the space allocated for sound trying to hook up the pre-amps to the power-amps. "I can't eat all this. You take some."

"Just a little." Marsha licked away all the swirls the machine had made pumping out the chocolate cone. "It's definitely not Häagen Dazs," she said, returning it half eaten.

"Baby, for not being good, you sure like how it tastes." Gussie pulls at the fly of her pants like a man. She spreads her legs a little as she walks, as if hiking up something that might get caught in the crotch.

"Will you stop that. . . . O look at that dress. It's on sale. They must have changed their windows last night. Have you ever worn a dress, Gussie?"

"What for."

"Just for the hell of it."

"It's not my style."

"O come on. . . ."

"You come on. I'm not so stupid that I fall for amateur hype."

"Well, if I'm so stupid why do you bother with me."

"I didn't say you were stupid, Marsha. You just never let on how freaky you are. It has to be sucked out of you." Gussie had her arm linked through Marsha's as the two stood in front of the Phase III window. She gently rubbed the back of her hand on the side of Marsha's breast.

"Cut it. Someone's going to see." The two started walking again.

"Why do you care?"

"I hate gossip."

"You talk about people you don't know." Gussie laughed and her chest started to jiggle under the tight-fitting red T-shirt that had Puerto Rico written on it in italic script.

"What's that supposed to mean?"

"Como sentimientos, bochincherita." Gussie squeezed Marsha's arm again.

"Cut it out. Why do you like to tease me. You want to be so superior."

"Me tease you," Gussie backed away. "You can't give me anything more than the back of your tit."

"O come on, I give you a lot. You don't know how to take me. But you always manage to get what you want, anyway. It comes around you."

"Like what. . . . O stop. Now I don't want to be talking like a kid. . . . What about tomorrow."

"What about it."

"Same time, same place."

"Maybe."

"Maybe. Maybe tease."

"Mañana, chica."

They had come to the foot of the main escalator and Marsha stepped on to make that climb to the third balcony. She worked as a salesgirl in the Flash and Funk Boutique. The clothes were hot and stylish sweatshop productions of a Jamaican designer, working for a Seventh Avenue import company, receiving fabrics from India and the Philippines for pennies a yard, from merchants who could hire whole villages to weave for food. The job was never very taxing except on Monday and Thursday nights when the shopping crowd was out till ten. The mall was a new three-level structure, like a big store whose departments were open, circling and overlooking a promenade and dining area decorated with plastic potted palms and tall dried birch tree limbs. There was no connection between the shops except they had space and paid rent. It was government subsidy's way of encouraging small business.

Gussie worked in the drug store on the main level. She was a cashier. She didn't especially like the job, making change, stocking cigarettes and cosmetics, but she had her own space behind the counter. Gussie always looked for her own place within the maze of wherever she found herself.

There had to be a corner she could claim as her own. She made herself at ease. People would mill and seethe around her, demanding Natural Wonder make-up and Sugar Daddy caramel candy sucker sticks. Sometimes she had to wash her hands after handling a couple hours' worth of money when things were busy. None of it touched her in her place, not even the comment that big gorilla Tony made, the time Marsha brought him down to buy cigarettes after work. Gussie was beyond the point of embarrassment at comments about the fuzzy shadow on her upper lip. "You know what they say about women with mustaches. . . ." and she clicked the heel of her red jazz shoes as she gave him her back to kiss Marsha good night. "Mañana."

Marsha liked working around clothes. She got a discount and first pick of all the new things that came in. She liked to think of herself as stylish, with her processed frizz hairdo, since the Rasta look had played out. Cocoa and plum were the make-up colors she wore these days. They complemented the dark rum tone of her skin. She was the girl who made a leap when Cosmopolitan Magazine said take a giant step and look sexy. She was made to be made up. If asked she'd show you her before and after pictures. She valued comments about her looks, especially when they compared her to images of famous personalities. "O you look just like a black Bette Midler," was her favorite.

She had met Gussie one day on her break, buying cosmetics at the drug store. She was taken by the look in the eyes. When she asked what kind of mascara she used, Gussie laughed and said she wasn't into it.

"You should try it. You'd be surprised what it can do."

"It's not my thing. I'm butch," said Gussie still laughing.

Marsha heard that last comment, but didn't let it register. She was too fascinated by the possibility of seeing this woman all done in make-up.

"Why don't you let me do you sometime?"

The eyes and the coloring intrigued her. Gussie's were almond-shaped light brown with thick black lashes and brows. The skin was smooth and seemingly transparent in the evenness of rich copper brown. The downy hair on the upper lip put the full soft mouth at the petulant extreme of sensuosity. When Gussie laughed she showed her even teeth and cut her eyes to Chinese slits. Her hair was short and naturally curly, except when she put olive oil on it and slicked it back in a D.A.

"You've got the kind of hair I wish I'd been born with," Marsha said one day as she combed it in the bathroom mirror. "Let me try this lipstick on you." It was a cocoa plum color, Born to Sin Plum.

"Now this is you," said Marsha, studying the effect of the color. "A dark crease in the eyefold . . . there."

"You want to smoke a 'J'? It's cool. I do it in here all the time. It makes the day fly." Gussie reached into her clutch bag for a small manila envelope. She pulled out one of the hand-rolled cigarettes, lit it and passed it to Marsha.

"I used to want to be a beautician," said Marsha, not giving up smoke to breathe in speaking. She savored the first rush.

"Fume, fume."

"I really want to take some courses and get a license."

"It's nice you know what you want to do. I only know what I don't want." Gussie watched herself in the mirror killing the roach. "This is me, after 'the before,' " and she laughed.

"You're gorgeous," said Marsha. "Every morning you walk out of your house you say, this is the first day of spring. No matter what."

Gussie looked skeptical. "Is that what you do?"

"No, I just give advice," and they both laughed and looked into each other's eyes. Then Gussie gently touched her lips to Marsha's and pulled back to see if there were some mistake.

"Why'd you do that?"

"I wanted to see something."

"Don't you like men?"

"Not too often. . . . That has nothing to do with it. . . . Did you mind?"

Marsha didn't speak, but continued to look at this beautiful face before hers. Gussie kissed her again. This time she allowed herself to let go a soft sweet juice of feeling that started to warm Marsha's blood.

"Let's get out of here before we start something we can't finish," said Marsha.

"I told you I was butch, so watch it, baby," and they laughed again as they returned to walking through the indoor avenues of the mall, back to their respective jobs.

It was after they discovered "the place" in the hallway of the emergency exit that Gussie asked Marsha if she believed in love.

"Sure I do. Someday I'll probably marry Tony and settle down and have kids."

"You don't have to feel anything to do that."

"We get along. That's more important."

"I want to feel easy," and she put her head on Marsha's shoulder and stroked her breast.

Tony was in training at the police academy. The professors from John Jay College of Criminal Justice would come over starting at 7:30 A.M. to begin classes. He was earning sixty college credits and getting paid for it. He was twenty-four and had avoided being "serious" with women. He'd known a few but always preferred sleeping out rather than having sleep-over company. He lived in a small garage converted to a basement apartment in the Canarsie section of Brooklyn, close to the Rockaways, close to the sea. A small yellow Ford Pinto was all paid for, but sometimes he liked to travel on foot. He would walk to the sea and study the waves. Sometimes rushing out of work he told his buddies he had an appointment with the devil. He would drive to the beach in winter and walk along the edge of the sea.

In the six months he'd known Marsha, he'd never explained these appointments he kept after work when he said he couldn't meet her. He didn't know if she'd understand. She'd probably want to come along when he wanted to be in his place alone with the sea.

He enjoyed the sensation of making love with her, but there was something inside her that wasn't full. Thinking maybe he could take her by surprise, he would rush in like the sea, trying to make the rhythm of a wave wash over the silence of that place inside her where she allowed him to wander alone, exploring his own skin on the walls of her womb.

"Why don't you give me a ring, Tony," Marsha said to him one day after he picked her up from work. They were driving at the edge of night in the cold before spring.

"What for? I can always pull you by the hair," and he laughed.

"As a sign of our feelings about each other."

"I told you how I feel, didn't I?"

"It would mean that we're engaged."

"Engaged for what?"

"Engaged to be married, of course."

"Why do you want to marry me?"

"I think we'd be good for each other, don't you?"

"I never thought about it."

"I'd like to have kids."

"Why, what's the rush?"

"I'm a year older than you."

"There's plenty of time."

"Maybe we should live together."

"You're talking about settling down?"

"In a way . . . getting closer."

"I thought we understood each other."

"We do."

"Well, that means we take things a step at a time."

"I'm going too fast for you?"

"You spend too much time comparing notes."

"I just want what any woman wants."

"What's that?"

"A place for myself."

Tony didn't answer. He kept his eyes straight ahead on the road and his two hands on the steering wheel. Marsha watched him drive the little Pinto over a series of treacherous potholes. Bronco style.

"Where are we going?" she asked.

"I thought we'd get some Chinese take-out and go up to your place."

Marsha's place was a fourth-floor walk-up in an old brownstone near Prospect Park in Brooklyn. There were two apartments on the floor. Her one-and-a-half rooms overlooked the backyard where an old tree grew tall and pushed its branches to scrape her windows when the winds were strong. When she opened the couch there wasn't much room to do anything else but lie in bed. She kept the couch open most of the time. She'd found this place a few years ago after she moved out of grandmother's apartment. Until then she'd always slept in a twin bed with the old woman on the other side of the room.

Pink with white trim. Red shag rug. Marsha had a habit of turning on the T.V. or radio as soon as she came in. Even with Tony the silence was too loud. Greasy brown sauce drying in plastic-coated containers. Floral sheets. In the dark there was silence even with the radio as she took off her clothes and felt him already hard without preliminaries. Silence as he shoved himself inside her.

"How was it, baby," he said after he came all over her, leaving her crotch soaking wet and feeling a draught.

"Mmmmmmm."

"Nothing special," said Gussie. She and Marsha were sitting in the stairwell of the emergency exit. "Just a plain ordinary life, only with too many people." Gussie lived with her sister and her sister's two boys.

"So why don't you move out. You've got a job."

"Millie and I, we help each other. You know her oldest kid was born the day abortions got legal. It freaked me when she said she was having a kid. I was small but we hung out sometimes. There was my big sister ready to be someone's mother. She thinks I'm a fast girl. I had to tell her I'm gay, and then all she could say was she used to feel uncomfortable when she first started being around men. But then you get used to it."

Gussie kept her friends away from the apartment she shared with her family. It was so crowded already, and then everyone always ended up around the dining room table looking in each other's faces and talking about what Tito did in school and how Laverne and Shirley would eventually find husbands.

"Do you ever go cruising, Marsha?"

"I don't like clubs by myself."

"There's this place called Serena's I go sometimes. You can go in the video room and make out. It's definitely class action. I always have a good time when I go. I'll take you there."

"Tony would dig it."

"Great, the three of us sitting around making wedding plans," and they both laughed. "You break my heart."

Heartbreak is a wild orchid crushed under heels in the night of a wet street. Lemon oil becomes musk on the skin. Compress the petals so there is no air for definition. Marsha opened a small vial of scent. She touched it to her throat, behind her ears, then put some at the nape of Gussie's neck. They were cuddled on the stairwell of the emergency exit. They smelled sweet in the dark.

Marsha liked being around Gussie. They had fun. Tony was picking her up and they were all going to meet at Serena's Palace on Flatbush Avenue. She was a little nervous. She wanted to look good. Gussie was so beautiful without even being interested in herself. Marsha didn't want Tony getting any ideas. She stood in her little pink bathroom and picked out her hair. She thought about the time they spent together in the emergency exit, hanging out. She didn't know why she talked Tony into going out tonight with her and Gussie.

When she and Tony got inside she saw it was a big place. They all wouldn't have to stick to each other. Gussie was standing at the semicircular bar against the mirrored wall under the balcony. The music made the free-form crystal chandelier vibrate.

"Isn't that your friend?" Tony saw her first.

Gussie was wearing a straight black satin skirt slit up the thigh, high-heeled black suede pumps and a gold sequined tube top under a black blazer. She was talking with a tall black woman in a man's tuxedo and a long red wig.

"Well, you're certainly dressed to kill." Marsha took Gussie apart with her eyes and put her back together again.

"You look great." Tony was smiling. His teeth were very white against his dark skin. "I hope you feel as good as you look." He was flirting.

"I figured since I'd be with friends, I'd be safe to feel anything." Gussie smiled back and turned to the woman at her side. "This is Haze. Marsha. Tony."

"How you all doing? Listen Gussie I got to split. Business uptown. Bye honey. Nice meeting you all." Haze rubbed cheeks with Gussie so as not to smear her with heavy red lipstick and was gone.

"Who was that?" Marsha watched her disappear through the exit marked Exit.

"An old friend who used to look out for me. She's really good people."

"Sure, as long as I don't find her working my streets. Everything in its place you know." Tony was laughing but no one joined him so he stopped. The music was thumping, but in the place where they stood together there was only silence.

"Let's get a drink." Marsha motioned the bartender and ordered a rum and coke.

"You can hold up the bar, but I'm going to dance." Gussie moved to the rhythm of the funky disco beat onto the color-lit Lucite floor. She didn't need a partner.

"Do you ever do that?" Tony kept his eyes on Gussie.

"Do what?" Marsha sipped her drink through a straw.

"Dance by yourself."

"Why should I dance by myself when I have you?"

"Just because you like dancing." Tony walked across the main room of Serena's Palace, crystal and deep red except for the dance floor that was rainbow lighted from beneath the surface. He brushed past Gussie who was feeling the funk and giving no mind to anything else. There were carpet-covered low benches around the edge of the room and exits with neon signs. He pushed open the black vinyl-padded and silver-studded door marked Gents in iridescent blue.

Marsha stood at the bar in her pink high-front, low-back jumpsuit. She sipped at the drink and chewed on the straw. Gussie had to touch the back of her neck with the coolness of a water glass to get her attention. Marsha's eyes were all over the room.

"You know how to hustle?" Gussie had to raise her voice in Marsha's ear.

"Can you lead?"

The two moved onto the dance floor and started doing some basic steps, getting into the groove of things. When he came out, Tony stood against the wall next to the Gents' door. He watched the women cut their turns hard. They did some spin-offs that sparked. The fever made their dancing speak. He wanted to be in the place where they moved, but he was too far away from delighting in the motion of sound. He watched them from his place. Running water and flushing toilet from behind the swinging door were sounds that mingled with the music.

Girls say they dance together for practice.

Women need the familiarity of sharing what is common among them.

He wanted to step back. Let it go for being a strange intruder, but the locker room isn't an easy place. Tony pulled out a cigarette and lit it. He smoked in the shadows, watching the two women dance.

The crowd started to sing along with the record:

> Put your hands up in the air.
> Shake it like you just don't care . . .
> Ain't nothing to it
> you got to do it . . .

Frenzy was building. It was almost 1:00 A.M. Marsha caught Tony's eyes through the dark and smoke as the D.J. did a mix. She came over and Gussie followed.

"Having a good time?" His expression was hidden. The air was thick.

"Let's check out the buffet," Gussie suggested. They made their way through one of the exits marked Buffet. Inside the redwood picnic tables were set up around a food bar with a red awning.

"How about an ice cream soda," said Gussie. "Chocolate works you up, right?" Marsha smiled and nodded.

"I'll get them. You girls grab a table cause I want a hamburger."

Gussie and Marsha faced each other across a table. Marsha kept her eyes on Tony.

"What's the matter with your boyfriend?" Gussie took off her jacket and exposed her bare shoulders.

"What's with you, dressing all sexy in front of him?"

"I'm not doing anything. You're telling me to look at him. You wanted to bring him."

"He's not having a good time. I can tell."

"So what are you going to do about it?"

"I don't know, maybe we should leave."

"Let him work it out. It's still early for bed." Gussie nudged Marsha's calf as she crossed her legs under the table. "Maybe we should both show him a good time."

"He's not into that."

"He's not into what?" Tony slid onto the bench next to Marsha and put the tray on the table. "Well, what am I not into?"

"Marsha doesn't think you'd dig making it with both of us together."

"Why not?"

"She thinks you're too straight but won't admit it."

"Since when are you into men, Gussie." Marsha chopped up the whipped cream on top of her soda before taking a sip. She rolled her eyes and started making footprints on Gussie's suede shoes.

Tony opened a packet of ketchup and fixed his cheeseburger. "You see, I'd get all the play. The question is could you two girls handle it?" His cheeks bulged out when he talked with a full mouth.

"Yea, I dig women. Marsha knows."

Marsha sat chewing her straw and watching Tony gulp down the burger in three bites. "You eat too fast."

Tony: "My mother doesn't even nag me."

Gussie: "That's cause he's such an industrious boy."

Tony: "Your friend here talks with a lot of experience."

Gussie: "I'm a fresh girl. Marsha knows how fresh I am."

Tony: "How fresh is she, Marsha?"

Gussie: "He thinks he can handle it. You don't know anything about women."

Tony: "I know when they hide."

Marsha sat chewing her straw in that place where silence is louder than words.

"I think I'm being had. You asked me out to play a bitches' game?" He wiped his mouth.

"I'm not playing. I'm serious about the three of us," said Gussie. "We'll take you someplace you've never been."

"Don't let's get into this." Marsha's eyes were swimming.

"We'll take you to the emergency exit."

"You are serious." Tony put his hands under the table between his legs as if to protect his balls, but they were in the way there too.

A tear rolled down from under the heavy mascara lashes and hung at the corner of Marsha's nose. Sometimes she can't help being shaken by how outside affects her insides. She heard Gussie's voice coming at her from beyond the place they had shared.

"You only get into it when there's nothing else. You take me, but that doesn't count for much." Gussie doesn't like to look at tears.

"I don't know what's going on. You two want to cut me up and play games. Well, it's late, I really didn't want to come out tonight, so you all can stay and enjoy your fun."

"Tony, I. . . . " Marsha didn't know what else to say, so she watched him walk away.

When Tony got home he realized he wasn't tired. He didn't know what to think about Serena's Palace, only that the music was too loud and the decor too red. Not his kind of place. He got back in his car and drove all the way out to Jones Beach. A solitary car on the expressway breaks the wind on a cold, clear night. He sat in the empty parking lot and watched the sun come up, seeing Marsha's face in all that pink. And the other one trying to tease him. Smart he hadn't taken her seriously. Smart he hadn't stayed. They probably had a good laugh anyway. Bitches' games. And then they want to hide. That Marsha, playing a full house.

It was Sunday and the mall didn't open up till noon. Gussie got there about 11:30 and went straight up to Funk and Flash. The young Pakistani manager was tripping over his platform shoes trying to be arty in setting out a display of some new T-shirts.

"She won't be in. She called in sick. You tell your friend if she leaves me short again, she's had it."

"You tell her yourself." Gussie went down the escalator. She was tired. She punched the time clock in the supply room of the drug store and took her place behind the cash register. Super slicker stick. Strawberry and champagne-flavored douche. Roulette red.

"Where are the Wipe and Dries?" The woman wore oversized tinted glasses and carried an oversized canvas bag. She made her purchase and was gone.

"Hey, your flowers." Gussie picked up the single tea rose, nestled in fern, haloed in baby's breath and wrapped around with florist paper. She made no further effort to go after the woman. Already she was intoxicated by the fragrance of the flower. Throughout the rest of the day she kept finding space to refresh herself with its scent. She told herself the flower wasn't hers. It would be retrieved. So, there was no thought given to possession, no thought to care. By closing time the rosebud had become a lifeless thing, wilted and unopened.

Helios and Athene · *H.D.*

Athens, 1920

I

The serpent does not crouch at Athene's feet.
The serpent lifts a proud head under the shelter of
her shield.

The serpent is marked with pattern as exquisite
as the grain of the field-lily petal. He is hatched
from an egg like the swan.

The baby Ion, son of Helios, was deserted by his
mother. She laid him among violets. Athene, the
goddess, sent serpents to protect him. These serpents
fed the child with honey.

When Helios the god slays the serpent, he slays in
reality not so much the serpent, as fear of the serpent.
The god learns from the serpent. Be ye wise as serpents.

The serpent lifts a proud head beneath the massive
shield-rim of Athene, guardian of children, patron of the
city.

On one of the remote altars of Demeter at Eleusis,
is a serpent carved beautifully in high bas-relief.

The Eleusinian candidate, it is thought, at one
stage of initiation, walked through a black cave,
the retreat of snakes.

The mind may learn, though the body cringes back.

Consider the birds. Be wise as serpents.

In Athene's hands is a winged creature, a Nike,
her own soul.

Consider the birds. Consider your own soul.

II

The naked Greek, the youth in athletic contest,
has set, accurately prescribed movement and posture.
This convention made of him a medium or link between
men in ordinary life and images of Pentallic frieze or
temple front. We gaze upon this living naked embodiment
of grace and decorum. We are enflamed by its beauty.
We love it.

When we have exhausted the experiences of personal
emotion, we gain from the statue the same glow of physical
warmth and power.

The statue of Helios on the Olympic frieze, as the
beautiful personality that once charmed us, acts as a
go-between.

The youth is a link between men (let us say) and
statues.

The statue is a link between the beauty of our human
lovers and the gods.

The statue enflames us. Its beauty is a charm or
definite talisman.

Our minds can go no further. The human imagination
is capable of no further expression of beauty than the
carved owl of Athene, the archaic, marble serpent, the
arrogant selfish head of the Acropolis Apollo.

No individual has created beauty like this. No
country or individual ever will.

But the Hellene did not throw down his chisel and
rest in self-complacent admiration.

His work began when his work was finished.

The priest at Delphi, the initiate, even the more advanced worshipper, began his work where the artist ceased his labour.

The statue was like a ledge of rock, from which a great bird steps as he spreads his wings.

The mind, the intellect, like the bird rests for a moment, in the contemplation or worship of that Beauty.

The mind grips the statue as the bird grips the rock-ledge. It would convince itself that this is its final resting place.

The mind, in its effort to disregard the truth, has built up through the centuries, a mass of polyglot literature explanatory of Grecian myth and culture.

But the time has come for men and women of intelligence to build up a new standard, a new approach to Hellenic literature and art.

Let daemons possess us! Let us terrify like Erinyes, the whole tribe of academic Grecians!

Because (I state it inspired and calm and daemoniacal) they know nothing!

III

It was in Helios' heart to break, in Athene's
not to be broken.

So Delphi and Athens stood, existent, gaining power,
gaining strength, through inter-dependence of hatred.

But this hatred was clear, defined, removed from
any hint of personal intrusion, intellectual, abstract.

If Athene's citadel broke, Helios' temple crumbled.
If Helios yielded to her, Athene herself was undone.

Delphi and Athens were thus allied forever.

Delphi, the serpent, the destructive heat, Delphi
the devastatingly subtle seat of oracles, Delphi whose
centre of religion was a centre of political intrigue,
Delphi the lie, the inspiration, the music, found in
Hellas, in the world, one equal: Athene.

Athene with silver line between eye-brow and ridge of
helmet could look with all the concentrated power of her
eyes and leave unscathed no God in the world but one:
Phoebus of Delphi.

The olive, turned from sombre gray to trembling silver
by the wind, sweeping from the snows of Pentellicus, the
imperishable silver of her helmet, the serpent whose belly
shone silver as she lured him by her daemoniac power to
lift his head from the black grass; the white silver of
the olive leaf, the white belly of the serpent were as
her guarded eyes.

To Helios alone could she open wide their splendour.

He hated her because she stood unconquerable: he loved
her as an equal.

We cannot approach her direct, so abstract, so cold, so beautiful.

We approach her, if at all, through the medium of the Mysteries and through the intercession of other Gods.

At the foot of the Acropolis, as a lover, waiting at the feet of his Beloved, is the theatre of Dionysius.

The Greek Drama, the outgrowth of the worship of Dionysius, is a means of approach to Athene.

The greatest Athenians of the greatest period were initiates of the Eleusinian mysteries. Those great mysteries were protected by the Love of Athene.

The Love of Athene is symbolized by the arch of wings, for Demeter by the cavern or grot in the earth, and for Phoebus by the very essential male power. Love for Athene is the surrender to neither, the merging and welding of both, the conquering in herself of each element, so that the two merge in the softness and tenderness of the mother and the creative power and passion of the male. In her hand is the symbol of this double conquest and double power, the winged Nike.

The winged Nike, the white sea-gull, the imperturbable soft Owl, the owl, whose great eyes search the night, the mind, the dark places of ignorance.

Athene, the maiden, Parthanos, is doubly passionate.

Reading H.D.'s "Helios and Athene" ·
Adalaide Morris

H.D.'S SIGNATURE, like her poems, is an energy bundle: a seed, a co-coon, a wrapped mystery. The initials condense the birthname, Hilda Doolittle, which in 1886 anchored her as daughter of Helen Wolle Doolittle, member of a prominent mystic Moravian family, and Charles Leander Doolittle, Professor of Mathematics and Astronomy at Lehigh University in Bethlehem, Pennsylvania. Her writings construct from history and mythology a series of selves which successively extend the figure of her initials: Helmsman, Huntress, Hippolytus, Hippolyta, Hermes, Hermione, Helios, Heliodora, and, throughout, her mother's namesource, Helen: Helen *Dentritis* (of the Trees), Helen of Sparta, Helen of Troy, and, at the center of her most complex and extended identification, Helen of Egypt. Each "Hermetic Definition," as the initial-bearing title of a late poem suggests, is a momentary manifestation of the mystery of identity, a butterfly released from the anagram, cryptogram, little box of her signature.

The signature was at first qualified by a poetic affiliation: "H.D., Imagiste." The poems it signed were until recently H.D.'s best known work, the brilliant imagist poems which began appearing in 1913. Cited by movement theorists as representing quintessential imagist qualities, these poems filled her first volume, *Sea Garden* (1916), and appeared prominently in each of the four successive movement anthologies. The imagists' resolve to strip poetry of what Ezra Pound called "slush" left their work laconic: hard, dry, factual, accurate, freshly recorded perceptions. H.D.'s imagist work has a radiant spareness. In these poems, pools quiver like sea-fish, sea-grass tangles with shore-grass, and wind-driven flowers drag up from the sand a bright and acrid fragrance.

In 1920, when she wrote "Helios and Athene," H.D.'s imagist period was over. The harsh years just preceding provided material which eluded imagist formulations and compressions, material she would work and re-work throughout her life. In London through most of World War I, H.D. had suffered a series of losses: in 1915, she gave birth to a stillborn child, the miscarriage caused, she felt, by the shock of the Lusitania's sinking; in 1916, her husband, Richard Aldington, entered the war with a passion which by 1917 had estranged them permanently; in 1918, her brother (and other self) Gilbert was killed in action in France, a loss that killed her father the following year; and finally, in 1919, H.D., so ill from double pneumonia that her landlady predicted immediate death, gave birth to a daughter, Perdita.

The story of H.D.'s resurgence begins with a young writer's response to *Sea Garden*. Winifred Ellerman, soon to take the name Bryher, came on H.D.'s work in the midst of the war. "There will always be one book among all others that makes us aware of ourselves," she wrote; "for me, it is *Sea Garden*. . . . I began the morning and ended the day repeating the poems." Bryher's passionate self-recognition in H.D.'s work became, when she knocked on her door, an equally intense recognition of the author: "The door opened and I started in surprise," Bryher recounts. "I had seen the face before, on a Greek statue or in some indefinable territory of the mind."[1]

Though she had never been there, H.D.'s poetry was saturated with the landscape, history, language, and mythology of Greece. Greece was, she says later in phrasing which echoes Bryher's, "the land, spiritually of my predilection, geographically of my dreams."[2] A territory of the mind, a geography of dreams, a recognized affinity—everything was in place for the interchange which occurred in spring 1919 when Bryher visited H.D. in the final stages of her illness and pregnancy. The words, Bryher reports, "seemed to come from somewhere beyond my brain":

> I was so alarmed by her appearance that I could only stumble through an itinerary of places. I have just found you, suppose I lose you, was the thought running through my head. . . . "If I could walk to Delphi," H.D. whispered with an intensity that I knew I was seeing for the first time, "I should be healed."
> "I will take you to Greece as soon as you are well."[3]

All commitments were kept: H.D. survived, Bryher negotiated the trains, steamers, and difficult postwar permissions, and, in the spring of 1920 they began the trip which generated not only "Helios and Athene" but, just after, on the island of Corfu, a vision which seems to have determined the course of H.D.'s poetic and spiritual development.

H.D. and Bryher traveled first to Athens and then set sail for Delphi, Apollo's shrine and their journey's main objective. For over one thousand years, from the 6th century B.C., pilgrims had brought their pain and confusion to Delphi, and Apollo's oracle—as history, legend, and mythology record—had responded with miraculously prophetic skill. H.D.'s determination to visit Delphi positioned her within this ancient tradition. Consciously or not, it seems clear that what she desired from her pilgrimage was prophecy: instruction about the sources of her survival, assurance of her vocation, perhaps even indication of her poetic direction.

What an immense disappointment, then, it must have been for H.D. and Bryher to be informed that it was impossible for two ladies alone, so soon after the war, to travel the dangerous mountain roads. Unable to disembark at Itea as planned, they were forced to sail on past Delphi to Corfu. But in Corfu something amazing happened. H.D. and Bryher in their hotel bedroom underwent an experience that both in substance and in form stood in place of a session with the Delphic oracle. It was a vision which both predicted and enacted a transcendence for H.D., a rebirth out of the ruins of World War I into a new spiritual dimension, the prophetic capacities from which H.D.'s greatest work emerges.

"Helios and Athene" is the meditative preparation for this revelation. Written in Athens, just before the journey past Delphi, the poem interrupts the generally placid, decorative, at times incantatory verse which just precedes and, for a while, follows it. In its long, rapt prose lines, H.D. has taken new and heretical models: the accreting structure and metrical thickening and thinning of the phrases recall Whitman, and the lilies, birds, and wise serpent recall Matthew and Luke, associations reinforced by the biblical arrangement of the verse units. Its most heretical aspect, however, is the stretch of its anti-imagist project. "Helios and Athene" is not an objective formulation of perception: it is impassioned mythology and history, biography and psychology, aesthetics, epistemology, and metaphysics.

Reading "Helios and Athene" is as rigorous a process as reading H.D.'s late long poems. As in decoding an inscription on a partially erased palimpsest or interpreting a particularly radiant and recalcitrant dream, the reader needs both patience and inspiration, both the skills of research and the arts of intuition. Surrounded by the labors of those H.D. calls "the whole tribe of academic Grecians"—tomes on the Delphic myth and its origin, the Delphic oracle and its pronouncements, pamphlets on the politics of the Greek city-states, debates over the reconstruction of the lost statues of Phidias, and essays with crackly pages and titles like "The Hermeneutics of the Eleusinian Mysteries"—the H.D. reader becomes, ready or not, a candidate for initiation.

The three bodies of knowledge one needs to read "Helios and Athene" involve Apollo/Helios, Athene, and Demeter. Like a good imagist in search of concision and pictorial clarity, H.D. makes Apollo, intellectualized deity of solar light, into Helios, the personified Greek sun. For the Greeks, Helios was not abstracted light but shining energy; he had little mythology beyond that which helps us see his rising and setting above us. Drawn in his swift chariot, he sheds light everywhere: his eyes flash from his golden helmet; rays glint from his breastplate; draped in wind-whipped gauze, he courses across the sky from eastern swamp to western darkness. While the shape of his name draws Helios close to H.D.'s obsessions (Hellas, Helen, her own initialed identity), the concreteness of the image gives new immediacy to the poetic and prophetic aspects of Apollo's mythology, aspects which H.D. appropriates for Helios. "God who is light, who is song, who is music, is mantic, is prophetic," she summarizes in *HERmione*, "that is what Helios means, a god who is prophetic."[4] Throughout "Helios and Athene" he is identified with Delphi and its oracle.

If one pole of the poem's spiritual territory is the enlightened, poetic, prophetic Delphi, the other is Athens, seat of wise and powerful governance, manifested here in Athene—not just the abstracted Athene, however, but the precise, forty-foot-high, gold-and-ivory statue, now vanished but once the most sacred, the most costly, and technically the most difficult of all the sculptures Phidias executed for the Parthenon. H.D. describes her with fresh, visionary fullness, as if the statue rose before her eyes. This is Athene Parthenos, the virgin Athene, her virginity signifying not abstinence but intactness: the entire-in-herself, the powerfully inviolate protector of the state. One hand rests on her shield; the other, outstretched, holds an eight-foot-tall image of Nike, the winged Victory. Her rich hair combs back over her temples; her eyes gaze forward with a brilliant thoughtfulness; strength flows through her broad-shouldered, slender-hipped stance. Though her calm seems opposed to the wheeling intensity of Helios, H.D. emphasizes their complementarity. As the stability of Athens was crucial to the survival of Delphi, Athene was necessary to Helios, a fact H.D. knew not only from history and mythology but also from immediate experience: the poet survives, if at all, in a precarious alliance of ecstasy and steadiness. As the poem puts it, "If Athene's citadel broke, Helios' temple crumbled. If Helios yielded to her, Athene herself was undone."

Through the winged Nike, the reach of the high-crested helmet, even the colossal upsweep of the statue itself, all energy in the figure of Athene rises. Balancing this ascent is the force embodied in the third presence in "Helios and Athene": Demeter at Eleusis. For over one thousand years, until roughly the same period as the Delphic oracle's collapse, the Mysteries at Eleusis enacted a drama of descent: Demeter's search for her vanished daughter, the lost half of herself, the ravished Persephone. So sacred and powerful were the Eleusinian rites that not one of the initiates—in some years numbering 30,000, a figure equivalent to the entire Athenian population—left a clear record of the proceedings. They seem, however, to have functioned much like the ritual at Delphi: under conditions that were kept strictly secret, after fasting, cleansing, and devotions that proved their worth across centuries, in sacred forms which it would have been godless to deny, the vision came again and again. Each initiate, possessed by and enacting the spirit of Demeter, witnessed Persephone's return from the underworld. This was loss restored, life regained, and light risen once again from darkness. It was faith in the possibilities of this moment that supported the linked worlds of Athens and Delphi.

So far, then, the poem superimposes three images. Like three scenes in a dream, they are dramatic, compact, interconnected, and haunting. The stories' most striking common element, the focal point on which H.D. makes them converge, is the serpent which in each embodies the profound forces of the subterranean. The poem begins with the serpent which, in Phidias's statue, "does not crouch at Athene's feet" but, in a rising twelve-foot-high s-shape, "lifts a proud head under the shelter of her shield." In her mythology, the serpent was said to have sprung from an attempted rape by Hephaestus. His seed fell to the ground, and from it rose a son who had at first either completely or partially the form of a serpent. Athene preserved and nurtured him, placing him, as she later placed Ion, Helios's son, in a basket encircled by serpents. He grew to be Erichthonius who, rising from violence and darkness, founded Athens and the worship of Athena.

Delphi's founding was also connected with a serpent, the Python, monstrous creature, death-dealer and chaos-demon, guardian of the sacred springs. Slain by Apollo/Helios, the serpent yielded the prophetic powers which named and flowed through Apollo's seer, the Pythia. In the prophetic session at the Delphic temple, the Pythia, intermediary between Apollo and the questioner, having fasted and prayed, mounted the tripod from which she spoke. She was attended by priests and temple-guardians, but the ceremony was simple: the consultant asked, the Pythia listened, and Apollo illumined her soul so that she knew the future and could, in her own words, reveal her vision to the petitioner. As talismans on her tripod, the Python's bones, teeth, and hide summoned the powers of the unconscious, the instincts which prepared the Pythia for prophecy.

There are countless myths of dragon-serpents which, like the Python, guard access to subterranean springs, to sources of knowledge which, subdued and used properly, turn darkness, disorders, and death into enlightenment, order, and resurrection. Everywhere in the Eleusinian rituals, the serpent is used to summon this dark, prophetic, rejuvenating power. Carried in a basket by Demeter's priestesses, entwining the winged chariot of the initiate, or carved in high relief on Demeter's altars, the serpent, "marked with a pattern as exquisite as the grain of the field-lily petal," embodies the great secret of resurrection and metamorphosis.

It is this, the serpent's knowledge, that H.D. sought in Greece. She needed to know how to bring order out of outrage, how to turn pain to prophecy, how, like Persephone, to rise from the depths of her darkness. If Parts I and III of "Helios and Athene" give us three talismans, three scenes to initiate us into the magic of the serpent, Parts II and IV suggest a method of knowing, embodying, and interpreting these scenes: an epistemology, an aesthetics, and a hermeneutics. Though she sends us ransacking reference works, H.D. everywhere subordinates fact-finding intellect to the possessed/possessing powers of imagination: "Let daemons possess us! Let us terrify like Erinyes, the whole tribe of academic Grecians!" It is worth remembering that Erinyes are, like Medusa on Athene's aegis, snaky-locked: bands of serpents encircle their heads and in their hands they bear snakes like torches. Their process of knowing, H.D. would remind us, is not through abstract thought but through passionate contact: embodiment and enactment.

Art—a statue, a play, a meditation like "Helios and Athene"—helps us do this. It is intercession. It is, H.D. reiterates, a medium, a link, a go-between, a means of approach. It stands between us and those powers which, unmastered, would overwhelm our too frail understandings. Like the Pythia, art joins speaker and spirit, question and answer; like Persephone, it circulates between loss and restoration, lack and amplitude; like Erichthonius, it leads us to the powerfully nurturing Athene. Such an art exacts a response—a responsibility—from its viewer. Where the artist ceases, in H.D.'s formulation, there the soul of the initiate must begin. The statue, poem, scene, or dream is, in her wonderful metaphor, but "a ledge of rock, from which a great bird steps as he spreads his wings."

The first part of "Helios and Athene" ends with the admonition "Consider the birds. Consider your own soul." The great bird's spread wings in Part II dissolve in the last section into the image of the winged Nike, cradled in Athene's hand, symbol of her mastery, symbol of her soul, and also, in an interesting and complex extension, a symbol of her centrality. In H.D.'s trinity, Athene is one of three, but at the end she becomes also three-in-one: her androgynous solitude combines Demeter's altruism and Helios's glorious self-absorption. This was a position which had great appeal for H.D. She was always fascinated by edges and intersections, and the sexual border between male and female was no exception. In her writing, she spoke as Hermes and as Hermione, as Hippolytus and Hippolyta equally. In her life, she maintained dual allegiances to men and women: to Ezra Pound and Frances Gregg, to Aldington or to Kenneth McPherson and, throughout her life, to Bryher. Always, in life, in art, or in mythology, she was compelled by the image of the two-in-one, the brother-sister unit: Hilda and Gilbert, Balzac's Séraphita and Séraphitus, the Egyptian Isis and Osiris, or, here, Zeus's children, Demeter and Helios. Athene in this poem is made to link qualities traditionally named "male" and "female." "Love for Athene," H.D. summarizes—thinking, as she always does, across many layers at once—"is the surrender to neither, the merging and welding of both, the conquering in herself of each element, so that the two merge in the softness and tenderness of the mother and the creative power and passion of the male." This empowering duality is perfectly figured by Nike's two wings, wings which working together lift, balance, and transport her. With this "double passion" H.D.'s meditation in "Helios and Athene" closes.

The vision in Athens is completed by the vision in Corfu where H.D. foresees her own entry into prophetic power. The Corfu vision is structured like a hermetic re-creation of the Delphic session. In it, H.D., attended by Bryher, is at once questioner and Pythia. As she describes it in *Tribute to Freud*, the vision came like a more orderly "Helios and Athene": a series of intense scenes which rise, one by one, with luminous, enigmatic clarity. H.D. compares them to playing cards, transfers, or slides. They are images traced in light which she, filled like the Pythia with prophetic illumination, projects outward onto the bedroom wall. Of the symbols, the majority recombine elements from "Helios and Athene": there is the warrior who has "a distinctly familiar line about the head with the visored cap," an abstracted androgynous figure who recalls not only her soldier-brother Gilbert but also the helmeted Athene; there is the Delphic tripod, familiar symbol of poetry and prophecy; there is a series of *s* or half-*s* shapes curved like the lifted serpent under Athene's shield; and, finally, there is the winged Victory, Nike, who in "Helios and Athene" represented the androgynous soul of Athene but now, fully possessed, becomes for H.D. "my own especial sign or part of my hieroglyph." The vision was an intense strain and, as H.D.'s part of it ends, she thinks, "I must hold on to this one word. I thought, Nike, Victory.' I thought, 'Helios, the sun.'" And then, exhausted, "I shut off, 'cut out' before the final picture, before (you might say) the explosion took place."

Once more Bryher comes to the rescue. She had seen nothing until H.D. closed her eyes, but then, suddenly, miraculously, she herself witnesses the last resonant image: "a circle like the sun-disk and a figure within the disk; a man, she thought, was reaching out to draw the image of a woman (my Nike) into the sun beside him."[5] In a moment which will have repercussions for H.D.'s subsequent work, the paradigm of the Delphic oracle is significantly transmuted. Athene Nike, the soul of the poet, becomes one with Helios. The woman, seen before as a type of Pythia or earthly channel for Apollo's vision, is now herself assumed into the disk of Apollo/Helios. No longer the speaker of someone else's vision, she too is a sun, a fully empowered source.

H.D.'s post-World War II poetry accomplishes the prophecy embedded in the twin visions which occurred in Greece in 1920. In her long poems, *Trilogy* and *Helen in Egypt,* H.D., like the Eleusinian Demeter, would witness rebirth out of devastating loss. Like Athene, she would bring power and wisdom to bear on the preservation of civilized life. And, finally, like the oracle at Delphi, she would connect us to a force that feels lost yet, as she came to know in Athens and Corfu, remains deeply within us: our own spiritual capacities, our ability to make the serpent the instrument not of darkness but of light, song, music, and life.

Notes

[1] *The Heart to Artemis* (London: Collins, 1963), pp. 187-88.
[2] *Tribute to Freud* (New York: McGraw-Hill, 1974), p. 41.
[3] *Heart to Artemis,* p. 191.
[4] *HERmione* (New York: New Directions, 1981), p. 110.
[5] *Tribute to Freud,* pp. 45-56.

Queen Charming · *Pamela White Hadas*

for Alice

A woman writing thinks back through her mothers.
—Virginia Woolf, *A Room of One's Own*

Dear Godmother, Another year and the annual
ball rolls round again; there's my pumpkin
taxi tick-tocking through its axle-turns for all
it's worth . . . the Pegasused rodents and the footmen

you ordered up from your sense of fittingness. . . .
They roll round in thought I mean. So it's time
for the anniversary letter. Not that I'm ever mindless
of the continued gift. My other given name

still flutters in the dark, repeating like a heart,
metering each costly mime. The royal pseudonym
meanwhile feathers me out of the grubby hearth
as pumpkin takes to the air. Then midnight: I'm

dumped back into the ashbucket, rags and all . . .
of course, you know. And the clock's recoil takes care
of your being there, as then, giving your soft call
from the garden's edge; it's unexpected as ever.

Again I fetch the pumpkin and find my sooty dress
transformed right down to the transparent shoe,
watch mice evolve to power as you put the harness
on their hack identities. Everything you do

momentarily to make me over, makes me more
or less myself. But which? Could I endure my wishes
made actual without the punctual nightmare?
Salt-watering the hazel, sorting piles of ashes

from lentils, fighting the rituals of narcissism
rejection demands, cindering the nest—can all this be
dropped for more than the briefest moratorium
of masquerade? Is it possible to unforesee

the midnight deshabille? Despite a number of years
between satin sheets, the rescue is as windfall as sun-
rise always is, drawn by phantom horsepowers
out of their mousy hearts, metronome-drawn.

All this rolls by in half-light, just before the King
knocks at my door with the breakfast tray.
My feet, still sheathed in solid tears, are kicking
free for the now daily dance, prosaic in its way,

like the shining tea poured out. I doubt my vision
still. Am I this or that? I stare into my cup.
Minute dark leavings—mice? A ghost's breath on
the glimmered surface—mother? I look up.

There is more than a ghost in the gilt-laden
mirror, of a chance. My rash weird sisters cut
off their toes and heels for this. Why am I chosen
who did nothing but comfort myself, poising my feet

over my mother's bones? The lucky doves
in the hazel tree took care of me pretty well,
seeing I was such a mess. Everybody loves
a self-effacer. Say, does your whole clientele

keep coming back this way, after you've sent them out
feet first into the fitting rooms? Do they come clean,
change in time, toss out the frowzy petticoat,
keep ashes out of the soup for good and dream

too deeply to remember? I suspect the pangs
of separation last. Today we hold an audience,
the King and I, for all our subjects—hopes, harangues,
funny stories, grievances; and then the dance.

Are you sending someone to dance with my grown son?
Grant me the grace to be kind, to be more than a mirror
with its black side hidden. May she be a vision
enacted by you and see how you put it all together

for us outside of us. I will tell her "nothing
is promised," and she will think me unpromising until
she sees the whole design. A charming title's nothing,
given life. It's for the vision I am grateful.

The Gaudenzia · *Gwen Head*

THE KISS had not gone well, remained a yearning, clumsy meeting of alien skin and membranes that refused to become anything more, arousing only that loneliness it had been intended to alleviate.

She had disengaged herself gently, letting her lips skim his cheek as if reluctantly, then shifted the strap of her big bag heavily up on her right shoulder again, and walked firmly away, neither looking back, nor letting her shoulders sag.

In the front hall her husband waited for her, seated on a small hard bench no visitor ever used, flipping through the pages of an old magazine as if she had been a dentist and he a suffering patient callously kept waiting. *Husband, yes, still,* she thought, astonished at seeing the strange man with the tight mouth and complaining voice, who began at once to upbraid her.

"It's nearly eleven."

"I wasn't aware I had a curfew."

"I assumed you'd be back earlier."

"You *pre*sumed, you mean."

"Where were you?"

"Out. With friends. *Plural* friends." The exact way in which *they* had become *we,* and then only *I* again was no longer any right concern of his, if it had ever been.

He stood up, confronting her by the door. She stepped aside, but he made no move to go. Instead, "Sarah called," he said, staring hard at her before he moved unexpectedly back toward the living room.

"Sarah who?"

"Sarah Medford. You remember Sarah. Abigail's teacher."

"Sarah! What on earth for? They're not having another of their horrible potluck dinners to raise money, are they? Not in the middle of the summer? I can't, I simply can't, make anything this time. I doubt I can even go, not with Abby's camp starting Sunday, and my trip—"

"Not that. She's calling all the parents. Bobby O'Day died."

"Oh, *no!*" Rocked by the first horrible assault of it, she could still notice the small satisfied upturn of his lips.

"I didn't know what I should tell Abigail, or when. And I couldn't think of much else after Sarah called. It was hard doing the Daddy bit all evening. I'd hoped you'd be back before Abby's bedtime."

"Just as well I wasn't, then. That would have been an awful time to tell her. She'd have stayed awake all night."

"You *will* tell her, though?"

"Of course. Tomorrow, I guess. I need some time to myself first. When—?"

"Last Tuesday, Sarah said."

"I can't believe it. He looked so *well*. He did everything the other kids did. He even had *hair*."

"Apparently they knew it was coming—had known since April. Sarah said they had one last drug to try—"

"His *shots!* Abby told me that Bobby had shots every Friday. It didn't even occur to me—"

"It got him through the end of school, at least. After that things apparently went downhill very fast."

"God, oh god."

She sat down abruptly, covering her face with both hands; from the hot reddish darkness behind her closed lids she could hear her husband's footsteps, going into the next room, pausing for a few seconds, returning.

"I wrote down the information about the services. Bobby was cremated. The remains will be buried tomorrow afternoon. There'll be a graveside service. Then there's a memorial service tomorrow evening. Seven, at Saint Patrick's. Sarah asked me to have you call her back and let her know if you and Abby can come. Apparently she's doing all the calling for the kid's parents, what are their names?"

"Ida is the mother, I think. The father's name I don't know. Of course we'll go. Bobby was—I don't even know what to call it, at ten. He was a special friend of Abby's. She really, *really* liked him."

The sobbing began then, a clenching at her deepest core, not far removed from nausea, rage, or terror. With her eyes clamped shut, she reached out, and found him standing above her, knew the familiar textures of cloth and skin, the little hairs of his forearms, so much thinner and wirier now. She rose up only high and long enough to draw him down beside her.

"Tomorrow I think we should all be together," she managed to say.

"It's so hard for Abby. First us. And now this. Now Bobby."

He held her then for a long time, in a way no longer sexual, but still personal and intimate in the extreme, their bodies falling together with thoughtless accuracy as they had always done. Her crying, the agonized grinding of her forehead against his collarbone, the grip and release of her hands on his shoulder and sleeve, came and went; and in their final, depleted ebb, she felt confusedly how pain had come to be their strongest bond, more final, perhaps even—the thought loosed a fresh swell of silent tears—more permanent than the child they so uneasily shared.

They were nearly late to the service because of the flowers.

All day long, in a way that made her think of a dress rehearsal, they had walked through the activities in which years of weekends had passed, producing a composite Saturday, a brief history of Abby's childhood performed again. Perhaps, indeed, this was no rehearsal, but rather a revival, a command performance to divert and solace their child.

At any rate they had heeded her every whim, perhaps even demanded whims where none existed, for their own grieved satisfaction as well as Abigail's. First came an hour of family bicycling, although Jed, who had come by car, had to take turns using hers, while whichever of them was without the bicycle trotted along beside Abby like a faithful dog, grinning and panting encouragement. Then an hour of collapse on one of the park's wide lawns, an exhibition of children's art, and finally, after hastily consumed hamburgers, the market.

Abby fidgeted while her mother bought, from sheer habit, the gallon can of olive oil, the frozen *pesto,* the pounds of real Parmesan cheese and bulk pasta, the rice, kasha, and exotic sweetmeats of apricot and pistachio that the two of them, light eaters and now near-recluses as well, would never manage to use up, but throw out finally, rancid, cracked, moldy, or shriveled to leathery sweetness. Meanwhile Abby nibbled the skin around her fingernails, or sucked at a strand of long, wheat-colored hair.

Jed took the heavy shopping bags uncomplaining, but bent to Abigail to ask, "What would you *really* like to do now, Abs?"

"Can we go to the Stamp Act?"

"Can you afford to buy anything?"

"I think so. Mom owes me my allowance."

"You're right, Abby. I forgot. You get another dollar for sitting yourself, too."

Jed's eyebrows shot up; determined to maintain their truce, she forced herself to explain. "Just a couple of hours in the afternoon. I had to go to the drugstore, check on my visas, get a typhoid shot, stuff like that."

They descended a ramp of gray, undulating planks, part boardwalk, part stationary roller coaster. On each side, tiny glassed-in shop fronts flanked it, fanning out along its leisurely curve of descent. Old books, records, clothes; shops for preserves, shops for soap, cheeses, candy; shops full of forlorn, ectomorphic plants, force-fed to a dense greenness as unhealthy as the pallor of newborn veal. At the Stamp Act, Abby lost herself at once in a world not of geography, tariffs, trade, or boundaries, but simply and blissfully, of horses.

This passion had begun almost in her infancy. When it became impossible to add more stuffed horses to the dozens that grazed on her bed all day, more model horses to the pens and stalls of her toy breeding farm, more volumes on horses to her bookcase, more news photographs and clippings of horses, or more exuberant drawings and paintings of them to the Scotch tape and thumbtack scarred walls of her room, the child had turned finally to stamps, seeing in each frail, exotic paper world only the flashing hooves, the wild eyes, the tossing manes and streaming tails, of horses. Her favorite stamp was a large, poorly printed commemorative, inscrutably captioned in Cyrillic letters, on which, in the extreme background of a mob scene of such turbid colors and careless registration that it could have represented anything from a coronation to a revolutionary riot, the dim and tiny figure of a stone horse, surmounting what appeared to be a triumphal arch, could be barely discerned, rearing wildly against a livid sky.

Now Abigail was admiring in miniature the park of some great country estate, where an elegant Polish lady, in a full black dress diagonally sashed with red, sat sidesaddle on a composedly cantering white horse. Next she fingered, coveted, marveled at an Italian stamp, depicting some golden mosaic in which a Roman centurion looked down from his prancing dapple-gray horse as Jesus was led to his cross; then a stamp of celestial blue across which two racing Arab colts exploded like silver comets; and, finally, most wonderful of all, a stamp depicting Eohippus, the primal

First Horse, with his gourd-shaped head and body, small laid-back ears, delicate legs, and tasseled, donkeylike tail.

It was the Polish lady in the mournful green park who reminded her of the flowers. Too late to call a florist; and in any case the stiff perfunctory sheaves of dyed carnations, scentless roses, and unyielding gladioli seemed all wrong for the memory of a child. Above her, near the market entrance (for the market buildings, on many levels, were terraced into a hillside so steep as to be almost a bluff) she remembered a flower stall, capricious, seasonal, full of unfamiliar, constantly changing marvels.

Leaving Jed and Abigail to correlate the aesthetic and equine merits of the stamps with their prices, she climbed a half-hidden flight of cement stairs, crossed an alley rumbling with truck traffic, passed a row of fish and seafood counters, and found herself in a small, stylized jungle, where tiers of green gallon cans arranged in pyramids rose on either side of her, their varied burdens of flowers and foliage exploding, cascading, twining, catching at her hair and clothing as she moved, so that she felt herself a giant, sterile, goggling insect among them. At her feet were cyclamens, hairy-leaved, bilabial, in astonishing shades of lavender and pink; huge blue alliums whose globular heads reminded her of dandelions gone to seed; gray lacy Dusty Miller; the kaleidoscopic foliage of tuberous begonias. Above dangled the shiny-leaved sprays and porcelain bells of fuchsias, and on either side were lilies: not mere day lilies, but lilies for each hour, each minute of light, from the first pale rose of morning to the deepest black-throated mauve, russet, and wine of approaching night.

A bearded assistant wearing a green canvas apron over his plaid shirt approached her. Wordlessly she pointed out her choices: the alliums, a selection of lilies, some narrow-leafed pink and purple flowers whose name she could not bring herself to ask, a flat white flower like a pincushion stuck full of tiny stars, a few gold and coral snapdragons, sprays of red and white honeysuckle for fragrance.

Later, at home, pushing their dinner plates aside unscraped, she thrust as many and varied flowers as she could into a common kitchen glass, not wanting Bobby's parents to have the trouble of returning a finer vase. She added only enough water to cover the stems, hastily twisted and torn to the right lengths. Then, crying "Abby, Jed, put on your coats," she rushed into her own garden, the disheveled bouquet in one hand, and as they passed out to the car, impulsively snatched up a few handfuls of daisies and some spires of orange montbretia. These, while Jed drove, she tucked into edges and bare spots, indifferent to their imperfections, and to the litter of leaves, torn stems, and fallen petals on the car floor.

The street in front of the church was full of cars but nearly empty of people. Across the street from their parking place she saw the church door just closing. She jumped out and began clumsily to run, leaving her family to follow, feeling her skirt spattered with drops of water shaken from the bouquet she clutched with both hands to her wet breast.

No one had thought to turn on the lights in the church entry hall. At seven, in summer, it was still mid-afternoon outside, and even after she had removed her sunglasses and begun to take in the constantly reforming lines and knots of large and small figures in the dimness, she saw few faces that she knew. Sarah, the children's teacher, embraced her, weeping; murmured "Lovely, lovely," brokenly over the flowers; and waved her toward a guest book on an ugly oak table, where she signed each of their three separate names. Briefly she thought of leaving the flowers there. Jed and Abby had already brushed past her, past Sarah, past the constantly changing group gathered around the small, pale, stunned-looking O'Days; and she would have joined them immediately, in spite of the rapid unseemly clicking of her high heels on the marble entry floor as she ran to catch up, had not Sarah deflected her, placed a hand on her shoulder, steered her past Bobby's parents, to whom she mumbled brief, fragmentary greetings and words of sympathy, and propelled her through the double oak doors, and into the center aisle of a nave glaringly high, stark, and flooded with ruthless late-afternoon light.

In all this space and clinical brightness, down the great length of varnished pine pews she passed, there could not have been more than forty people. Nor were there any flowers; instead the altar was dominated by a large, flimsy-looking easel displaying a portrait in brown chalk, evidently drawn from a photograph, of the dead Bobby, crew-cut and wearing a T-shirt, relentlessly smiling.

She placed her flowers on the altar rail beside it, then rejoined Jed and Abby, who moved over, leaving the aisle seat to her. She had not entered a Catholic church, nor attended a mass, since the gilt, marble, and jeweled-glass cathedrals of her junior year in Europe, dark, mysterious, and grand, heady with incense, reverberating with organ music and chanted Latin.

Now only the uncomfortable length of the service remained. Except for herself, in a printed silk dress normally reserved for luncheons with friends, the mourners wore everyday clothes, shirt-sleeves, cotton frocks, even blue jeans. Rendered in language as bare and, to her ear, graceless, as the plain pews and high white walls that surrounded her, the magnificent words of grief and consolation, the tremendous promises of rest, resurrection, and triumph had become small, shopworn, and trivialized; so that time and again, as she glanced from the dead child depicted before her, to the delicate pale profile, inquisitive, tearless blue eyes, and fine, freshly brushed, light hair of the living child at her side, tears sprang to her own eyes, not at the truth of the words, but at their bald, evident, hopelessly flimsy and yearning falsity.

Walking between them back to the car, Abby turned first to Jed.

"*You* don't believe it, do you?"

"Believe what?"

"All that resurrection and life after death stuff?"

"I don't necessarily *dis*believe."

"Then why were you making jokes?"

"Yes, why were you, Jed? Whether *you* believe or not, simple respect for the child's parents—"

"No one could hear me but you and Abby. I was just trying to lighten things up a little for the kid."

"Maybe she doesn't want things lightened up. Maybe she needs to understand."

"Does anyone understand?"

"Mommy, do *you* believe it?"

"I don't know, Abigail. I guess deep down everyone *wants* to believe it, or something like it. Nobody can prove it *isn't* so."

"Nobody can prove it *is*, either."

"I can't argue that, Jed. But Abby, the world can be a hard place, as well as a joyous and beautiful one. And I think it's wrong to make fun of anything that gives people some comfort, some strength."

"Even if it isn't true?"

Abigail, in the front seat between them, looked again from one to the other.

"Even if it's true only for them. In their hearts."

Jed corrected her. "In their imaginations, you mean."

"I suppose so."

And then, thinking of their remote idolatrously loving past, she added, "I don't think anyone lives life as it is, Jed. I don't think anyone is strong enough."

"You believe in delusions, then, and in deliberately lying, even to children?"

"I believe in whatever I need to believe in to keep on living."

"But Mommy," Abby said, looking up at her perplexed. "*You* cried. All the way through the service. And Daddy didn't."

"I still don't believe it," Abby said over their special Saturday breakfast of French toast, bacon, and the fresh orange juice it was Abby's task to squeeze.

"Well, you don't have to," her mother said wearily, wondering how other parents managed to skim so lightly over the sheer drops and hidden quicksands of their children's lives. "Neither your father nor I has ever tried to sell you on religion. His *or* mine. But it doesn't do any harm to know what other people believe, then decide when you're older. You can believe whatever you want, Abby, and that includes not believing anything at all."

"That wasn't what I meant."

"Then what—"

"I mean I just don't believe Bobby is *dead.*" Abby put down the gnawed rind of a slice of French toast.

"That's one thing you *do* have to believe."

"I didn't even know he was sick!"

"I was surprised too, Abby. Shocked, really. I didn't know he was *that* sick either."

"Did you know he was going to die?"

"I knew he might. I knew he had been very, very seriously ill. But I guess I thought—at least I hoped—that he was cured. And not just in remission."

"What does that mean?"

"Remission? It means being better, even almost well. Sometimes for quite a long time."

"I thought he was cured. I saw him at school every day, and I played with him. He was the only boy in my club. We drew pictures for each other, and wrote stories together, and traded horse stamps."

"Oh, Abby!"

What could she do but open her arms and gather in the lovely, awkward, mysteriously changing body of her daughter, letting the lengthening legs dangle over her own rounded knees. "Abby, Abby, I'm so sorry."

If the body altered so visibly each day, what went on in the invisible mind and spirit of this, of any child beginning to grow up? Her eyes began to prickle with unshed tears, even as her arms tightened, and her back bent to the timeless familiar rocking. But the child, still a child, slipped away from her.

"It's only been a couple of weeks since I saw him. My *brain* believes it. But—"

"But what, Abby?"

"But I keep wanting to call him up. To tell him what's happened. *To tell Bobby he's dead.*"

Now Abigail was in motion, even in flight, circling the dining room table again and again, a habit she had had, when angry or bewildered, since infancy. Abruptly she stopped, confronting her mother across the full width of the table, clutching a sketch pad and pen she had picked up while she prowled as if they had been a small shield, a short sword.

"Mommy, that's crazy, isn't it? Isn't it?"

Her mother waited a moment for the right answer to come, letting the words collect in some hidden hollow of her mind, as if seeping one by one from a cold subterranean spring.

"I don't think so, Abby. I've felt the same way myself."

"When someone died?"

Again she considered. "Not so much then. Perhaps because when people close to me have died, my own mother for example, they've been very old, or so sick it was obvious they could never get well. And when it's that kind of death, as it usually is, the personality, the mind, the spirit—whatever it is you really know and love—goes long before the body. But Bobby—"

"Then when *did* you feel that way?" Abby asked again, urgently.

"When your father and I—" she began helplessly.

"*What?*"

"When we decided we couldn't live together any more."

"When you decided to get divorced!" Abby said, a new brutality in her voice.

"Yes. Abby, you know the reasons. You know I didn't want it to be this way. But still I kept wanting to call up Jed because he was the only person who could understand how sad I was. And why."

"I know, Mommy. I'm sorry."

Abby came round behind her chair, gave her a quick, hard, choking hug, then sat down before the sketch pad, a little girl again. Her mother tried to return to her reading, but instead found herself watching covertly as a form of great intricacy, lightness, and speed took shape on her daughter's sketch pad, half hidden between the soft side curtains of light hair that trailed over the page as she bent to it.

"What are you drawing, Abby?"

"Nothing, Mother."

But a few moments later, without looking up from her work, Abby began to speak, one of the long strangely learned monologues she sometimes offered spontaneously on any matter that had been the object of her impassioned curiosity. Most often, lately, these lectures dealt with horses: their breeding, lineage, training, or legendary exploits.

"Do you know what a gaudenzia is?" Abigail asked.

"No, Abby."

"But you've heard of the Palio? In Siena?"

"Of course. I've even been in Siena, Abby. The square isn't really a square. And the color of the brick—"

"Gaudenzia," Abigail interrupted impatiently, as she often did when intent on her own thoughts, "was a mare, a beautiful white mare who won the Palio three times, three years in a row, more than any other horse ever. When she was a filly, she was playful and wild, and her owners called her Farfalla, which means Butterfly, because she was so silly and lazy, and they thought she wouldn't ever amount to much.

"But then they broke her, and began to train her, and she changed. She learned to run, really run, and to love running; and they entered her in the Palio and she won it. She was the first and only mare *ever* to win it. And she won again and again."

"Why did they change her name? I think Farfalla is a pretty name."

"It's all right, I guess," Abby said. She lifted her head, looking past her mother, her blue eyes wide, her nostrils dilated. "But after she learned to run, she needed a new name, a great name. So they called her Gaudenzia."

"Meaning?"

"Joy of Life," Abby said softly, bending to her paper again. "The joy of being alive."

They were silent for a few minutes, the mother turning again to the photography magazine in which a recent exhibition of her own work was featured, noting with irritation, but without real interest, that several of her best photographs accompanying the article had been quite poorly reproduced. Some larger, elusive question, however, stuck at the back of her mind, something she restlessly sidestepped, shied at, returned to against her will. Finally she recalled the one word Abigail had left unexplained, as troubling as a small stone that could not be dislodged.

"Abby," she said, "you told me all about Gaudenzia. But didn't you say you were drawing *a* gaudenzia? What is that?"

"I'll show you," Abby said, coming round to her mother's place at the table holding her finished drawing, which she laid on top of the magazine with the perfect assurance of the loved. Before her the mother saw depicted a wondrous, airborne horse with an elaborate mane and tail, and an assortment of fluttering decorations or streamers whose meaning was obscure.

"Explain it, Abby," she said. "Tell me what I'm seeing."

"This is a gaudenzia, of course," Abigail said, speaking at first in the superior, teaching tone she reserved for well-meaning but slow-witted adults.

"A gaudenzia is an enormous white horse that flies through the sky forever. A gaudenzia has huge dark eyes like mirrors, a mane and tail of albino peacock feathers, and a forelock made out of the eyes of peacock feathers. There are tiny wings on each hoof. And these—" Abby pointed to what seemed a pair of long banners, or a double train flowing from the wonderful horse's shoulders, "—these are streams of water, pure sparkling water, bubbling up and out into the sky like fountains, or cold, icy springs, or a trail of shooting stars."

Now Abigail stood erect, looking away from her mother, fingers alternately crumpling and smoothing one corner of her drawing.

"When I die," she said, in a small, resolute voice, from which all trace of conceit or pedantry had abruptly vanished, "I will be a gaudenzia. Bobby is a gaudenzia. There are many angels, I think, but only a few gaudenzias. Bobby and I are both gaudenzias."

Then she was gone, and in the speed and suddenness of her going the drawing fluttered to the floor like a feather of spun silver.

Preoccupied and tired—her plane from Bogotá had finally come in nearly five hours late, leaving no time at all for sleep—she twice took wrong exits from the freeway. She had forgotten the map included in the camp literature, and although Abby was a second-year camper, she realized that Jed must have driven last year to pick Abby up, for she had only a general sense of direction and distance, and a vague recollection of the low, rambling suburban school building of glass and yellow brick, sprawling the length of an enormous parking lot.

When finally she found the place, it was already nearly a half-hour past the scheduled rendezvous. But although the baggage truck had come, and trunks, sleeping bags, backpacks, suitcases, and an odd assortment of miscellaneous unmarked pillows and stuffed animals had been unloaded on the wide sidewalk, the camp buses had not yet arrived. She considered a narrow but shady parking spot at the far end of the crowded lot; but then, remembering the weight of Abigail's trunk, she reconsidered, and as another car pulled out, slid immediately into a vacant space almost next to the baggage truck.

She loaded the smaller items first, amused by Abby's sloppily rolled sleeping bag, her half-empty pack, and the pillow in its flowered case, marked as Abby's by the green felt frog in the pillow case, blunt nose, white button eyes, and front legs protruding as if he had been tucked into bed there.

The trunk was another matter. She squatted, hot and sweaty in the many-pocketed designer khakis she wore when traveling on assignment, and tested the weight of it. Too heavy to carry any distance, unless she hefted it onto one hip; and then she would risk aggravating her old, tedious back problem, perhaps being laid up for days, even weeks. No, she would drag it; damage to the trunk's scarred blue paint was definitely a secondary consideration. But the noise of heavily weighted metal rasping over rough concrete was startling even in the crowded parking lot, filled with the sound of automobiles and shouted greetings, and she had taken only a few hobbled, breathless steps before she found one of the junior counselors who had ridden ahead with the baggage truck at her side, offering to help. She unlocked the car's trunk and raised the lid, pushing aside a jack, tools, safety flares, a blanket, some clothes she had forgotten to take to the cleaner. Then together they tipped Abby's trunk over the car bumper and into the tight but adequate space she had cleared.

Slamming the lid, looking up to thank him, she saw the first of the fat-tired, battered yellow buses pull in at the far end of the lot, heard the camp songs break up into a shower of greetings and cries of recognition, and an instant later saw Abigail running toward her, and felt the surprisingly large, solid, and vigorous body land hard in her outstretched arms.

"You've grown," she said, joyfully aware of the immemorial banality of the statement, "and you must have gained five pounds."

"Nah. You're just getting old and decrepit, Mumsy."

She held the child briefly at arm's length, studying the mobile sun-burned face, the blue eyes and the light hair under the lacy shadow of an openwork straw hat with blue ribbons that tied under the chin. Jed had bought the hat for Abby in the Caribbean; she noted with pleasure the oddity and charm it lent to a costume otherwise consisting of a sweat shirt, tattered cords, hiking boots, and an unseasonable goosedown vest. No marriage, she thought, no love that had made so beautiful a child could ever be said wholly to have failed.

"So how was camp?"

"It was fine. Mommy, I can dive now, and do the elementary back-stroke, and float on my stomach *and* my back! And Annie says my breathing on my crawl is getting really good."

"That's wonderful, baby. What else? What about your riding?"

"Well, Pogo isn't there any more."

"Oh, he was your *favorite!* What happened?"

"He got thrush and they had to sell him."

"Thrush! I thought that was a bird, or some dumb thing babies got."

"It's a horse disease too. He'll be okay, Georgie says, but he can't work as hard as a camp horse has to, so they sold him."

"Do you have another favorite horse, then?"

"Oh, maybe Rainbow. She's a palomino, very smooth-gaited, and I guess she's a little nervous or something, because she's never tied up in the pasture. They let her wander around loose, but she's a troublemaker. She likes to nip at the other horses, and then back away very fast before they can kick her."

"She sounds too wild to ride."

"She needs a good, strong rider, Georgie says. *I* got to ride her twice."

"That's terrific, Abby. I'm very proud of you."

They were driving now, along wide, almost empty streets without sidewalks, bordered by rough cedar and redwood fences, or uneven hedges of laurel or juniper. Behind lay low, sprawling houses, only their roofs, television antennas and utility lines clearly visible. Now and then she steered toward the center line to avoid children on bicycles, or bored, wildly barking family dogs idling away the Sunday afternoon in the suicidal pursuit of passing cars.

"Do you think you want to go back next year?"

"Oh, yes! Could I go second term too?"

"Well, we could think about it. You know most of the kids will be different?"

"Oh, that's okay. Susie will be staying, and so will Rachel. And Annie's going to be our counselor again, she says she's almost sure of it."

"Well, that's great. I'd miss you, of course, but I don't see any real reason you couldn't go both terms, if you still feel the same way when it's time to reserve a place for you. I'm glad it was so much better than last year."

"Oh, it was."

"You weren't homesick?"

Abby shook her head.

"Well, *I* was. Or maybe just Abby-sick. I really missed you. I kept waking up in the middle of the night in these weird hotel rooms with strange plumbing and lizards crawling up the walls, and wishing I had someone with horrible sharp elbows and big feet to hug."

Abby giggled dutifully.

"So there wasn't *anything* you didn't like? Not even the food?"

"I didn't like the mosquitoes. I've got bites all over."

"So do I, only some of mine are ticks. I'll probably get Chagas disease."

"What's *that?*"

"Not really, Abby," she said hastily, aware that hypochondria could be both hereditary and highly contagious. "Anything else you didn't care for? Especially anything I could do something about?"

This time, somewhat to her surprise, her daughter did not answer; and in the sudden lapse of conversation, she had time to notice that they were passing a small park near the water. Beyond the promenade that meandered along the shore, sailboats dipped and veered like white sulphur butterflies, and in the park itself, part landscaped and part wild, the last fireweed towered above beds of marigolds and zinnias. She slowed the car, noting a small playground at the far end. Perhaps Abby, cooped up in a bus for nearly three hours, might like to stop, interrupting the long drive home with a run. Impulsively she pulled into the narrow parking lot that ran the length of the park, noting, as she cruised in search of a parking place, that except for children Abby's age or younger, there seemed to be no individuals there, but only halves of couples: young couples exuberantly playful or languidly sauntering, deep in animated conversation or deeper still in mute embrace; parents leaning against each other as they bent over the redwood rail of the sand-floored play area watching their children; or very old couples, silent and stationary, who seemed to her own hopelessly single vision not so much exhausted, as valiant, enduring, and enviable.

The full weariness of her travels rose up in her, and with it the pain of reunions that seemed always the prelude to further separations. Above all, she felt rage at the elusive, ineradicable contagion of love that she now saw all around her. Suddenly she realized how reclusive, apart from her work, she had become, how resolutely she avoided such places, places which, for all their loveliness in the ripe golden light of summer's end, might as well have been malarial swamps as far as she was concerned, infected with a pestilential miasma of loneliness.

"Why are we stopping here, Mommy?"

"There's a nice playground, Abby, see? No, down that way. There's a huge climbing rope, and a merry-go-round of inner tube swings—"

"Let's just go home, Mommy."

"Why, are you hungry or something?"

"No. It's just that there are too many families here."

Startled by the exactitude with which Abby had read her thoughts, and by the realization that she was inescapably half, if not of a couple, at least of a pair, it was the mother who now made no reply, but pulled out of the parking lot at the playground end, and moved again into the light fast traffic along the lakeshore boulevard. The park continued for some miles as a narrow border of grass along the water; in its scalloped inlets grew tall stands of cattails, or flat intricate mats of water lilies; and beyond swam an occasional female mallard trailing an obstreperous, insubordinate brood of half-grown ducklings.

"Are you a good dancer, Mommy?" Abigail asked suddenly.

"Okay, I guess. At least I used to be."

"Well, I'm not."

"Abby, that's silly. I couldn't *ever* have done half the things you do in your modern dance class."

"You know that's not the kind of dancing I'm talking about."

"Well, but all dancing is the same, basically. You're light and agile — what's all this about anyway?"

"They have dances at camp."

"They do? For the high school kids?"

"No. For everybody."

"Well, I'm sure you dance at *least* as well as anybody else your age."

"I don't really know," Abigail said, turning to her window to stare out over the water. "I never got to try."

"Didn't anyone ask you to dance?"

"No," softly. "Nobody. And there was a dance every week."

Mindful of Abigail's unpredictable fits of shyness and stubbornness, and the necessity, for herself, of those few unencumbered summer weeks on which a substantial part of their income depended, the mother steeled herself against a too ready sympathy.

"Well, you're a liberated kid," she said. "You could have asked one of the boys to dance."

"I did."

"How many times?"

"Once," Abby said reluctantly.

"And he wouldn't?"

"No."

"Did he say why?"

"He said a horse stepped on his foot."

"Well, it may *have*, Abby. That place is *overrun* with horses. That's one of the main reasons you kids like going there."

"No."

"No, what?"

"That's not why he wouldn't dance."

"Oh, Abby, how do you know?"

"I just do."

Again there was silence between them, an inconclusive silence that unrolled before them like the asphalt ribbon of the road and its green border vanishing into a blind curve some distance ahead.

"What did you do at the dances, then, Abby, if you didn't dance?"

"I brought a horse book along to read."

"Oh, Abigail, no wonder! If you just sat there with your nose in a book and didn't even look at anyone, how did you expect them to know you even *wanted* to dance?"

"Why couldn't someone be interested in my book? And come over and talk to me? And maybe *then* dance?"

"Do you think you really looked like you *wanted* someone to talk to you?"

Abby's eyes snapped forward, and the line of her round chin hardened.

"*Bobby* would have come over and talked to me," she muttered.

Bobby. The two syllables were like two lurching steps interrupting a long untrammeled run through a field suddenly perceived to be full of hidden burrows and sinkholes, each with the potential to maim.

"Yes, I think he would have, Abby," she said slowly. "He was that kind of little boy. I think he really understood what other people were feeling, really thought about them. You know, sometimes when he came over to play with you, he'd get tired after a while and I'd find him down on the living room sofa, just quietly reading a book. And when he saw me, he'd put the book down and we'd have the *nicest* conversations."

"What about?"

"Whatever he was reading, or thinking. What I was doing. Or you. He loved hearing about you."

"He knew all about me."

"At school, maybe. But the rest of your life was—a kind of fairy tale to him. He had to spend so much time resting, Abby. And going to doctors."

Abby was sitting uncharacteristically straight and still, hands primly folded in her lap; and with the same quick glance away from the road that took in these details, her mother noted as well a single enormous tear, jerkily sliding along the faint shadow at the inner corner of Abigail's left eye, down the side of the sunburned nose and cheek, until it hung, mournful and faintly ludicrous, above the girl's upper lip. Always in the past Abigail's crying had been noisy, wholehearted and simple, accompanied by stamping, thrashing, and great, rending, soul-satisfying sobs. The new composure of her grief was chilling, and remained so even when the tear, as she opened up her mouth to speak again, slid over the pink cornice of her upper lip, and dissolved on her tongue.

"Mommy," very quietly, as if from a great distance, "I had a crush on Bobby."

"I know, Abigail. I'm very sorry."

"You *knew*? How did you know?

"I thought he was so nice, Abby. When I told you about talking to him, what I was trying to say was that it was almost like talking to you. I felt *that* close. He was a fine, a dear little boy. He would have grown up to be a wonderful man. I guess I had kind of a crush on him myself."

Quickly they glanced at each other, the mother taking in her child's matted lashes and red eyelids, and the branching revival of glistening tracks on her cheeks.

"Abby, Abby, I'm so sorry."

"Mommy, it's not just that I'm sad."

"Then what?"

"I'm afraid."

"Darling, please, please don't. You *will* get over it. People get over worse things, things so terrible you or I couldn't even begin to imagine them. Life—"

"You don't *understand!*"

Shocked into silence, she noted mechanically their approach to the free-way entrance, downshifted, checked her outside rearview mirror as she slid the car across two lanes of heavy traffic. In a few minutes they would be home, and she could hold her child, watch over her undistracted, be the saving raft in the breaking storm of her grief. If she had time; for in a soft, ferocious whisper, Abigail went on.

"I *know* Bobby is dead. But I'm still not sure sometimes. At camp, when we went on hikes, there were places on the trail where I thought I could almost see him. Just out of the corner of my eye. But I'd look again, and nothing was there—not even a bird, or a funny shadow in the tree."

I am lost, her mother thought, *we are lost,* although not half a mile away she could see the long arch of the familiar overpass toward home.

Relentlessly, Abigail continued. "And the real reason I hated the dances was that sometimes I felt sure Bobby was there. Not on the tennis court with the other kids, but maybe a little way back, by the horse corrals, watching. And I thought if I sat in the corner where it was darkest, with my book, that he might come talk to me. Oh, I knew it wasn't true, that I was just pretending. But I don't want to dance with anybody else, Mommy. Not ever."

How could she save her child from this grief, reassure her that life was not short, but long, various, rich in the unexpected, when her own life was so channeled and diminished into an unending series of duties, one of which even now held them separate? The car began to ascend the long straight ramp, and for a moment she felt the machine as a living, willful creature in exhilarating motion, rising exuberantly above the noise and brown stench of the freeway.

"Abigail," she said suddenly, desperately, jolted by an awful mingling of terror and relief, but hanging on, barely, "Abby, what about the gaudenzia? Don't you believe in him any more?"

"That was just a stupid story, Mommy," Abby said. "I made it up to go with my dumb picture."

But the sky above them was a celestial, an empyrean blue; and the ramp, rising, swept into a wide, perfectly banked curve, sensuously slow and controlled even at the little car's top speed.

Then she knew that their road could never end, nor would either of them ever again find the words, for what soared tirelessly, watched sleeplessly over them both, their guardian and doom, invisible, radiant with loss.

Indulgence and Accidents · *Judith Hemschemeyer*

. . . *These 7 years were full of indulgence and accidents. A doughnut or two a day wasn't unusual and I demolished a 57 Chevy, which was just the beginning of a horrible driving record. Adding to the trouble my brother Guy drove over me with the Massey-Ferguson. Didn't hurt me much and all in all the years went very well.*
               —from Aura's autobiography

then marriage, the baby
and making him so mad
in that N.Y. apartment

he threw the phone
and broke the wall
but I got up

at dawn to write
so he did too
and woke the baby

then Greece, and baby #2
and my breasts got hard as stone
and so the midwife milked me

as gently as she could
staring out the window
dreamy-eyed

talking to the other women in the room
for such a long sweet time
I went to sleep

and woke up in Connecticut
with something wrong with me
the need to tell the truth

and be a perfect human being
so I started writing poetry
my brother Guy

"Is the poem so transparent
that it will reveal my failings?"
is my first official entry

*Didn't hurt me much
and all in all
the years went very well*

until my brother turned
and saw I was still moving
and swung the Massey-Ferguson around

Getting To Know, or Stepping Out in an Entirely Different Way · *Akua Lezli Hope*

for Swan

Still, it's *how* we negotiate
not *that*. style yet. rule
and measure deep the interface. just
Don't say the concrete alchemies night
like grassbreeze and palmetto sea
or sand-sting and dune-dance.

Where is your body wired? to
telegraph the moment.
coiled-lock conductors
spark fresh air, sear
space with pigment's trace and linen stretched
pinned flags on backyard line
tiered gravity defiers, signal clean

Massacre meaning's first blush
spread soil with this fleshy compost
and alter sacrificial curtsies to don
the bloodfruit's leather skin. Live.

July 1980

Gowanus Canal (because you said look again) · *Akua Lezli Hope*

Another loneheart evening
watched your murktide tire and gasp
like Harlem's greater body once
you breathed with fishes. children
sought you for their play
they say the sins of fathers
are polluting choice of sons
what fools go slaughter water
that needed balm for pain

yet romance remains on Union Street,
on Third where girded squatting bridges
lie above your mournful sludge

i sip the blur by full moon:
low horizon night of azure periwinkle
brownstone skyline lights and cobbled
streets of industry are still.
long brick, darklid glass, the silent
buildings wink at you, european
shadows by the amerind shore. no more.

i sip the blur by full moon:
crane or derricks hulk
above you, dinosaur and dragon bone
see only multicolor in twisted metal litter
and renascent spring sails perfume
on the kissy wind, and think you beauty.

Spring 1980

Mouse · *Laura Jensen*

Mother picked up the fantastic cup,
washed the idea of dishes, hovered over
the stove-notion behind a make-believe curtain.
Saw her children not-wake, go away asleep
wearing coats like their blankets. And not aware
of much but the tender feel at the edge
of the evergreen, the pout of the fattening berry.

Eyes spending butter on a clock
cannot make their own way up to midnight, up to noon,
or the falling,
crying mamma, mamma,
I do not want to go on.
There's a song from the bottle,
from the seashell, from the sharp beak
of the sea-gull: *pain be gone.*

Autumn, and the pear skin does not want to curl.

Mother pear, mother pearl, can you follow
what I am telling? Mother, the idea of love
wraps around us like a quilt of old morning,
like a horseshoe of flowers.

Ah, they are small, small, sleep in the stomach.
Ah, they are small, small, little rodents of love.

Whale · *Laura Jensen*

The oars are silenced.
The silenced oars silence the echoing
darkness and water, unscrew
the lightbulbs of the phosphorescence.

You have shut your eyes to the sureness
of that tactile evening, the whale
like an old thumb-print of presence,
the gray canvas damp at the surface,
dark and enormous with a small, small eye.
The digits at the shovel of the hand
always knew they could not quite place it.

Listen. Echo is twining on stone.
Marginal, intact, virtual, virtuous
coracle. Rainbow arcs into the ear
like old dry beans, like Mother's warning,
like Wrath of Uncle, "What have we here?"

The vine holds on to what comes next, what
happens: though the stone may crumble
in Hellenic ruin; or be parked by the
Empire mile, carved into, dumb, columbine-
fresheted; or stacked up, handled, managed
and bandied by the Old Man of the Wall;
or cobbled into overshoes and sunken
down, hauling bones by the tarsals,
hauling Zoot suit and cigar
and meeting silt exploding
where it must moan many years.

There the stone dreams of a center sun
that blushes on the east at the skyline
a branch that opens up a flower by blinking,
a flame that rushes to the stove without thinking,
without saying, "I don't know. . . . "

There it dreams that echo swims by now,
dreams echo says to the stone,
you will once again see daylight,
there, there. Believe me,
echo only need hear.

Problems of Translation: Problems of Language · *June Jordan*

dedicated to Myriam Diaz Diocaretz

I

I turn to my Rand McNally Atlas.
Europe appears right after the Map of the World.
All of Italy can be seen page 9.
Half of Chile page 29.
I take out my ruler.
In global perspective Italy
amounts to less than half an inch.
Chile measures more than an inch and a quarter
of an inch.
Approximately
Chile is as long as China
is wide:
Back to the Atlas:
Chunk of China page 17.
All of France page 5: as we say in New York:
Who do France and Italy know
at Rand McNally?

II

I see the four mountains in Chile higher
than any mountain of North America.
I see Ojos del Salado the highest.
I see Chile unequivocal as crystal thread.
I see the Atacama Desert dry in Chile more than the rest
of the world is dry.
I see Chile dissolving into water.
I do not see what keeps the blue land of Chile
out of blue water.
I do not see the hand of Pablo Neruda on the blue land.

III

As the plane flies flat to the trees
Below Brazil
Below Bolivia
Below five thousand miles below
my Brooklyn windows
and beside the shifted Pacific waters
welled away from the Atlantic at Cape Horn
La Isla Negra that is not an island La
Isla Negra
that is not black
is stone and stone of Chile
feeding clouds to color
scale and undertake terrestrial forms
of everything unspeakable

IV

In your country how
do you say copper
for my country?

V

Blood rising under the Andes and above
the Andes blood
spilling down the rock
corrupted by the amorality
of so much space
that leaves such little trace of blood
rising to the irritated skin the face
of the confession far
from home:

I confess I did not resist interrogation.
I confess that by the next day I was no longer sure
of my identity.
I confess I knew the hunger.
I confess I saw the guns.
I confess I was afraid.
I confess I did not die.

VI

What you Americans call a boycott
of the junta?
Who will that feed?

VII

Not just the message but the sound.

VIII

Early morning now and I remember
corriente a la madrugada from a different
English poem
I remember from the difficulties of the talk
an argument
athwart the wine the dinner and the dancing
meant to welcome you you
did not understand the commonplace expression
of my heart:

the truth is in the life
la verdad en la vida

Early morning:
Do you say *la mañanita?*
But then we lose
the idea of the sky uncurling to the light:

Early morning and I do not think we lose:
the rose we left behind
broken to a glass of water on the table
at the restaurant stands
even sweeter
por la mañanita

Abishag · *Shirley Kaufman*

*. . . and let her lie in thy
bosom that the lord my king
may get heat.*

−1 Kings 1:2

That's what they ordered
for the old man
to dangle around his neck,
send currents of fever
through his phlegmatic nerves, something
like rabbit fur, silky,
or maybe a goat-hair blanket
to tickle his chin.

He can do nothing else
but wear her, pluck at her body
like a lost bird
pecking in winter.
He spreads her out
like a road map, trying
to find his way from one point
to another, unable.

She thinks if she pinches
his hand it will turn to powder.
She feels his thin claws, his wings
spread over her like arms, not bones
but feathers ready to fall.
She suffers the jerk
of his feeble legs. Take it easy,
she tells him, cruelly

submissive in her bright flesh.
He's cold from the fear
of death, the sorrow
of failure, night after night
he shivers with her breasts
against him like an accusation,
her mouth slightly open,
her hair spilling everywhere.

from Claims · *Shirley Kaufman*

Look at the map. If you forget
the scale there's no way to measure
how far you have traveled
from there to here.

I roll out the strudel
as she taught me, pulling the dough
until it's thin enough to see through
all the way back.

Strangers open the door. They show me
into the room I slept in
next to their big one,
somebody else's crib, the wallpaper new
where I slipped my finger under the seam
and tore the roses.

I lay on my left
side next to their wall
to hear her whimper in bed,
or was it some immoderate
noise that scared me
from my sleep and made me
cry I'm afraid of the dark
till he stamped in the doorway
and switched on the light.

* * *

My mother remembered how she sat
in the cart beside her father
when he rode through the lands
of the absent landlord collecting the rents.

It was near Brestlitovsk,
the names kept changing and the peasants
would stare at them and pay.

Peasant to grandfather, Jew to Pole,
each greasing the other,
steps that went nowhere
like the road to the border.

When the Cossacks came charging through the town
they bolted the doors and windows
and hid under the beds. They put pillows
over the children's mouths
to stop their cries.

There was no summer in this landscape,
even the language disappeared.
Fifty years later all she remembered
was her father's white shirt,
that he was always clean.

* * *

Snow in the winter,
pillows of goose down
where my mother still walked
on the underside of sorrow,
thick braids splashing between her shoulders,

or sat by the lamp they lit early
while the young man read Pushkin
leaning against her knees.

It rained in Seattle even in June.
She made fine stitches in her sheets
and waited. French knots and gossip.
The distance between them
was a hole through the center of the world
the rain kept filling. The rain
made a river in her ribs
on which her sad heart drifted.

There are words that can't travel,
threads that have lost their way home.

I wanted to grow up somewhere else.
Not in the living room
where no one lived, the dark oak
smelling of polish, untouchable doilies,
and the sun stopped back of the curtains
so the upholstery wouldn't fade.
Not in the kitchen where she skimmed
the fat off the soup like fear
left over from the first life.

* * *

I might have had a sister
mother told me only she lost her
down the toilet at three months.

She grew so pure in her grieving
she no longer saw the blood.

Hunger forgets what it came for
when the fingers won't tighten
around a spoon and the food
is sawdust in the reluctant mouth,

chewing and chewing what I fed her,
refusing to swallow
the lump on her tongue.

Her hands with their patient knuckles
are lighter than anything she held.
They are obsequious as aliens,
swabbed clean, exiled
even under the ground.

Philosophy in Warm Weather ·
Jane Kenyon

Now all the doors and windows
are open, and we move so easily
through the rooms. Cats roll
on the sunny rugs, and a clumsy wasp
climbs the pane, pausing
to rub a leg over her head.

All around us physical life reconvenes.
The molecules of our bodies must love
to exist—they whirl in circles
and seem to begrudge us nothing.
Heat, Horatio, *heat* makes them
put this antic disposition on!

This year's brown spider
sways over the door as I come
and go. A single poppy shouts
from the far field, and the crow,
beyond alarm, goes right on
pulling up the corn.

Briefly It Enters, and Briefly Speaks · *Jane Kenyon*

I am the blossom pressed in a book
and found again after 200 years . . .

I am the maker, the lover, and the keeper . . .

When the young girl who starves
sits down to a table
she will sit beside me . . .

I am food on the prisoner's plate . . .

I am water rushing to the wellhead,
filling the pitcher until it spills . . .

I am the patient gardener
of the dry and weedy garden . . .

I am the stone step,
the latch, and the working hinge . . .

I am the heart contracted by joy . . .
the longest hair, white
before the rest . . .

I am the basket of fruit
presented to the widow . . .

I am the musk rose opening
unattended; the fern on the boggy summit . . .

I am the one whose love
overcomes you, already with you
when you think to call my name. . . .

The Pond at Dusk · *Jane Kenyon*

When a fly wounds the water the wound
soon heals. Swallows tilt and twitter
overhead, dropping now and then toward
the outward-radiating signs of food.

The green haze on the trees changes
into leaves, and what looks like smoke
floating over the neighbor's barn
is nothing but apple blossoms.

But sometimes what looks like disaster
is disaster. Then the men struggle
with the casket, just clearing the pews;
then long past dark a woman sits,
distracted, over the ledger and the till.

Restaurant · *Maxine Hong Kingston*

for Lilah Kan

The main cook lies sick on a banquette, and his assistant
has cut his thumb. So the quiche cook takes
their places at the eight-burner range, and you and I
get to roll out twenty-three rounds of pie
dough and break a hundred eggs, four at a crack,
and sift out shell with a China cap, pack
spinach in the steel sink, squish and squeeze
the water out, and grate a full moon of cheese.
Pam, the pastry chef, who is baking Choco-
late Globs (once called Mulattos) complains about the disco,
which Lewis, the salad man, turns up louder out of spite.
"Black so-called musician." "Broads. Whites."
The porters, who speak French, from the Ivory Coast,
sweep up droppings and wash the pans without soap.
We won't be out of here until three a.m. In this basement,
I lose my size. I am a bent-over
child, Gretel or Jill, and I can
lift a pot as big as a tub with both hands.
Using a pitchfork, you stoke the broccoli and bacon.
Then I find you in the freezer, taking
a nibble of a slab of chocolate big as a table.
We put the quiches in the oven, then we are able
to stick our heads up out of the sidewalk into the night
and wonder at the clean diners behind glass in candlelight.

Absorption of Rock · *Maxine Hong Kingston*

We bought from Laotian refugees a cloth
that in war a woman sewed, appliquéd
700 triangles — mountain ranges
changing colors with H'mong suns and seasons,
white and yellow teeth, black arrows,
or sails. They point in at an embroidery,
whose mystery seems the same as that posed
by face cards. Up close, the curls and x's do
not turn plainer; a green strand runs through
the yellow chains, and black between the white.
Sometimes caught from across the room, twilighted,
the lace in the center smokes, and shadows move
over the red background, which should shine.
One refugee said, "This is old woman's design."

We rented a room to a Vietnam vet,
who one Saturday night ran back to it —
thrashed through bamboo along the neighborhood
stream, then out on to sidewalk, lost the police,
though he imprinted the cement with blood
from his cut foot. He came out of the bathroom
an unidentifiable man. His strange
jagged wound yet unstaunched, he had shaved.
Yellow beard was mixed with blood and what
looked like bits of skin in the tub and toilet.
On the way to the hospital, he said, "Today
the M.C. raised his finger part way.
They're just about ready to gong my act."

We search out facts to defend a Vietnamese,
who has allegedly shot to death a Lao
in Stockton, outside a bar. It was in fear,
we hear him say, of a cantaloupe or rock
that the Lao man had caused to appear
inside him. One anthropologist testifies

that Vietnamese driving in the highlands
rolled up the windows against the H'mong air.
The H'mong in Fairfield were not indicted for
their try at family suicide; there was a question
of a Lao curse or want of a telephone.
Three translators have run away—this fourth
does not say enough words.

Eager Street · *Kendra Kopelke*

I drag my shirt across the floor
with my foot, kick the shoes
under the couch and everything
is out of order. Even the goldfish
plant is growing in wrong directions,
its pot too close to the window,
leaves rotting on the sill to dust.
Everyone knows the women in Baltimore
wash their front steps each week.
On their knees, on Saturday,
they rub their palms hard against
the marble, as their children play
together on the sidewalk. But you and I
share another kind of order,
when you're gone, I can see
where you've been, which towel
you dried your hair with, what magazine
you read at dinner. Some weeks
we barely speak, but if we're lucky,
by morning our bodies drift together,
our talk curls to the center of the bed
like a daughter. And the clothes
covering the furniture are forgiven.
Forgiven, yet still not put away,
it's how we live through each
unfolding season. We drive
our guests down Eager Street,
point out the marble stairs,
the strong women, the generations
of commitment. It's a good story.
These things out of order make
a difference. There is a dream
inside each glass on the dresser,
each book on the floor. Cleaning
would be a lie.

But tonight, I remember back
to our first winter on a southern coast,
you were picking the beach clean
of shells, stuffing them in your pocket,
you were just a little ahead of me
when you spotted a flat shell shaped
like a fish and you tossed it hard
into the waves. You kept your back
to me a long time. You must have been
wishing hard then, for something
like our lives, to matter.

Leaving My Daughter's House · *Maxine Kumin*

I wake to the sound of horses' hooves clacking
on cobblestones, a raucous, irregular rhythm.
Mornings, the exercise boys, young Algerians
from the stable next door, take their assigned
animals into the Forêt de Soignes for a gallop.

In Belgium all such menial work is done
by Arabs or Turks. Barefoot, shivering
in the north light of 8 A.M., I stand
twitching the curtain aside to admire
the casual crouch of small men in the saddle,
their birdlike twitters, their debonair
cigarettes, and the crush of excitable horses
milling about, already lather-flecked.

I know that these skinny colts are second-rate runners.
They'll never turn up in silks at Ascot or Devon.
The closest they'll get to the ocean
is to muddy the oval track at Ostende
for the summer vacation crowd braving the drizzle
to snack on waffles or pickled eel between races.

And no matter how hard I run I know
I can't penetrate my daughter's life
in this tiny Flemish town where vectors of glass
roofs run to the horizon. Tomatoes climb
among grapes in all the greenhouses of Hoeilaart.
Although it is March, the immense purple faces
of last summer's cabbages, as if choleric
from the work of growing, still loll in the garden.

At odd hours in the rain (it is nearly
always raining) I hear the neighbor's rooster
clear-calling across the patchwork farm
where I walk among sheep the height and heft
of ponies. Their gravelly baas rumble
an octave lower than their American cousins'.

What a Crusoe place this is, juicily rained on,
emerald-thick! What a bide-a-wee I visit
playing a walk-on part with my excursion ticket
that does not prevent my caring with secret frenzy
about this woman, this child no longer a child.

The horses are coming back now, making a calmer
metrical clatter in 4/4 time. Tomorrow
when they set out again, arching their swans' necks,
I will have crossed the ocean, gone beyond time
where we stand in a mannerly pose at the window
watching the ancient iron strike flint from stones,
balancing on the bit that links us and keeps us
from weeping o God! into each other's arms.

Upstairs · *Marlene Leamon*

Why do you always live upstairs? she asks, showing the same
mother's care she always has. I tell her it's the view, seeing
everything spread out and in proportion, the people eating
meals or leaving home, small dogs escaping traffic, even the arc
of news hitting a neighbor's porch.

Up here, her face can be
large or small, its lines like the wires in my sky, carrying
messages to strangers, calls for help, maybe just supporting
birds.

She can be anything I like, a small woman in a gingerbread
house, quite harmless, simple, really. She will touch me
the way that fairy tale figures do by standing outside her door,
offering to let me in, to warm me with stories of her
life.

There once was a man on a hill, someone who relished
views. He is the man I most clearly resemble, our eyes the same
steely blue, our heartbeats irregular. She tells me of his love
of reduction, how he would squint in the scope of his gun,
lining up hearts and brains.

He gave her the kill, some-
thing even now she can see. On her hearth, the soft
bodies of rabbits, of deer, maybe pheasant, the wealth
of a hunter's wife. It was never just food, but a kill bringing
marriage to life.

Here in her gingerbread, in her house
close to the ground, everything lives out
of time. The stories are real, the hunter gone, and she
an old woman making peace with herself.

                                    She will die
negotiating stairs, perhaps to my house. I will wait
for her here, composing the sky, the absence of clouds, the view
from the hill.

A Sequence for My Mother · *Jan Heller Levi*

Formal Feeling

After a great pain, a formal feeling comes—
—Emily Dickinson

I

September. The rabbi didn't know her.
All day I expect her, look for her in every room.
I have so much to tell her now.

Orange strands from the carpet cling to my feet.

Where is she?
Where is she?

2

Now let me tell you about minutes of lead,
the color blue. Blue is the color of her
fingernails, her lips, my father's wet eyes.
Blue is the color of some other world I insist
she sees. Blue is their language, their children,
their future, dissolving.

Now let me tell you what we can tell the dying:
nothing.
Now let me tell you about a kingdom, about transformations,
about a healing, about a radio turned full volume
for which she would not turn her head.

8:40. 8:41.
I begin the slow, proud walk into motherless America.

3

October. Now I dream
dreams of perfect love and almost understand her.
She is the river
upon whose separate banks my father and I appear,
mouthing the words to a standard tragedy.

During the day I walk with ghosts—
all women, all ages,
all her.
She is everywhere.

Where is she?

4

In wood, in vault, in Baltimore.
Please omit flowers.

They say it will be a cold winter, colder than last.

I have her coat.

My Father's Wedding

Then the moment
slips away from you, an unanswered prayer.
Your father takes you aside,
throws his heavy arm across your shoulder,
tells you everything he thinks you want to know:
I'll never love like that again, but. . . .

A year ago, from California,
you called your radioactive mother,
came home in time
to watch her turn blue at the ends and die.
Now, back in New York,
the telephone rings

and you stop imagining,
for a moment,
the novel of grief and redemption
you should have written last year,
or the year before.

It was all right, it was
lovely, you tell your friends who predicted
depression, or the black tongue of anger,
but nothing like this cool breeze,
this clean page
of nothing.

After Her Death

1 *I Lie Awake Listening to Ken's Breathing*

For weeks my heart has been camping out.
He shifts, the down quilt slides
across our bodies, we curve into one another.
Dear friend, sleep-as-conversation,
witness.

2 *The Father Goes Out on Dates*

In these, my father and mother are divorced.
I am an angry teenager and live
with my father.
I visit my mother.
We sit at an unfamiliar table, beautiful
in its strangeness.
(Our hands are the same. They are *her* hands.)
Outside the window, trees.

At first I am worried about her:
how will she live alone?
Soon I realize she is happy with her new life.

3 *The Father Remarries*

And this is death's gift-dream to me:

She comes back.

We all sit in a small room,
chattering, embarrassed.
Sara kisses my father.
My mother lowers her eyes.
Her lashes are dark, soft, almost wet.

She who all her life angered me by obsequiousness
stuns me now with this gesture.

4 *If We Could Speak to Death, What Would We Say?*

(I have come to His press conference, or
He is a guest on a TV talk show.
There are questions from the audience.)

There is so much I want to say:

that death is political;
that it is necessary;
that it is unnecessary;
that it follows me all the days of my life;
that it is my life;
    I eat it,
    I drink it,
    I breathe it;
that I dream and undream it;
that it is the unspeakable space between myself and others;
and that it is the soft black cushion, like velvet, upon which we all rest;
that we have infringed too far on God's authority
and this is his last remaining power over us;
that there is no God;
     that the sun rises in cancer;
        I wake from cancer;
        I brush my cancer;

I wash my cancer;
I put on my cancer;
I sit at my cancer;
I write my cancer;
I am married to cancer;
I meet my friends in cancer;
that the sun sets in cancer;
that through a tunnel of blue light, I hear
the silence of the dead,
and this is music;
that across a wide river, I cannot see
the shadow of myself,
but know it is there, and this
is poetry:
not beauty, not order, not burden, not legislation, but
consciousness,
the dream of dreams,
the only connection between fathers and daughters,
generations,
the woman rocking you to sleep
and the woman who sleeps.

(I say: How is my mother? Does she need anything?)

A Poem for Women in Rage ·
Audre Lorde

A killing summer heat wraps up the city
emptied of all who are not bound to stay
a black woman waits for a white woman
leans against the railing in the Upper West Side street
at intermission
the distant sounds of Broadway dim to lulling
until I can hear the voice of sparrows
like a promise I await
the woman I love
our slice of time
a place beyond the city's pain.

In the corner phone booth a woman
glassed in by reflections of the street between us
her white face dangles
a tapestry of disasters seen
through a veneer of order
mouth drawn like an ill-used road map
to eyes without core, a bottled heart

impeccable credentials of old pain.
The veneer cracks open
she lurches through the glaze into my afternoon
our eyes touch like hot wire
and the street snaps into nightmare
a woman with white eyes is clutching
a bottle of Fleischman's gin
is fumbling at her waistband
is pulling a butcher knife from her ragged pants
her hand arcs backward "You Black Bitch!"
the heavy blade spins out toward me
slow motion
years of fury surge upward like a wall
and I do not hear it
clatter to the pavement at my feet.

Gears of ancient nightmare churn
swift in familiar dread and silence
but this time I am awake, released
I smile. Now. This time is
my turn.
I bend to the knife my ears blood-drumming
across the street my lover's voice
the only moving sound within white heat
"Don't   touch it!"
I straighten, weaken, then start down again
hungry for resolution
simple as anger and so close at hand
my fingers reach for the familiar blade
the known grip of wood against my palm
for I have held it to the whetstone
a thousand nights for this
escorting fury through my sleep
like a cherished friend
to wake in the stink of rage
beside the sleep-white face of love.

The keen steel of a dreamt knife
sparks honed from the whetted edge with a tortured shriek
between my lover's voice and the grey spinning
a choice of pain or fury
slashing across judgment like a crimson scar
I could open her up to my anger
with a point sharpened upon love.

In the deathland my lover's voice
fades
like the roar of a train derailed
on the other side of a river
every white woman's face I love
and distrust is upon it
eating green grapes from a paper bag
marking yellow exam-books tucked into a manila folder
orderly as the last thought before death
I throw the switch.

Through screams of crumpled steel
I search the wreckage for a ticket of hatred
my lover's voice
calling
a knife at her throat.

In this steaming aisle of the dead
I am weeping
to learn the names of those streets
my feet have worn thin with running
and why they will never serve me
nor ever lead me home.
"Don't touch it!" she cries
I straighten myself
in confusion
a drunken woman is running away
down the West Side street
my lover's voice moves
a shadowy clearing.

Corralled in fantasy
the woman with white eyes has vanished
to become her own nightmare
and a french butcher blade hangs in my house
love's token
I remember this knife
it carves its message into my sleeping
she only read its warning
written upon my face.

Abortion · *Audre Lorde*

from *I've Been Standing on This Street Corner*
a Hell of a Long Time: A Bio-mythography

HALF-REMEMBERED information garnered from other people's friends who had been "in trouble." The doctor in Pennsylvania who did good clean abortions very cheaply because his daughter had died on a kitchen table after he had refused to abort her. But sometimes the police grew suspicious, so he wasn't always working. A call through the grapevine found out that he wasn't.

Trapped. Something—anything—had to be done. No one else can take care of this. What am I going to do?

The doctor who gave me the results of my positive rabbit test was a friend of Jean's aunt, who had said he might "help." This doctor's help meant offering to get me into a home for unwed mothers out of the city run by a friend of his. "Anything else," he said, piously, "is illegal."

I was terrified by the stories I had heard in school and from my friends about the butchers and the abortion mills of the *Daily News:* cheap kitchen table abortions. Jean's friend Francie had died on the way to the hospital just last year after trying to do it with the handle of a #1 paintbrush.

These horrors were not just stories, nor infrequent. I had seen too many of the results of botched abortions on the bloody gurneys lining the hallways outside the Emergency Room.

Besides, I had no real contacts.

Through winter-dim streets, I walked to the subway from the doctor's office, knowing I could not have a baby and knowing it with a certainty that galvanized me far beyond anything I knew to do.

The girl in the Labor Youth League who had introduced me to Peter had had an abortion, but it had cost $300. The guy had paid for it. I did not have $300, and I had no way of getting $300, and I swore her to secrecy telling her it wasn't Peter's. Whatever was going to be done I had to do. And fast.

Castor oil and a dozen Bromo-Quinine pills didn't help.

Mustard baths gave me a rash, but didn't help, either.

Neither did jumping off a table in an empty classroom at Hunter, and I almost broke my glasses.

Ann was a Licensed Practical Nurse I knew from working the evening shift at Beth David Hospital. We used to flirt in the nurses' pantry after midnight when the head nurse was sneaking a doze in some vacant private room on the floor. Ann's husband was in Korea. She was beautiful and friendly, small, sturdy and deeply black. One night, while we were warming the alcohol and talcum for P.M. Care backrubs, she pulled out her right breast to show me the dark mole which grew at the very line where her deep-purple aureola met the slightly lighter chocolate brown of her skin, and which, she told me with a mellow laugh, "drove all the doctors crazy."

Ann had introduced me to amphetamine samples on those long sleepy night shifts, and we crashed afterward at her bright kitchenette apartment on Cathedral Parkway, drinking black coffee and gossiping until dawn about the strange habits of head nurses, among other things.

I called Ann at the hospital and met her after work one night. I told her I was pregnant.

"I thought you was gay!"

I let that one pass. I asked her to get me some ergotrate from the pharmacy, a drug which I had heard from nurses' talk could be used to encourage bleeding.

"Are you crazy?" she said in horror, "you can't mess around with that stuff, girl, it could kill you. It causes hemorrhaging. Let me see what I can find out for you."

Everybody knows somebody, Ann said. For her, it was the mother of another nurse in Surgery. Very safe and clean, foolproof and cheap, she said. An induced miscarriage by Foley catheter. A homemade abortion. The narrow hard-rubber tube, used in post-operative cases to keep various body canals open, softened when sterilized. When passed through the cervix into the uterus while soft, it coiled, all 15 inches, neatly into the womb. Once hardened, its angular turns ruptured the bloody lining and began the uterine contractions that eventually expelled the implanted fetus, along with the membrane. If it wasn't expelled too soon. If it did not also puncture the uterus.

224

The process took about 15 hours and cost $40, which was a week and a half's pay.

I walked over to Mrs. Munoz's apartment after I had finished work at Dr. Sutter's office that afternoon. The January thaw was past, and even though it was only 1:00 P.M., the sun had no warmth. The winter grey of mid-February and the darker patches of dirty Upper East-Side snow. Against my peacoat in the wind I carried a bag containing the fresh pair of rubber gloves and the new bright-red catheter Ann had taken from the hospital for me, and a sanitary pad. I had most of the contents of my last pay envelope, plus the $5 Ann had lent me.

"Darling, take off your skirt and panties now while I boil this." Mrs. Munoz took the catheter from the bag and poured boiling water from a kettle over it and into a shallow basin. I sat curled around myself on the edge of her broad bed, embarrassed by my half-nakedness before this stranger. She pulled on the thin rubber gloves, and setting the basin upon the table, she looked over to where I was perched in the corner of the neat and shabby room.

"Lie down, lie down. You scared, huh?" She eyed me from under the clean white kerchief that completely covered her small head. I could not see her hair, and could not tell from her sharp-featured, bright-eyed face how old she was, but she looked so young that it surprised me that she could have a daughter old enough to be a nurse.

"You scared? Don't be scared, sweetheart," she said, picking up the basin with the edge of a towel and moving it onto the other edge of the bed.

"Now just lie back and put your legs up. Nothing to be afraid of. Nothing to it—I would do it on my own daughter. Now if you was three, four months, say, it would be harder because it would take longer, see. But you not far gone. Don't worry. Tonight, tomorrow, maybe, you hurt a little bit, like bad cramps. You get cramps?"

I nodded, mute, my teeth clenched against the pain. But her hands were busy between my legs as she looked intently at what she was doing.

"You take some aspirin, a little drink. Not too much though. When its ready, then the tube comes back down and the bleeding comes with it. Then no more baby. Next time you take better care of yourself, darling."

By the time Mrs. Munoz had finished talking she had skillfully passed the long slender catheter through my cervix into my uterus. The pain had been acute but short. It lay coiled inside of me like a cruel benefactor, slowly hardening and turning angular as it cooled, soon to rupture the delicate lining and wash away my worries in blood.

Since to me all pain was unbearable, even this short bout seemed interminable.

"You see, now, that's all there is to it. Now that wasn't so bad, was it?" She patted my shuddering thigh reassuringly. "All over. Now get dressed. And wear the pad," she cautioned, as she pulled off the rubber gloves. "You start bleeding in a couple of hours, then you lie down. Here, you want the gloves back?"

I shook my head, and handed her the money. She thanked me. "That's a special price because you a friend of Anna's," she smiled, helping me on with my coat. "By this time tomorrow, it will be all over. If you have any trouble you call me. But no trouble, just a little cramps."

I stopped off on West 4th Street and bought a bottle of Apricot Brandy for 89¢. It was the day before my 18th birthday and I decided to celebrate my relief. Now all I had to do was hurt.

On the slow Saturday Local back to my furnished room in Brighton Beach the cramps began, steadily increasing. Everything's going to be all right now, I kept saying to myself as I leaned over slightly on the subway seat, if I can just get through the next day. I can do it. She said it was safe. The worst is over, and if anything goes wrong I can always go to the hospital. I'll tell them I don't know her name, and I was blindfolded so I don't know where I was.

I wondered how bad the pain was going to get, and that terrified me more than anything else. All pain was unbearable and I had no measure. But the terror was only about the pain.

I did not think about how I could die from hemorrhage, or a perforated uterus.

The subway car was almost empty.

Just last spring around this same time one Saturday morning, I woke up in my mother's house to the smell of bacon frying in the kitchen, and the abrupt realization as I opened my eyes that the dream I had been having of having just given birth to a baby girl was in fact only a dream.

I sat bolt upright in my bed facing the little window onto the airshaft, and cried and cried and cried from disappointment until my mother came into the room to see what was wrong.

The train came up out of the tunnel over the bleak edge of South Brooklyn. The Coney Island Parachute Jump steeple and a huge grey gas storage tank were the only breaks in the leaden skyline.

I dared myself to feel any regrets.

That night about 8 P.M., I was lying curled tightly on my bed, trying to distract myself from the stabbing pains in my groin by deciding whether or not I wanted to dye my hair coal black.

I couldn't begin to think about the risks I was running. But another piece of me was being amazed at my own daring. I had done it. Even more than my leaving home, this action which was tearing my guts apart and from which I could die except I wasn't going to, this action was a kind of shift from safety toward self-preservation. It was a choice of pains. That's what living was all about. I clung to that and tried to feel only proud.

I had not given in. They hadn't gotten me. I wasn't being a pebble in somebody else's ocean, washed along by any wave that came along.

I had not been the eye on the ceiling, until it was too late.

There was a tap on the alley door, and I looked out the window. My friend Blossom from school had gotten one of our old High School teachers to drive her out to see if I was "okay," and to bring me a bottle of Peach Brandy for my birthday. She was one of the people I had consulted, and she had wanted to have nothing to do with an abortion, saying I should have the baby. I didn't bother to tell her that black babies were not adopted. They were absorbed into families, abandoned, or "given up." But not adopted. That was just another little piece of that secret knowledge which later came to be known as cultural differences. But when I saw Blossom, nonetheless I knew she must have been worried to have come all the way from Queens to Manhattan and then to Brighton Beach.

I was touched.

We only talked about inconsequential things. Never a word about what was going on inside of me. Now it was my secret; the only way I could handle it was alone. Somewhere they were both grateful.

"You sure you're going to be okay?" Blos asked. I nodded.

Blossom knew how to make anybody laugh. Miss Burman suggested we go for a walk along the boardwalk in the crisp February darkness. There was no moon. The walk helped a little, and so did the brandy. But when we got back to my room, I couldn't concentrate on their conversation any more. I was too distracted by the rage gnawing at my belly.

"Do you want us to go?" Blos asked with her old characteristic bluntness. Miss Burman, sympathetic but austere, stood quietly in the doorway looking at my posters. I nodded at Blos gratefully. Miss Burman lent me $5 before she left.

The rest of the night was an agony of padding back and forth along the length of the hallway from my bedroom to the bathroom, doubled over in pain, watching clots of blood fall out of my body into the toilet and wondering if I was all right, after all. I had never seen such huge red blobs come from me before. They scared me. I was afraid I might be bleeding to death in that community bathroom in Bright Beach in the middle of the night of my 18th birthday, with a crazy old lady down the hall muttering restlessly in her sleep. But I was going to be all right. Soon this was all going to be over, and I would be safe.

I watched one greyish mucous shape disappear in the bowl, wondering if that was the embryo.

By dawn, when I went to take some more aspirin, the catheter had worked its way out of my body. I was bleeding heavily, very heavily. But my experience in the OB wards told me that I was not hemorrhaging.

I washed the long stiff catheter and laid it away in a drawer, after examining it carefully. This implement of my salvation was a wicked red, but otherwise thin and innocuous looking.

I took an amphetamine in the thin morning sun and wondered if I should spend a quarter on some coffee and a Danish. I remembered I was supposed to usher at a Hunter College Concert that same afternoon, for which I was to be paid $10, a large sum for an afternoon's work, and one that would enable me to repay my debts to Ann and Miss Burman.

I made myself some sweet milky coffee and took a hot bath, even though I was bleeding. After that, the pain dimmed gradually to a dull knocking gripe.

On a sudden whim, I got up and threw on some clothes and went out into the morning. I took the bus into Coney Island to an early morning foodshop near Nathan's, and had myself a huge birthday breakfast, complete with french fries and an English muffin. I hadn't had a regular meal in a restaurant for a long time. It cost almost half of Miss Burman's five dollars, because it was Kosher and expensive. And delicious.

Afterward, I returned home. I lay resting upon my bed, filled with a sense of well-being and relief from pain and terror that was almost euphoric. I really was all right.

As the morning slipped into afternoon, I realized that I was exhausted. But the thought of making $10 for one afternoon's work got me wearily up and back onto the Weekend Local train for the 1¼ hour's trip to Hunter College.

By midafternoon my legs were quivering. I walked up and down the aisles dully, hardly hearing the string quartet. In the last part of the concert, I went into the ladies' room to change my tampax and the pads I was wearing. In the stall, I was seized with a sudden wave of nausea that bent me double, and I promptly and with great force lost my $2.50-with-tip Coney Island breakfast, which I had never digested. Weakened and shivering, I sat on the stool, my head against the wall. A fit of renewed cramps swept through me so sharply that I moaned softly.

Miz Lewis, the black ladies' room attendant who had known me from the bathrooms of Hunter High School, was in the back of the room in her cubby, and she had seen me come into the otherwise empty washroom.

"Is that you, Autray, moaning like that? You all right?" I saw her low-shoed feet stop outside my stall.

"Yes mam," I gasped through the door, cursing my luck to have walked into that particular bathroom. "It's just my period."

I steadied myself, and arranged my clothes. When I finally stepped out, bravely and my head high, Miz Lewis was still standing outside, her arms folded.

She had always maintained a steady but impersonal interest in the lives of the few black girls at the high school, and she was a familiar face which I was glad to see when I met her in the washroom of the College in the autumn. I told her I was going to the College now, and that I had left home. Miz Lewis had raised her eyebrows and pursed her lips, shaking her grey head. "You girls sure are somethin'!" she'd said.

In the uncompromising harshness of the fluorescent lights, Miz Lewis gazed at me intently through her proper gold spectacles which perched upon her broad brown nose like round antennae.

"Girl, you sure you all right? Don't sound all right to me." She peered up into my face. "Sit down here a minute. You just started? You white like some other people's chile."

I took her seat, gratefully. "I'm all right, Miz Lewis," I protested. "I just have bad cramps, that's all."

"Jus' cramps? That bad? Then why you come here like that today for? You ought to be home in bed, the way you eyes looking. You want some coffee, honey?" She offered me her cup.

" 'Cause I need the money, Miz Lewis. I'll be all right, I really will." I shook my head to the coffee, and stood up. Another cramp slid up from my clenched thighs and rammed into the small of my back, but I only rested my head against the edge of the stalls. Then, taking a paper towel from the stack on the glass shelf in front of me, I wet it and wiped the cold sweat from my forehead. I wiped the rest of my face, and blotted my faded lipstick carefully. I grinned at my reflection in the mirror and at Miz Lewis standing to the side behind me, her arms still folded against her broad short-waisted bosom. She sucked her teeth with a sharp intake of breath and sighed a long sigh.

"Chile, why don't you go on back home to your mama, where you belong?"

I almost burst into tears. I felt like screaming, drowning out her plaintive, kindly, old-woman's voice that kept pretending everything was so simple.

"Don't you think she's worrying about you? Do she know you in all this trouble?"

"I'm not in trouble, Miz Lewis. I just don't feel well because of my period." Turning away, I crumpled up the used towel and dropped it into the basket, and then sat down again, heavily. My legs were shockingly weak.

"Yeah. Well." Miz Lewis put her hand into her apron pocket. "Here," she said, pulling 4 dollars out of her purse. "You take these and get yourself a taxi home." She knew I lived in Brooklyn. "And you go right home, now. I'll cross your name off the list downstairs for you. And you can pay me back when you get it."

I took the crumpled bills from her dark, work-wise hands. "Thanks a lot, Miz Lewis," I said gratefully. I stood up again, this time a little more steadily. "But don't you worry about me, this won't last very long." I walked shakily to the door.

"And you put your feet up, and a cold compress on your tummy, and you stay in bed for a few days, too," she called after me, as I made my way to the elevators to the main floor.

I asked the cab to take me around to the alley entrance instead of getting out on Brighton Beach Avenue. For the first time in my life, I was afraid my legs might not take me where I wanted to go. I wondered if I had almost fainted.

Once indoors, I took three aspirin and slept for 24 hours.

When I awoke Monday afternoon, the bedsheets were stained, but my bleeding had slowed to normal and the cramps were gone.

I wondered if I had gotten some bad food at the Foodshop Sunday morning that had made me sick. Usually I never got upset stomachs, and prided myself on my cast-iron digestion. The following day I went back to school.

On Friday after classes, before I went to work, I picked up my money for ushering. I sought out Miz Lewis in the Auditorium washroom and paid her back her 4 dollars.

"Oh, thank you, Autray," she said, looking a little surprised. She folded the bills up neatly and tucked them back into the green snap-purse she kept in her uniform apron pocket. "How you feeling?"

"Fine, Miz Lewis," I said jauntily. "I told you I was going to be all right."

"You did not! You said you *was* all right and I knew you wasn't, so don't tell me none of that stuff, I don't want to hear." Miz Lewis eyed me balefully.

"You gon' back home to your mama, yet?" she asked, dryly.

The River Honey Queen Bess ·
Cynthia Macdonald

I

In May it drops down fresh from the mountains,
Dashing silver flakes of water like mica in the air.
Such abundance foils the stones' and hearts' resistance.
   The five dare not broach their wish to dance with water.
   This is the season of their odes.

Early July and not much rain. The pulse slows. Rocks still
Force froth, but the rush is spent. Puckering white
At the selvedge, its weave of blue and green unfurls.
   Three men, two women are rapt in it.
   This is the season of their proposals.

August, and what has always been at the bottom is seen:
Tires, shoes; water moccasins, coral snakes
Braiding in the mud; and what is culturing in
The mirror plates now glazed false blue?
   "A pox on rivers; we always knew," they say.
   This is the season of their attempted escapes.

After the swellings and fevers abate
The suitors drape themselves in velvet blue and green
To conceal August scars, and order spring-bottled water,
Hoping glass will contain the uncontrollable.
Before they can begin to drink, a swarm escapes —
Gold-dazzle, noise, honey, sting — a circle
Around each head, a crown of May bees.

Truth has been concealed, like 15th-century meat
Rotting under its fabric of spices. Seasons
Have their progression and this is misleading:
The fool's-gold suitors believe if May had lasted
They would have found their beloved. Four leave,
Mourning the march of months, the thwarting procession.
But Will stays, through winter's seeming stasis
When blood becomes manageable, to have the Honey Queen again.

This year, no one knows why—a record snowfall? the drift of
Lava ash over the sun? fatigue, sheer as
The cliff beside the river? —June does not begin
On its appointed date. He has not only the month
But its extension to try to pull the river's winding sheet
Through his gold ring, the wedding band which
Plays *The Water Music*. But though he cannot handle
The river which refuses to be treated like
A scarf, he finds he knows her.

August discoveries are not the fault of August. Under
The river's cloak, under the course of its blue blood
Is a slut, a gutter of water and men. The thirst of love
Is slaked by cloacal knowledge. What should Will do?
Cross himself or the river? What can he afford?

He goes to Raleigh to buy the river valley, to build
The Mother Goose Enchanted Village. No more brooding.
Between "The Queen is in the parlor eating bread and
Honey Golden Manse" and "The Jack fell down
And broke his crown Hill," the water wends. Will has it
Paved with silver glass, assuring safe reflection; he bends
To face himself. Through flowered banks the mirrored river curves;
Underneath, Honey Queen Bess sings her sting green music.

My Familiar Lover · *Cynthia Macdonald*

All too. We ran away from the burrow of family
To meet at the Continental Divide. Apart
The pieces had fallen into place; together, they fall apart.
Yet from all that tearing up and down and in and out of
Passion's landscape, finally a sigh escapes its prison of ribs
As the awe-full snow-capped Rockies are glimpsed, then
Confronted. At the pinnacle there is division, of course:
Water flows in opposite directions, blue arteries,
East and West. And snow replaces green as
Rock's embellishment. We stand on the ridge watching
A single mole, a hairy beauty spot against the white
Below. Here, together, our penny dreadful melodramas—
Gaslight flicker, Noh or Passion play, Peking or
Puccini opera—will be played up and down and out and over.

The worst of what is familiar is less likely to maim
Than the moderately bad of what is not. So we
Make neither up nor out nor over, just make sure to guarantee
The worst as we set out—the picnic. For me, because my family
Came from Alsace, Weiss and Campagne; for you, from Gdansk,
Kielbasa. Spreading the cloth, you state this is no picnic
And turn to put on the ritual paint, red silk kimono.
Gilt fan in hand, you exhale the gasping music speech as
I dress in lampblack satin, jet beads, a crow boa
And paste a heart-shaped mole on my left cheek. The play
Begins: you use blocks; I, faints. Nothing
Meets; we slice the sausage into familiar declarations.

In spite of the gloss of the scenery, perhaps because of it
There is something sinister here which even the best paraphrase
Cannot put into words, a certain spitefulness thickens
The exhilarating air. Moles thread the snow,
Suggesting subterranean terrors better left unmolested.
Old enough to know it is impossible to change weather or
Landscape, we look at today's parts and try to change them,

Try to braid the twain. Compromise: *Turandot.* You, still in
Eastern garb, lie down in the snow to ice for the role,
Impressing a perfect Asian angel. I suit up as Calaf who,
Though he won the Empress, his Turandot, would not claim her till
She loved him, too. We perform in Asian fashion:
Man becomes woman, woman, man though your heavy beard,
My wide hips become neither part. Puccini's music echoes against
Channels of rock, flows with water into clefts.
Only when the sky's scar, a lightning bolt, strikes me as
You raise your hand do I realize I am no Calaf but a common suitor
Who does not wish to die for love and therefore will.
Turandot hits high B-flat conveying the rules and penalties.
After the first act we sit down to recast, struggling
For something easy. Making mountains into molehills is not,
Especially when Wagner shimmers in the distance like
Forest fire without trees. Impossible immolation.

Black-brown fur blinks in the drifts. We stop
Counting down and up and in and out to push the snow aside
Revealing the squirming litters, dark, moist, quickly
Increasing. Let's take cover in the pulsing, moving bed.
They weave around us, licking, softly probing, warm nest
Of fur, nothing molten. Music: breath in thin air,
A hum, small scale, piano practice instead of
Pageant. We pull up the blanket of snow and cleave together.
Such familiar comfort, my love, we forget what we know.

On Faith · *Heather McHugh*

They couldn't see the future
for a fact. Imagination
of oatmeal, room of mush,
it wasn't that they hadn't seen
the blackening and ironing
around the lungs, the celebrations
in a raw heart, how the bullets
were put to bed in a chamber.

They just didn't believe
that they themselves could be
knocked off to the nearest star.
They didn't believe what they saw
was gone. The red shift was, at worst,
a dress away at the cleaners.
Invisible ink had to be kept
in bottles, and that took space.
They added attics in the event,
sperm banks in the bomb shelter.

And though the self was always
arriving late, they saw it, at best,
as a friendly ghost, one of the wise men
making a point
of carrying diamonds to stars
or being a shade in the dark.
The substance of the argument was pure
spirit, the drink was drunk, the rock
miraculously gone, and why not,
once you saw it come to life,
live with yourself?

The past was another story, they said.
You couldn't imagine the past.

Asthma · *Lynne McMahon*

Tremors, and yet my daughter
    Demands to play, to climb
Onto my knees, her Everest.
    The air begins thinning out

In white sockets around her eyes
    Which closes my throat too. *Rest now,*
I want to tell her, which only makes her angry
    And scared. I have gasped that way

In nightmares, muffled in feathers and wool,
    But my bones never took on
Such prominence. Her shoulders work
    Their wingbones and her ribs

Open and close like palm fronds
    In some terrible fan and still she rises
Putting her hand against my face
    And finding my lap two logs

On which to roll, not falling.
    Her small heart and my larger one
Jerk out their mismatched rhythms
    But now it is my breath

Which begins the hard ascent.
    I am the mountain after all
Locked by the snow's embrace, and the blue veins,
    And remote clouds which are not moving.

Utanikki, August 1978 · *Sandra McPherson*

for A. K.

The summer heat dries the partitions of the fallen
honeycomb—so thin, one emptiness hears another.

> Beneath the roof,
> Drops of spring rain
> Trail slowly
> Down the honeycomb.
> — *Bashō*

> Warmed honey,
> Soaking through the wall,
> Drops in
> On my pillow.

The old hive falls indoors and outdoors. It is
sorted into crusts of combs and spillways of honey.
Who chose to settle in the seams of this house, to
frighten the landlord?

You and your husband are sitting naked with my
husband on a stair. Our daughter?—

> Her door is closed,
> She's sleeping sound,
> Painting the night
> To show me later.

The men bellow and swear. They are not angry, or at
least that is not the reason they bellow and swear.
They are full of feeling. Since they have adopted a
language like animals', it can't be understood any
more exactly than animal cries.

> Is it the cats?
> Or a rabbit torn by an owl?
> Or another choice—
> The cry of the poisoned bees.

This morning I took snapshots of our only child in
her slip in front of the mirror. She leaned and
turned, bent forward and touched the mirror. Tonight,
with the film that remains, I surprise the two men and
you. I say that the camera's eye is only my eye, its
blink my blink.

In the morning, when all are dressed and you continue
your journey, I find that someone has exposed the
film to the light.

The wall must be full of eternally sleeping bees. I
tasted the honey before I knew it was poisoned.

> Wasn't I lucky?
> It didn't hurt a bit.
> Not like this,
> Not like this. . . .

Afternoon Walk · *Josephine Miles*

There is this old man, wistful, hungry, peaked,
Going to mail his letters,
Formerly a governor of some renown.
Good morning, I see you are going to mail your letters.
Yes, I am going to mail my letters.

This peaked old man, suddenly
He looks out of the profiles, out of the eyes of friends,
Smiling, what strained happening.
Mortality, are you going to mail your letters?
Yes, I am going to mail your letters.

Doing Time · *Sara Miles*

for Michael Fury

Too tough
too tough
I must have tugged at your thumb wincing
for half an hour as the splinter worked loose. It's
nothing you said, and told me
stories: romances: how the girl
screamed get away get away from me down
on Delancey Street last Christmas how the snow came
then the cops came: to tell me how
the redhead inbred islanders
backed off in St. Croix when you broke the bottle on the bar
to tell me stories
how they rode you late one night ("two other
Irish guys but big")
from the lobby to the fourteenth floor
of the projects up and back up and back beating
you senseless against the walls of the elevator "yeah I
was drunk but swear to God" you leaned closer, confiding, "all
I said getting in was don't
start anything jack": romance
romance means time makes
telling it better
than living it was.
You turned forty in a Louisiana jail
in the perpetual present tense of prison
you turned too tough with six
bullets in your knees and lungs to tell me over
the station house phone anything
resembling a blaze of glory: just how
it hurt.
How it hurts. "I'm sitting here speeding
my brains out on coffee" you wrote, "once again watching
the Yankees blow it as they come down to the wire.

All I ever wanted was a woman to love and a job
I didn't hate. So two of my biggest problems—oops
the Yanks just went down well fuck 'em—have been lust
and fear. These are my constant companions. And armed
robbery but I have been a thief as long
as I can remember."
As long as I can remember you
have been a liar.
Too scrupulous to say you've been unlucky
too sentimental not to say
you've been unloved
too tough
too tough
you must have known romance means doing time, makes
living it
a better deal.

First Intimation · *Vassar Miller*

My body and her pleasure
no longer clap each other on the back
or fall into each other's arms,

but greet warily
as two old friends
who have grown fragile,

or maybe even hostile,
each carrying a razor
in her purse,

the death seed stirring
in flesh folds since birth,
to dawdle along my tall and narrow bones.

Meditation on Friendship: Getting Lost in the Woods with Deena—Jamesville, NY ·
Judith Minty

You think I am like your grandmother
because I've been so far
North. But even a wolf marks territory, even she
sets her teeth, lets no one beyond.

We stand at the edge
of winter. The desert beats in your blood.
I haven't lived here
long enough, though I tell you
I've been here before, though in fact
not exactly here. These are civilized woods.

You try to put on
the skin of this place, but it doesn't fit, the pelt
stretches and binds. Oh friend, we aren't animals after all.
We're troubled women, unable
to see clearly.

These are the oaks where, in October,
migrating robins rested. Now chattering half-truths,
we step off the path into mud. We know better,
still we wander a thread of a creek
to bark and dead leaves, musty soil.
We've not been touched for so long.

Almost dark, and we're turned
to repeating mistakes. I'm ashamed of my feet
stumbling, snapping twigs, grown clumsy as old women.
They sense the circles we've made.

We're lost and we know it.
There's no farmhouse, no cabin. We're locked in
these woods, the trees our markers,
the setting sun our compass.

We need to speak from the heart again, to listen
for the river. It's our way out, that water
flowing. We need to be led
downstream to the bridge, we need
to reach the other side touching.

Key West (Triple Ballade with Enjambed Refrain, plus Envoy) · *Judith Moffett*

for David Jackson

The garden's shading. Let there be
Tea in the deck-and-louvre tent
Begun, degree by slow degree,
Upon its languid, smooth descent
Toward eighty. Rose and succulent
Look up from blooming peatbeds thick
With strangeness, lush, ebullient
Displayed against white-sand-and-brick

Paving. From frond to shrub to tree
(So *that's* what Orphan Annie meant!)
Lizards are leaping—skittery,
Dirt-colored, slim, belligerent,
Each furnished with a prominent
Accessory featured in their shtick,
Unvocal, yet grandiloquent
Displayed against white sand and brick.

Say X has accidentally
Invaded turf big Z has spent
His little life defending; Z
Does jerky push-ups, does Present-
Throat-flat (inflated? through a vent?),
Out-in, out-in, erotic tic
Of warning—Pounce! and *skitter* went
Displayed-Against. White sand and brick

Are not much less intelligent,
Frankly. They'll "flap" a leaf or stick,
Bright membrane flashing Go! Repent!
Displayed against white sand and brick.

The reptile brain is cold and small,
No space, no need for judgment there.
Watch. In the deepest Turtle Kraal
A monstrous head pokes up for air,
Lairpet of Grendel's, chased from lair
To scare up dinner. Jaws of dread
Gasp open. Eyes of earthenware
Identify. The loggerhead

Lunges on cue; the guide will trawl
A chunk of rotten lobster where
He'll strike. Abruptly I recall
The moth aflutter on the bare
Floorboards, the little lizard's stare,
Fixed, from the threshold, how it sped
Across the varnish . . . yes. Compare?
Identify? the loggerhead

Who wallows, tries to climb the wall,
Whose ton of crushing-power can tear
A man in chunks and eat him all,
Whose fins thrash up the mal de mer,
Who now, with all that force to spare,
Crushes the bait and sinks like lead.
A blond child shrieks. These kinds of scare
Identify the loggerhead

And lizard with its charming flare
Round as a flannel tongue and red.
Look long, think well before you dare
Identify the loggerhead.

A green iguana spined with plates
Blinks at the tourist with a ques-
Tion not these flattened welterweights':
Where are the dinosaurs of yes-
Ter-Age? New Zealand and Loch Ness,
Pygmy Iguanodon, poor thing.
That clockwork, kneejerk, passionless
Instinct persists, but Reason's king.

It's Sophosaurus rex who baits
The sea-troll Instinct now. I guess
I'm glad—though how he tolerates
That filthy pool—! (As Freud would stress,
Whatever dragon we repress
Befouls its prison.) Evening
Brings us to ours, we both undress,
Instinct persists . . . but Reason's king

Here where a white bar melts, and spates
Of filtered water effervesce,
Pure azure balm that liquidates
Disturbing thoughts, the turtle mess,
The saurian heat, the— S.O.S.?
Again? This same dumb lizardling
Keeps trying, with the same success—
Instinct persists (but Reason's king

Or else)—to scale the tiles. Noblesse
Oblige, a royal palm's frayed wing
Retrieves him from a giantess.
Instinct persists but Reason's king.

These trinkets, David—waterslick
Pool tiling, tiny splayfeet spread
On surface tension (rhetoric?),
Sea monster in his muckbath fed
On rot, display in tropicbed—
All thanks to you. The length of string
They're threaded on is only thread:
Instinct-persists-but-Reason's-king.

In *Mrs. N's Palace* · *Honor Moore*

Louise Nevelson retrospective
Whitney Museum, 1980

An hour I waited for you. And her. Gold. Black. *First*
   Personage. Shreds of what would happen here
      would piece with how we had loved,
    altering it. Waited. Black boxes, black
finials screwed to knobs and buttons, naked spools,
      gold fluted columns. Waited
    until you came, until there were three to walk
    the black rooms. *Night Presence, Cascade* feeling you
all mine: *Dawn's Wedding,* white air as I would kiss and kiss. Now
    her presence: lids pulled from barrels, tops without
      baskets, black hooks lifted, poised,
    painted to the sides of so many black boxes—
nothing to fasten. You loved her first. Shapes tilt. Harsh
    ripple of washboard white makes serene. Red
    silk blouse, light in the room like moon. Slats
      cut from white wood pleat until
they drape. We could have been serene. You move toward her, your
    face toward me. I wore red to stand out. In gold,
      whispering, you repeat I
    want   you; in black; I want her. Spools, finials,
chaos flattened with paint. You shimmering in profile,
      she at an angle looking.
    It looks like a breastplate. If it weren't
    art, I could take it, wear it. Black boxes stacked,
teeth on a stem. Buttons. Brushes. All this in boxes
    held. Hold. Out of black to free standing
      black on white so black looks saw-
    tooth sharp. Hold me. Edges. Is it light spilling
or are we crying? Wood feather-shaped, swirl of tools screwed
    still, black. Knob without a door. I show you
    black reeds bending from barrels, a knob shaped like
      your breast. *Royal Tide.* No door

to prepare us. *Moon Garden.* We've come this far. Bend
with me, loosen your shoes. Let your feet fall
with mine, naked to the black mirror floor.

First Personage, Night Presence, Cascade, Dawn's Wedding, Royal Tide, Moon Garden: titles of Nevelson scupture.

Stone Soup · *Lisel Mueller*

So easy to stir up a feast
with only a random, unmagical stone
or, in some versions, the nail
we happen to carry around in our pockets.
It takes nothing more than hope
and, being persuaded, our natural gift
for persuasion to bring out the neighbors
with carrots and onions and parsley
and finally even with meat and salt.
We are standing in front of the window
behind which a nurse lifts you up,
newborn. We are holding
the ingredients for your future.
Already you have been given a name,
a second skin, more durable than the first.
Now your father is adding his vision
of you in twelve years, your beauty,
a long-term stowaway, hinted at;
your grandmother offers her trust
in your resilience, your aunt her assumption
of your genius for love.
And you, our odd-shaped, sea-worn stone,
our gleaming, crooked nail—
you let it happen, let the savor
of your life begin to simmer.

Fracture · *Lisel Mueller*

Hard way of learning
legbone connected to the kneebone
et cetera, up the spinal ladder
and out past the shoulder hinges
to the delicate crowns of the wrists,
removed, like monarchs in exile,
from the revolt of the bones.
Even they ring small bells of pain.

The burly shin bone that started it
is incarcerated in plaster.
Mend your ways, the doctor says.
Meanwhile it strikes me with what he calls
dependent pain, as I slide into
a wheelchair, my infant's gown
with its stamps of blue flowers
tied behind my back.
This is a hospital by the Pacific,
two thousand miles from home.
I depend on strangers, wheels turning,
your nightly phone call.

This morning I rode to the sun-room.
The gold sky folded flat
to glaze the water, sweep
the heads of seals in their brush with air.
I was holding a pink sweet pea,
a Sunday gift from the kitchen.
The straight, elegant legs
of fir trees floated toward the sawmill
unhurriedly, orderly. One of them
will turn itself into crutches
for me to lean on when I depart
this month of Sundays on my own two feet.

Fairy Tale · *Carol Muske*

In that country sacred to the wolf,
the mill no longer grinds out
its dull bread and duller proverbs.
The unshepherded flocks complain
in the empty fields. In the dead
branches sit crows too exhausted to fly.

It's November, as it has been for years.
In the kitchen of the lonely palace
one chop hobbles into the skillet.
The barrel staves split, and stack.

High on the landing of the great staircase
above the ballroom, the chandelier
rattles its glass skeletons and
the cobweb's drawn back:

here is the illegitimate daughter of the king
standing the way she stood
the night he banished her,
cold-eyed, her grey cloak slipping
from her shoulder as she strikes
her open palm with the butt of the riding crop—

to emphasize each point she is making.
According to the story—it is her job,
now that she's back—to make the leaves
regrow, to unfreeze the waterfall.
Why does she wait?

All she has to do is speak the ancient name
of each predator
                    and he will open his eyes,
walk on his hind legs through the gate,
looking right and left, clean-shaven,
utterly certain of a second chance.

Even Before the Mirror Myra ·
Gerda S. Norvig

You coil
like strips of a clay bowl
around yourself,
not wheeled, but pinched
with strong and intimate fingers,
     eccentric,
drunk with your jut and texture,
coy of the well forming
     within.
Then blinded by the dazzle
and the glaze,
     thrown off,
feeling invisible, despite yourself,
you breed, you grow.
You grow stalks, swirls, foliage,
     poems.
Everybody sees.

Hand Fantasy · *Gerda S. Norvig*

I followed the ink-blue water of the glove.
The water of the glove had run out to the sea.
The ocean rolled like a lioness receiving her cubs,
and her white caps shed abundant milk
into the ink-blue water of the glove.

Two tall white brood mares came down to the surf
and I in my bare feet and ragged pants
led them, then let them go
watching them run off, run out
into the blue and over the water of the glove.

Admiring the lions and the horses,
merging with them, I too rode the waters.
And on the other side, an island with a tiny pool
of tiny horseshoe crabs rose up before me
containing the transparent, ink-blue water of the glove
in the shape of its crabby fingers.

Final Anatomy · *Diana Ó Hehir*

The light goes pale in the lenses of the eyes,
The blood pulls away, leaves the face a folded cloth.
We walk sideways, crabs. All the fingers and toes
Are drained like kosher meat.

Then the little torso, bent like a mushroom, becomes
A child that is not a child;
It creeps around the edge of the room
Careful as a spider,
Tests the floor like the skin on water.

But inside the skull a tiny spark
Still hisses, a pilot light.
That's the soul, the immortal soul:
Flutter of air, uneasiness, shifting lists of memories,
It wants to spread itself flat across spaces,
Thin, thinner, a woven layered screen.

Hold me tight.
It's getting impatient now, trying to find its way out;
It tests with its mouth the backs of my tired eyes.

Pilot Captured by the Japanese, 1942 · *Sharon Olds*

They are holding his arms, bringing him off the plane,
leading him away. The black blindfold
covers his eyes. Their white gloves
hook around the leather of his flying-jacket,
lapels turned back, sheepskin lining
exposed like an inner layer of the body.
His arms dangle. His mouth is open
in a half-smile, still hoping to be liked.
The guards look down, lips curled.
They are touching something they would rather not touch.
They are ashamed to be seen with a man who has surrendered,
a man who has let himself be taken alive.
He towers between them, smiling as if
telling a joke. They lead him on his long
American legs to his forty months
alone in a tiger cage. He preferred
life to honor: now let him taste it
slowly, by itself, this thing he sets
above all else, this life.

History: 13 · *Sharon Olds*

When I found my father that night, the blood
smeared on his head and face, I did not
know who had done it. I had loved his body
whole, his head, his face, untouched,
and now he floated on the couch, his arms
up, like Mussolini hanging
upside down in the air, his head
dangling where they could reach him with boards and their
fingernails, those who had lived
under his tyranny.
I saw how the inside of the body could be
brought to the surface, to cover the skin,
his heart standing on his face, the weight of his
body pressing down on his head,
his life slung in the bag of his scalp,
and who had done it? Had I, had my mother,
my brother, my sister, we who had been silent
under him, under him for years? He lay in his
gore all night, as the body hung all
day outside the gas station in
Milan, and when they helped him up and
washed him and he left, I did not see it —
I was not there for the ashes, I had been there
only for the fire, I had seen my father
strung and mottled, mauled as if taken and
raked by a crowd, and I of the crowd
over his body, and how could anything be
good after that, how could anything be good
in such a world, I turned my back
on happiness, at 13 I entered
a life of mourning, of mourning for the Fascist.

The Takers · *Sharon Olds*

Hitler entered Paris the way my
sister entered my room at night,
sat astride me, squeezed me with her knees,
held her thumbnails to the skin of my wrists and
peed on me, knowing Mother would
never believe my story. It was very
silent, her dim face above me
gleaming in the shadows, the dark gold
smell of her urine spreading through the room, its
heat boiling on my legs, my small
pelvis wet. When the hissing stopped, when the
hole had been scorched in my body, I lay
crisp and charred with shame and felt her
skin glitter in the air, her dark
gold pleasure unfold as he stood over
Napoleon's tomb and murmured *This is the
finest moment of my life.*

The Meal · *Sharon Olds*

Mama, I never stop seeing you there
at the breakfast table when I'd come home from school—
sitting with your excellent skeletal posture
facing that plate with the one scoop of cottage cheese on it,
forcing yourself to eat, though you did not want to live,
feeding yourself, small spoonful by
small spoonful, so you would not die and
leave us without a mother as you were
left without a mother. You'd sit
in front of that mound rounded as a breast and
giving off a cold moony light,
light of the life you did not want, you would
hold yourself there and stare down at it,
an orphan forty years old staring at the breast,
a freshly divorced woman down to 82 pounds
staring at the cock runny with milk gone sour,
a daughter who had always said
the best thing her mother ever did for her
was to die. I came home every day to
find you there, dry-eyed, unbent, that
hot control in the breakfast nook, your
delicate savage bones over the cheese
curdled like the breast of the mother twenty years in the
porous earth,
                    and yet what I remember is your
spoon moving like the cock moving in the
body of the girl waking to the power of her pleasure,
your spoon rising in courage, bite after bite, you
tilted rigid over that plate until you
polished it for my life.

The House of Fecundity · *Sharon Olds*

After my girl's first gerbils die,
the tumors sprouting like purple broccoli on their stomachs,
after she gets the new gerbils and we
hang over their cage, watching them
rub their dark hairy faces with their
miniscule hands,
after my boy gets his first mice and they
fight, one going for the other's belly,
throat, jaws, horrible squeaks
cracking the air, after he gets his
second pair and we hang over their cage,
watching the shuddering noses, delicate
gluey toes, long raw
tendon of the tail, I have had it! Thirty-two
tiny hands and feet, sixteen
soft bellies in danger, this mixture of
pus and blood and excrement and
love is all too much for me, it
takes me back too far, stomach and
nose and the back of my mind like the battered
blackness behind the moon, to those years of the
animal, those years I was six feet
under in dark motherhood, my
mind a flooded field, the water
going down slowly. Now the children's
rooms begin to reek gently of
maternity, paternity, I
tell you I cannot sink down again, I
cannot do it, I have got to rise from
childbed at last, wipe the scarlet
mucus off my thighs, I've got to
get on with it. I have done my time in the
breaking-shed, the birthing-room, the
slaughterhouse, the pit, I walk

away through a haze of cedar chips, the
gold dust of life, a free
woman at last, a rational guide to the universe.

Sex Without Love · *Sharon Olds*

How do they do it, the ones who make love
without love? Beautiful as dancers,
they glide over each other like ice skaters
over the ice, fingers hooked
inside each other's bodies, faces
red as steak, wine, wet as the
children at birth whose mothers are going to
give them away. How do they come to the
come to the   come to the   god   come to the
still waters, and not love
the one who came there with them, light
rising slowly like steam off their joined
skin? These are the true religious,
the purists, the pros, the ones who will not
accept a false Messiah, love the
priest instead of the God. They don't
mistake the lover for their own pleasure,
they are like great runners — they know it is a matter of
the road surface, the cold, the wind,
the fit of their shoes, their overall cardio-
vascular health — just factors, like the partner
in the bed, and not the truth, which is
the single body alone in the universe
against its own best time.

The Birthmark · *Merrill Oliver*

There used to be a second dark bag
when I was small—not near the eye
like this. It stuck to my nose like gravel.

Mama would spit for luck and say, "Thank God
it disappeared, because no man
marries a girl who'd maybe curse their sons
with such a face. Like that you would have shriveled
alone and empty." First she scrubbed,
then tried bleaching it clean with vinegar.
Joseph unwrapped the cloudy bottle
a city doctor gave him years before
and made her spoon from it each day
for a month. The smell drove Papa into the street.

—But listen to what next: they used
"the hand of a dead person" to wipe at it
and that's what worked. The story goes
some neighbor died in childbirth, and when the news
came to my mother, like a hawk
she snatched me and went flying to the house.
The mark fell like a rotten tooth.

This here was larger, but she wouldn't have
fingers from a dead hand touching
close to the eye. You're never sure how much
the dead remove, or what they leave.

At That Time, or
The History of a Joke · *Grace Paley*

AT THAT TIME most people were willing to donate organs. Abuses were expected. In fact there was a young woman whose uterus was hysterically ripped from her by a passing gynecologist. He was distracted he said, by the suffering of a childless couple in Fresh Meadows. The young woman said, "It wasn't the pain or the embarrassment, but I think any court would certainly award me the earliest uterine transplant that Dr. Heiliger can obtain."

We are not a heartless people and this was done at the lowest judicial level, no need to appeal to state or federal power.

According to The Times, one of the young woman's ovaries rejected the new uterus. The other was perfectly satisfied and did not.

"I feel fine," she said, but almost immediately began to swell, for in the soft red warm interior of her womb, there was already a darling rolled-up foetus. It was unfurled in due time and lo! it was as black as the night which rests our day-worn eyes.

Then: "Sing!" said Dr. Heiliger, the scientist, "for see how the myth of man advances on the back of technological achievement and behold without conceiving a virgin has borne a son." This astonishing and holy news was carried to the eye of field, forest and industrial park, wherever the media had thrust its wireless thumb. The people celebrated and were relatively joyful and the birth was reenacted on giant screens in theaters and small screens at home.

Only on the underside of several cities, certain Jews who had observed and suffered the consequence of other virgin births cried out (weeping) (as usual) "It is not He! It is not He!"

No one knew how to deal with them; they were stubborn and maintained a humorless determination. The authorities took away their shortwave and antennae, their stereo screen TV and their Temple video tapes. (People were not incarcerated at that time for such social intransigence. Therefore, neither were they rehabilitated.)

Soon this foolish remnant had nothing left. They had to visit one another or wander from town to town in order to say the most ordinary thing to a friend or relative. They had only their shawls and phylacteries, which were used by women too, for women (by that time) had made their great natural advances and were ministers, seers, rabbis, yogi, priests, etc. in well-known as well as esoteric religions.

In their gossipy communications, they whispered the hidden or omitted fact (which some folks had already noticed): The Child WAS A Girl, and since word of mouth is sound made in the echo of God (in the beginning there was the Word and it was without form but wide), ear to mouth and mouth to ear it soon became the People's knowledge, outwitting the computerized devices to which most sensible people had not said a private word for decades anyway.

Then: "O.K.!" said Dr. Heiliger. "It's perfectly true, but I didn't want to make waves in any water as viscous as the seas of mythology. Yes, it is a girl. A virgin born of a virgin."

Throughout the world, people smiled. By that time, sexism and racism had no public life, though they were still sometimes practiced by adults at home. They were as gladdened by one birth as another. And plans were made to symbolically sew the generations of the daughters one to another by using the holy infant's umbilicus. This was luckily flesh *and* symbol. Therefore beside the cross to which people were accustomed there hung the circle of the navel and the wiggly line of the umbilical cord.

But those particular discontented Jews said again, "Wonderful! So? Another tendency heard from! So it's a girl! Praise to the most Highess! but the fact is, we need another Virgin Birth like our blessed dead want cupping by ancient holistic practitioners."

And so they continued as female and male, descending and undescending, workers in the muddy basement of history, to which, this very day, the poor return when requiring a cheap but stunning garment for a wedding, birth or funeral.

One Blue Flag · *Linda Pastan*

One blue flag
is the only color left
on the frozen lake.
If the water was blue once
the color has been leached
out of it.
If the flag was once red
it was in another dream,
another country.
For blue is the color I know best:
it stares back at me from mirrors;
I lie gazing up at it;
and when the lake melts
I will swim submerged
only in blue . . .

Only . . .
That word
has so much longing in it:
if only I had done things
differently;
it's only me.
And what does only long for?
A flag perhaps,
that piece of brave cloth
that needs only
the smallest breeze
to give it hope,
even alone —
one blue flag.

In the Middle of a Life · *Linda Pastan*

Tonight I understand
for the first time
how a woman might choose
her own death
as easily
as if it were a dark plum
she picked
from a basket
of bright peaches.

It wouldn't be despair
that moved her
or hunger,
but a kind of stillness.
The evenings are full
of closure: the pale flowers
of the shamrock fold
their fragile wings, everything
promised has been given.

There is always
that moment
when the sun balanced
on the rim
of the world
falls
and is lost at sea,
and the sky seems huge
and beautiful without it.

I lie down on my bed
giving myself
to the white sheets
as the white sheets of a sloop
must give themselves
to the wind,
setting out on a journey—
the last perhaps,
or even the first.

Spaces of Work · *Padma Perera*

(India — USA — Greece)

a personal essay from a book of
nonfiction titled *Sumi Spaces #1*

Poona (India)

THE FICTION I'm beginning to write here *(Afternoon of the House)* focuses, intensifies, my usual preoccupation with fusion and antithesis: space/substance, stasis/movement, silence/sound. I need to bring them down to their stringency, that uncompromising level of a human touchstone, without which they are merely so much verbiage.

This book has to be written in the spaces between the words, the spaces between incidents, so that even if I do deal with factual detail, even if I do delve into physical and mental landscapes, my concern is to try and speak without speaking. I want to get to the beginnings of definition. What is "holy" . . . ? What is "mad" . . . ? What is "healing" . . . ? What is "thief" . . . ? Eliminate all notions of *prowess* with words. Do away with that spurious, retrospective headiness of being articulate. Get down to the sources instead. Wrest them out of that silence/cry from which you experience is born. PUT INTO WORDS THAT MOMENT BEFORE YOU CAN PUT IT INTO WORDS. And of course that's an impossibility. How can I presume to try? But there's the monkey on my back, saying: "How dare you not risk it?"

Not just a question of technique: of demarcating that tightrope, perilous here, between *simplicité* and *simplesse,* between real simplicity and its sophisticated semblance. More. It's trying to keep that connection, in work as in life, between inner and outer — so that any epiphanies I have the temerity to attempt can truly become moments of extended privacy. . . . Extending into insight. And I hope into art. Even saying it here is spurious. In the book, of course, I haven't that recourse, I have to *do* it. But how? is the question. Can I? is the question. And the monkey says: "So what's another pitfall? Stake your life."

271

Bombay (Elephanta Caves)

India for me is where these inner-outer connections keep, strongest, and are also most capable of being frayed, simultaneously reinforcing and undermining that private mantra: the line from the Hopkins sonnet: *what I do is me, for that I came.* There is no upholstery here. Against the constant surrounding hunger and deprivation, you can't raise your voice in the most justified complaint, from a personal cry to a metaphysical protest, without feeling reduced to a *kvetch.* To have a roof over your head, a desk, a typewriter, is to go from guilt to fruitless apology. There is a point after which it's no use saying "O.K., we all have our sources, we all have our strictures." Won't wash.

Yet here, where bellies have to be filled first, art still has roots. In Elephanta, Ellora, Belur, Halebid, Mahabalipuram, it isn't the obvious genius and grandeur and scope of the finished caves and temples that prove it, as much as those abandoned and time-blurred carvings where your eye completes what the sculptor's hand began, what no one else perhaps can see quite as you do, so that the very seeing of it becomes an act of creative complicity between the past and the present, between the visible and the possible.

Poona

The book again, which I seem to unwrite as fast as I write. . . . Struggling with its spaces even as I keep a wary eye on the external spaces that bring it to birth, to make sure even tangents won't ring false, won't be just tangents. Taking the manuscript from context to context — the watcher-in-the-head never falling asleep. Yes. Insomnia. "Many have it."

How fortunate to be able to hole myself here and work every day. A conch shell blows for somebody's morning prayer; children and neighbours come around, peering through the windows at this weird anomaly of a woman closeted with her typewriter, under a sky illimitably full of sun. Subservient to my monkey, I want to scratch and ask for peanuts.

Outside, the hills around town change all day, from blue to lavender to a deep drenched purple and then, after dusk, to the exact tinge you see in the smudges of fatigue beneath a child's eyes. It is June; we are waiting for the monsoon to break. It has hit Ceylon. It has rounded the tip of the southern coast. Then the wind drops. How to describe it? —Day following hot, breathless day; the inexorable parching, all colour drained from the earth and the sky and the hills; the unspoken anxiety in everyone's eyes: "Please don't let the rains fail, please don't let the crops fail, please let our bellies be filled. . . ."

The wind picks up, reaches Cochin on the west coast, gets up as far as Bombay, and then stops again.

Early morning, my mother and I go up to the roof to watch a cloud above the mountains—small, purple-grey, no bigger than the proverbial man's hand. And there it stays. "You might as well get back to work," my mother says.

In my work room, at some point, I realize I need to turn on the light. Clouds have massed overhead. Suddenly, a breath of coolness courses through the trees . . . there's a roll of thunder (incredible timing) . . . and then *down* comes the rain. A roar rises from the whole neighbourhood, as if from one throat. Street vendors put down their baskets, college students put down their books, everyone links arms and they go singing and dancing and clapping down the street. Children rush out into the yard, or up on to the roof, whirling round and around like little dervishes, arms flung wide open, lifting their heads to drink the new rain as it falls.

Delhi

The Raos come to visit when they hear I'm back in India. They have two children since last we met, down south: a girl of seven, a boy of five, whose names—Kavita and Anand—translate to Poetry and Bliss.

Their parents have saved, to read to these children, a story of mine published when I was in college here, about what our concept of divinity seems to a child. Moved and amazed, I tell myself that we Hindus, like heffalumps, have long memories. But the kids themselves are reassuringly themselves.

Poetry says: Did you write it all yourself?

I say yes.

Then she says: Do you collect feathers?

I say no.

So she goes off, hoping to gather some left by a parrot, a pigeon, and two crows, and doesn't succeed.

Bliss, meanwhile, leans out of our second-floor window and spits strategically at intervals to discourage any passing thief who might steal their car, parked below.

—Roots beyond blurred carvings now, and not indigenous to us alone by any means: this rootedness in living, which creates around it the ambulant space of a perspective where I take my oath again on what I have always felt: that I can never be a Writer, capital W, only me writing, like me breathing or me puking.

And to say that is not to skim the agonized awareness of prices paid—the relentless and irretrievable cost. Odd, inevitable, and no doubt repeated to extinction by now: how, when the sources of being human and being an artist are the same, their practice should have to be so compartmentalized. So damnably difficult bringing the two together; such (perhaps self-defeating) effrontery to demand the kind of totality that some of us do. Wanting fusion, you can become a battleground; trying to live completely, you can die in bits. But the necessity never stops. I have earned myself, strengths and vulnerabilities inextricably allied; it is only from there I can speak.

New York

J. says: "How can I stand up and say another word, if I don't live what I believe?"

I think back, then, on the two-odd years I stayed in this city, the "literary" names known and met. My own naive perfectionism, perhaps, in wanting artists to be custodians of a cultural conscience, aghast at the discrepancy between the quality of their character and the pretensions of their talent . . . a monstrous imbalance, palpable as a cripple's limp.

Now at the Chelsea (with plaster falling off the ceiling), J. speaks of the difference between "having a value, and pursuing it."

And by now too I know full well the ways in which art can arise out of a sense of deficiency—for without that mindful, tangible handhold on the human, we are perhaps amorphous creatures who take form when we make form.

Boulder

Our conversations in front of the fire, where one completes a sentence that the other began:

"The inwardness of me—"
                    "has to become the outwardness of art."

And speaking of how, when all your pores are open, so much bad can come in with the good:

"The easiest learners . . ."
                    "are the ones most harshly taught."

(Which is perhaps why non-essentials can also build around us?)

Referring to the kind of poets who "don't leave tips," J. says: writing is gratuitous when two words/sentences put together can penetrate life, and don't.

It is not so much the hacks you mind, then, as the intelligent ones who have deliberately vacated themselves to shine up a surface. Yet there are those of us for whom, for better or for worse, the basic problem of art is at what level you take life.

On the boat from Santorini to Crete

Warm sweet wind. Standing on deck at nightfall—feeling utter and uncluttered—we watch the wake from the side of the boat: the way it swirls and spreads, thinning out into a fringe of foam . . . just one line of awareness against the encompassing dark.

(Until another wave, slantwise from the stern, intersects and disperses it.)

Delhi

two months later. Scuttling around, running some errand, I realize for the first time in what seems like centuries that I am not bone-tired. Something is getting put back together. Perhaps a return to familiar, slow, deep rhythms: a kind of physical certitude: the look of the land and the ones I love—light falling over cheekbones and hills in the same language, defining its durability.

Not to deny lacunae, difficulties; but having access now to weld them into a known perspective against which it is possible, briefly, to rest. Meanwhile the wary watcher-in-the-head watches out against lapsing back into any old states of domiciled intelligence.

I don't want to locate myself only by geography (however strongly I acknowledge its power and point), or books, or beliefs. I want to be located in every breath I take.

So, . . . still, . . . and any other guards and prepositions that come my way, being rested and rooted and strangely at peace now is like an extrapolation of that moment on the boat to Crete.

Here's a stillness too requisite, too voluntary, to be merely acquiescent. A living necessity, all too often denied to all too many of us: these moments of poise, balance, between taking in . . . and giving out.

To me it has always been a very specific, though nameless dimension between what is fully received, and how you respond to it, what you *do* with it. Space for physical/mental/emotional impacts to make connection with what is called "the life of the mind." Space that delineates too, I think, the difference between an abeyance and an abdication of intelligence:

Where you can afford to wait, open-eyed, open-pored, and *in* yourself totally—clear of any preoccupations that could blur a direct seeing. From where, having brought your whole unimpeded self to the moment, you can then carry your perception of it beyond the moment and beyond the self.

Started to spell it out—this region of absolute focus—and its place in my own life, for one, that night on the boat to Crete. But we docked and I couldn't follow it through. Now I think a real quest for metaphor (among so many other things) is tied up with it: nothing to do with verbal embellishments; not even merely expressing the abstract in terms of the concrete; but more: *a noting, a tracking down, of process into significance.* As with the line of foam on the sea to Crete that night, and its directing me (for one) to our edges of awareness in the dark.

Homage to Lucille, Dr. Lord-Heinstein
Marge Piercy

We all wanted to go to you,
even women who had not heard
of you, longed for you, our
cool grey mother who would
gently, carefully and slowly using
no nurse but ministering herself
open our thighs and our vaginas
and show us the os smiling
in the mirror like the moon.

You taught us our health, our sickness
and our regimes, presiding over
the raw ends of life, a priestess eager
to initiate. Never did you tell us
we could not understand what you
understood. You made our bodies
glow transparent. You did not think
you had a license to question us
about our married state or lovers' sex.

Your language was as gentle and caring
as your hands. On the mantle
in the waitingroom the clippings hung,
old battles, victories, marches.
You with your flower face, strong
in your thirties in the thirties,
were carted to prison for the crime
of prescribing birth control
for working class women in Lynn.

The quality of light in those quiet
rooms where we took our shoes off
before entering and the little
dog accompanied you like a familiar,
was respect: respect for life,
respect for women, respect for choice,
a mutual respect I cannot imagine
I shall feel for any other doctor,
bordering on love.

Laocoön is the name of the figure ·
Marge Piercy

That sweet sinewy green nymph
eddying in curves through the grasses:
she must stop and stare at him.
Of all the savage secret creatures
he imagines stealthy in the quivering
night, she must be made to approach,
she must be tamed to love him.
The power of his wanting will turn
her from hostile dark wandering
other beyond the circle of his
campfire into his own, his flesh,
his other wanting half. To keep her
she must be filled with his baby,
weighted down.
               Then suddenly
the horror of it: he awakens,
wrapped in the coils of the mother,
the great old serpent hag,
the hungry ravening witch who gives
birth and demands, and the lesser
mouths of the grinning children
gobbling his substance. He
must cut free.
               An epic battle
in courts and beds and offices,
in barrooms and before the bar
and then free at last, he wanders.
There on the grassy hill, how the body
moves,
        her, the real one,
                  green
as a Mayfly she hovers and he pounces.

self-criticism · *Monica Raymond*

it was a mistake to pretend that
we were on intimate terms
with wildlife

and fling words
like scarlet tanager
into our poems

this was at best a pretense
at worst a deception
we got them from books

and the names
of the constellations
spattered and starry

do you think poets
see all that differently
from you really

no   headlights
blunt the night sky
in the same way   I assure you

I can tell you
a pigeon   a squirrel
a tree in its nest of concrete

but the rest is technical vocabulary
typefaces   machines
with their intricate molded parts

there are experts
even for this leaf
fraying the edge of the concrete

remedy probably
for some disease
we have forgotten the name of

The Thread · *Monica Raymond*

LUCIEN MET an old high school friend in a gay bar. The friend is a hot shit television producer now, Lucien is an out-of-work academic, and Lucien's lover, who has the frail face of a calculating cherub, is an actor. "Twenty thousand dollars for an hour script," Lucien says. "Seriously, Monny, I'd like to work in television." Fourteen years ago, when Lucien was too squeamish to even be straight, and ran to the priest to confess every self-abuse, the man who is now the television producer wanted him. "He says I put him through hell," Lucien says with relish. "I didn't like him. He was dumb. Shrewd, but dumb. He wants me. He said I was one of the most influential people in his life. He said . . . I let him kiss me. He's obviously a much more experienced fellow than I am." "Are you attracted to him?" I ask. "Well, there are exciting kisses and not so exciting kisses. This was an exciting kiss."

Lucien tells me this over breakfast, the blank eggs staring up at us, their splishy yolks. In the park, even nature seems worldly, the wild cherry knobbly and shameless. The piles of leaves like dried-up roses in potpourri, and darting out of them, single, yellow ginkgoes, the parasols. Sixteen years ago we walked in threes to the park to draw them, every day a different species, and later—was it among the pin oak red oak elm or maple—we laughed uncontrollably at the old ladies complaining about their feet, their livers. Serious we were supposed to be and demure, little girls drawing the leaves over and over with our hard pencils and erasing until the paper wore thin. With Wendy and now Wendy uses words like dialectical objective scientific petit bourgeois, I am petit bourgeois, although she doesn't say so to me. I am not nostalgic. When I was in high school I was more elegiac than I am now, I wrote stories about young girls who had to put away childish things, I believed puberty was death. Now I believe things open and open, sometimes there is a feeling like destiny if you can get the edge of the thread. Only what am I to make of time? They are all there—the cycles and the spreading time like water, the heaping crush of revolution and the closed corridor of time, the underground safe I grew up with. It is November, I am twenty-seven, and I need to know—is this early or late?

I am living in a kind of stopped time this week because, for reasons too complicated to explain, I agreed not to see or speak to a woman I love for two weeks. Or perhaps this is putting it badly, maybe "love" confuses the issue. When I think of telling you how I feel about this woman, I think of this—there is a deep crevice in her skull, like the line where the lobes come together on a peach or apricot, and one of the lobes swells slightly above it. The skull itself is covered with crinkly brown hair. It is not that I feel particularly dear about this crevice, actually I don't, it makes me uneasy, like the sight or idea of any head wound. Using it as evidence that she is something other than ordinarily human, I can frighten myself with it. The last time I saw her, we were sitting in the kitchen of the house she was moving to. I was fasting and she was frightened, the dense pasty yellow of the walls seemed to zap into me like a tab in a slot. I stroked her head then, I ran my fingers along the cleft and the bulging hemisphere to one side of it, tenderly, feeling the strangeness, the strangeness of my tenderness.

The television producer is taking accordion lessions from Lucien's roommate, a rawboned woman singer. "He wanted me to sit there, *watch* him take the lessons. I said 'I'm not going to do that, it sounds boring.' He said 'But you're the reason I'm taking them!' I said 'Now you know learning an instrument is very difficult, it takes a lot of concentration, you wouldn't want distraction.' 'But I want you to, I want you to. You know I'd do *anything* you want, anything you want. . . .'" Lucien mimics him fiercely. "He had quite a little tantrum there." "Did you say anything?" "I didn't. But suppose the next time I were to say 'I'd like a friend to have a part in the next television pilot?' I think it could be arranged. Oh, I know, Monny," he says, admonishing himself as if he were me. "I should be careful, I get too caught up in these things. He wants to play with me awhile, have me as a toy. Why shouldn't I play back a little, if I want to?"

Sometimes I lose the thread, then I don't know what comes next. My friend Louise thinks she is the Virgin Mary, I saw her face today among the leaves, her high white forehead as if it were wrapped in gauze. In the bookstore a woman talked about looking for fossils, chipping and chipping away at rock, she said, without thinking of anything except finding something wonderful. A possible question—how many times can you pick up the thread and put it down again? Another question—are the times when the thread's lost part of the thread? A possible example—this pair of men's black leather shoes on a waist-high wall in the middle of the empty park, looking as if someone had just stepped out of them.

I had a theory about time, that it pours like honey, so the points that are far apart on the original strand lap over and touch one another. It turned out I couldn't say any more about the theory than this. I was talking to the woman I care for, the one I had promised not to call, the woman with the cleft in her skull. We were eating hamburgers and drinking water because we did not have enough money to pay for drinks, and she said "What's wonderful is that human beings have conversations like this." She didn't understand the metaphor of the honey, so I did a demonstration with the ketchup in one of those aluminum ashtrays stained with the specks of old butts.

Last night I wanted to call this woman terribly, terribly, and I had lost her number. I had scribbled it on an envelope in a panic. She had just moved. So I had to live up to the agreement after all. This is a funny story, in a way.

Lucien kisses me goodbye, he puts his tongue in my mouth, a tongue like footed pajamas or rice pudding. "We'll have to get married someday. When I'm thirty-three." "How old will I be?" "Thirty-one." "I have this fantasy," I say, "that when I'm thirty-three I'll be living on this women's commune and go off and seek the father of my child." "Then you'll have to do it twice," he says. "You'll have to be the mother of mine." There were more children in this story once, in the earlier drafts. There was Louise's little boy dreamily flinging his toast on the floor, and the son of the bookstore lady, picking up fossils along the surface of the ground.

When they said the trees were turning, I imagined the trunks rotating slowly as if an invisible motor moved a turntable under them, like trees on a music box, holding their branches out to the sun. It was forbidden to take the leaves from off of the trees, you had to find one from among those that had already fallen on the ground. Wendy and I laughing at the women so black and white with skulls the grey pink of monkey lips under their furls of white hair, the horned lumps of their shoes, the tubular glint of the wheelchairs, and when we turned around, the teacher, usually so severe, was laughing too. We had to draw the ginkgo in hard pencil so it would not blur, over and over, the veins, the thin lines.

It is November, I am down by the water. Yellow flowers like thistles grow out of the concrete of the bank. On a metal box by the shore, a pair of men's khaki pants and a cotton T-shirt, balled up, as if he had just stepped out of them. The woman I love has another lover. Last night I was desperately unhappy. If you see me like that again, remind me that it changes. The masts of the boats make strings in the water. The gulls make a ripple like a forceps as they swim.

For Ethel Rosenberg · *Adrienne Rich*

convicted, with her husband, of "conspiracy to commit espionage"; killed in the electric chair June 19, 1953

I

Europe 1953:
throughout my random sleepwalk
the words

scratched on walls, on pavements
painted over railway arches
Liberez les Rosenberg!

Escaping from home I found
home everywhere:
the Jewish question, Communism

marriage itself
a question of loyalty
or punishment

my Jewish father writing me
letters of seventeen pages
finely inscribed harangues

questions of loyalty
and punishment
One week before my wedding

that couple gets the chair
the volts grapple her, don't
kill her fast enough

Liberez les Rosenberg!
I hadn't realized
our family arguments were so important

my narrow understanding
of crime   of punishment
no language for this torment

mystery of that marriage
always both faces
on every front page in the world

Something so shocking   so
unfathomable
it must be pushed aside

II

She sank however into my soul   A weight of   sadness
I hardly can register how deep
her memory has sunk   that wife and mother

like so many
who seemed to get nothing out of any of it
except her children

that daughter   of a family
like so many
needing its female monster

she, actually wishing to be   *an artist*
wanting out of poverty
possibly also really wanting

revolution

that woman   strapped in the chair
no fear and no regrets
charged by posterity

not with selling secrets to the Communists
but with wanting   *to distinguish*
herself   being a bad daughter   a bad mother

And I   walking   to my wedding
by the same token a bad daughter   a bad sister
my forces focussed

on that hardly revolutionary effort
Her life and death   the possible
ranges of disloyalty

so painful   so unfathomable
they must be pushed aside
ignored for years

III

Her mother testifies against her
Her brother testifies against   her
After her death

she becomes a natural prey for pornographers
her death itself a scene
her body *sizzling*   *half-strapped*   *whipped like a sail*

She becomes the extremest victim
described nonetheless as *rigid of will*
what are her politics by then   no one knows

Her figure sinks into my soul
a drowned statue
sealed in lead

For years it has lain there   unabsorbed
first as part of that dead couple
on the front pages of the world   the week

I gave myself in marriage
then slowly severing   drifting apart
a separate death   a life unto itself

no longer *the Rosenbergs*
no longer the chosen scapegoat
the family monster

till I hear how she sang
a prostitute to sleep
in the Women's House of Detention

Ethel Greenglass Rosenberg   would you
have marched to take back the night
collected signatures

for battered women who kill
What would you have to tell us
would you have burst the net

IV

Why do I even want to call her up
to console my pain   (she feels no pain at all)
why do I wish to put such questions

to ease myself   (she feels no pain at all
she   finally burned to death   like so many)
why all this exercise   of hindsight?

since   if I imagine her at all
I have to imagine first
the pain inflicted on her   by women

her mother testifies against her
her sister-in-law testifies against her
and how she sees it

not the impersonal forces
not the historical reasons
why they might have hated her strength

If I have held her at arm's length till now
if I have still believed it was
my loyalty, my punishment at stake

if I dare imagine her surviving
I must be fair to what she must have lived through
I must allow her to be at last

political in her ways   not in mine
her urgencies perhaps   impervious to   mine
defining revolution as she defines it

or, bored to the marrow of her bones
with "politics"
bored with the vast boredom of long pain

small; tiny in fact; in her late sixties
liking her room   her private life
living alone perhaps

no one you could interview
maybe filling a notebook herself
with secrets she has never sold

Mother-in-Law · *Adrienne Rich*

Tell me something
             you say
   Not: What are you working on now, is there anyone special,
   how is the job
   do you mind coming home to an empty house
   what do you do on Sundays
Tell me something . . .
                Some secret
   we both know and have never spoken?
   Some sentence that could flood with light
   your life, mine?
Tell me what daughters tell their mothers
everywhere in the world, and I and only I
even have to ask. . . .
Tell me something.

   Lately, I hear it: Tell me something true,
   daughter-in-law, before we part,
   tell me something true before I die

   And time was when I tried.
You married my son, and so
strange as you are, you're my daughter
Tell me. . . .
                I've been trying to tell you, mother-in-law
                that I think I'm breaking in two
                and half of me doesn't even want to love
                I can polish this table to satin because I don't care
                I am trying to tell you, I envy
                the people in mental hospitals their freedom
                and I can't live on placebos
                or valium, like you

A cut lemon scours the smell of fish away
You'll feel better when the children are in school
        I would try to tell you, mother-in-law
        but my anger takes fire from yours and in the oven
        the meal bursts into flames
Daughter-in-law, before we part
tell me something true
        I polished the table, mother-in-law
        and scrubbed the knives with half a lemon
        the   way you   showed me to do
        I wish I could tell you—
                Tell me!

They think I'm weak and hold
things back   from me.   I agreed to this years ago.
Daughter-in-law, strange as you are,
tell me something true

tell me something
        Your son is dead
        ten years, I am a lesbian,
        my children are themselves.
        Mother-in-law, before we part
        shall we try again? Strange as I am,
        strange as you are? What   do mothers
        ask their own daughters, everywhere in the world?
        Is   there a question?
                Ask me something.

Integrity · *Adrienne Rich*

the quality or state of being complete;
unbroken condition; entirety
               — Webster

A wild patience has taken me this far

as if I had to bring to shore
a boat with a spasmodic outboard motor
old sweaters, nets, spray-mottled books
tossed in the prow
some kind of sun burning my shoulder blades.
Splashing the oarlocks. Burning through.
Your forearms can get scalded, licked with pain
in a sun blotted like unspoken anger
behind a casual mist.

The length of daylight
this far north, in this
forty-ninth year of my life
is critical.

The light is critical: of me, of this
long-dreamed, involuntary landing
on the arm of an inland sea.
The glitter of the shoal
depleting into shadow
I recognize: the stand of pines
violet-black really, green in the old postcard
but really I have nothing but myself
to go by; nothing
stands in the realm of pure necessity
except what my hands can hold.

Nothing but myself? . . . My selves.
After so long, this answer.
As if I had always known
I steer the boat in, simply.
The motor dying on the pebbles
cicadas taking up the hum
dropped in the silence.

Anger and tenderness: my selves.
And now I can believe they breathe in me
as angels, not polarities.
Anger and tenderness: the spider's genius
to spin and weave in the same action
from her own body, anywhere—
even from a broken web.

The cabin in the stand of pines
is still for sale. I know this. Know the print
of the last foot, the hand that slammed and locked that door,
then stopped to wreathe the rain-smashed clematis
back on the trellis
for no one's sake except its own.
I know the chart nailed to the wallboards
the icy kettle squatting on the burner.
The hands that hammered in those nails
emptied that kettle one last time
are these two hands
and they have caught the baby leaping
from between trembling legs
and they have worked the vacuum aspirator
and stroked the sweated temples
and steered the boat here through this hot
mist-blotted sunlight, critical light
imperceptibly scalding
the skin these hands will also salve.

Laura Riding Roughshod · *Jane Marcus*

DRIVEN OUT of idyllic Mallorca, where she and Robert Graves wrote poetry and published small volumes of esoteric writing at the Seizin Press, the poet Laura Riding wrote a manifesto. There is nothing odd about a poet writing a manifesto in the thirties. It would be an odd poet who didn't. This three-page document was recently on exhibit at the New York Public Library among a remarkable collection of manuscripts from the Berg Collection in "The Thirties in England," organized by curator Lola Szladits, famous for her acquisition of modern British writers' papers.

Across the room in another glass case were the drafts and typescript of Virginia Woolf's *Three Guineas* (1938). What's odd is how alike the two manifestoes are in theme and argument, though Woolf's pamphlet is written with a speed and grace of symbol and metaphor, sensuous appeals to the eye and ear and every literary trick in the bag—which Laura Riding, purest of pure poets, would have abhorred.

Woolf's anti-fascism was a tri-partite political stance of socialism, pacificism and feminism, her original contribution being the argument that the origin of fascism was not in nationalism but in the patriarchal family. Laura Riding also believed in women's superiority, but in her case it was linked to a belief that because of their domestic isolation, women are better at *thinking* than men. Because of female rationality, men, she suggests, ought to leave the running of the world to women so that war may be abolished and aggression stopped, locally and internationally.

Few feminist protests were heard in what Auden called that "low dishonest decade," especially when they were as high-minded and ferociously honest as Woolf's and Riding's. The last thing that men wanted to hear as they mounted the barricades in a fight for freedom was that war was related to irrational male sex drives. Riding did not get much response to her plea and she and Robert Graves left London for New Hope, Pennsylvania, where their last literary experiment in living broke up in a personal debacle, and Laura Riding married the poetry editor of *Time* magazine, Schuyler B. Jackson. She gave up poetry as too impure a medium for the pursuit of truth, and domestic *thinking* and linguistic study have been her occupation ever since.

Chicago critic Joyce Wexler, who teaches at Loyola University, has written the first book on this important and influential American poet: *Laura Riding's Pursuit of Truth* (Ohio University Press, 1980). Laura Riding's critical essays and her several volumes of poetry, published from 1926 through 1938, reveal a powerful mind and an authoritative talent. "You are the one to save America from the Edna Millays!" wrote Allen Tate in 1925, commenting enthusiastically on how intellectual, ironic and original her poems were. But the very authority of her intellectual and poetic presence militates against historical recognition of her achievements. She is one of those figures, harsh and splendid in rigor and discipline, whom one would rather read than speak to. The public personalities of her former students and disciples, from Ransom to Tate, now considered to be the founders of American New Criticism, to that grand old man of English letters, Robert Graves, have obscured not only her influence on them, but her original contribution to literary criticism.

Joyce Wexler documents in detail Laura Riding's method of close textual analysis and the way she taught this doctrine to the Southern Fugitives, Ransom and Tate. Wexler also traces the argument which Graves and Riding developed in *A Survey of Modernist Poetry* (Hogarth, 1927), an argument William Empson claims inspired his famous *Seven Types of Ambiguity*. Wexler has rescued one of those "stranded ghosts" from literary obscurity and has told a fascinating story as well. But just as Riding's poetry has been forgotten, Wexler's book has been ignored by American journals. Irony is one of history's games, too, not just poetry's. For the timing of a Riding revival coincides with the rebellion of feminist critics against the too formal demands of New Critical exegesis. Will we be forced to acknowledge that it was a woman who invented Chinese footbinding of the critical imagination?

Riding's reputation raises many provocative questions, not the least of which are biographical. "Riding's poems portray a mind locked in combat with words and winning," Wexler writes. And so they do. But where did such an original mind come from? How did a Jewish girl from Brooklyn, Laura Riechenthal from Girls' High, become Laura Riding the queen of modernist poetry, reigning secure in the twenties and thirties over the Seizin Press and her London and Mallorca disciples? Her sceptre was invisible, but she actually wore a gold wire crown which spelled out LAURA, and no one found it odd at all.

Naming names is of course what poetry is all about, ever since Adam. In one of Riding's poems she shows her concern about the poetic and human act of naming: "I am because I say / I say myself / I am my name / My name is not my name / It is the name of what I say. / My name is what is said. / I alone say. / I alone am not I. / I am my name. / My name is not my name, / My name is the name." This puzzling "truth-telling" is Riding's definition of the poetic act. And though she won't admit comparisons, that poem was clearly begotten by a literary daughter of Emily Dickinson. Dickinson was a truth-teller too, but canny New Englander that she was, she demanded that the poet "Tell all the truth but tell it slant" for the "Truth must dazzle gradually / Or every man be blind."

Riding, however, didn't want the truth of her poems to dazzle gradually, and she has been impatient with the blindness of critics. Her Jewish socialist father had wanted her to be an American Rosa Luxemburg. But Laura Riechenthal went from Girls' High to Cornell, married a history instructor, became briefly Laura Gottschalk, and went to New York to write poetry. The admiring Hart Crane first called her "Rideshalk-Godding," then, cooling at her authoritative ways, termed her "Laura Riding Roughshod." "Riding" was the name she chose for herself as poet, though now she wishes to be known as Laura (Riding) Jackson. That parenthesis around her chosen name is as distancing as the famous parenthesis in which Mrs. Ramsay's death is revealed in Virginia Woolf's *To the Lighthouse*.

Riding was a good choice. For "riding-rhyme" is the name of the heroic couplet that Chaucer used, and Chaucer's Cressida is one of the domestic heroines she admires. Her disciples thought of her as Cassandra, but it was Cressida she held up to glory in *A Trojan Ending* (1937) in which we see a woman retelling the tragic tale from a domestic angle as a quarrel between Helen's husbands. Cressida says it is refreshing to get off the subject of victory, "bloody cartsful of it off the battlefield." Riding says she wants to redeem the story of Troy "from its association with schoolboys who do not weep when their mothers die." Her Helen is a housewife who works her cloth as if every stitch brought the war nearer to an end. In *Lives of Wives* (1939), a historical fiction about the ancients, she says that the "male characters are here written of as husbands rather than as heroes."

Riding ought to be restored to the ranks of writers like Hart Crane and Gertrude Stein, where she belongs as a shaper of our speech, a poet of powerful and original irony. In what Riding calls "the stuttering slow grammaring of self," it is language which makes us human. She is the least sentimental of love poets. For her, words are superior to acts:

> And I shall say to you, "There is needed now
> A poem upon love, to forget the kiss by
> And be more love than kiss to the lips."
> Or, failing your heart's talkativeness,
> I shall write this spoken kiss myself,
> Imprinting it on the mouth of time . . .

"Riding" is a name not only for a rhyme but also for districts or jurisdictions in a county. And since she named the press she ran with Robert Graves, Seizin Press, we could guess that another territorial imperative was being expressed, for "Seizin" means legal possession of freehold property. Both a "seizin" and a "riding" are far bigger chunks of territory for a woman writer to claim than the "room of one's own" Woolf modestly demanded. Is Riding's cult of domesticity feminist? Or does it simply lead to the inequalities of worship that cause poets like Robert Graves to make White Goddesses out of women?

"Analogy is always false," Riding argued, and tried to purge poetry of metaphor, symbol and myth. What else is left but pure language and thought? If, as she claims, things cannot be known by their resemblance to other things, then the poet is left with a purged language. The reader often finds the poems too abstract, but Riding would claim that thinking itself is not abstract. The title of her second volume of poems, *Love as Love, Death as Death,* conveys what she means. Riding published Gertrude Stein's poems at the Seizin Press in 1929, and her kinship with Stein is clear. In *Survey of Modernist Poetry,* a major influence on "the Auden generation," she praised repetition in Stein's work as having "the effect of breaking down the possible historical senses still inherent in the words." Since so much poetry alludes to past poetry, this is a revolutionary approach. Riding's abstract poetry reads like an extreme Modernist manifesto. It resembles nothing so much as the Russian revolutionary early Cubist/Constructivist paintings of Goncharova and Alexandra Exter.

These lines from "In the Beginning," about a daughter's "unpentateuchal genesis," for example, might be painted by a surrealist: "She opens the heads of her brothers / And lets out the aeroplanes. / 'Now,' she says, 'you will be able to think better.'"

The life of the Riding/Graves circle in London in the late twenties consisted of couples, triangles, rectangles, and great bursts of creative activity. It included Robert Graves's wife, Nancy Nicholson, on a barge in the Thames with the children, the disruptions of the Irish poet Phibbs, the erring disciple, and Laura Riding's attempted suicide. She jumped out a window and broke her back but survived to pursue truth in words, an authoritative poet and critic, retreating from the limelight to the solitary pursuit of linguistic purity. Graves and her ex-disciples quarrel about her influence. In an early poem, "Forgotten Girlhood," Riding answers them:

> But don't call Mother Damnable names.
> The names will come back
> At the end of a nine-tailed Damnable Strap.
> Mother Damnable, Mother Damnable
> Good Mother Damnable.

Laura Riding's *Selected Poems* (Faber and Faber, 1970) or her *Collected Poems* (Random House, 1938) are good places for the reader to start. Joyce Wexler does not discuss the prose, but both *Lives of Wives* (1939) and *A Trojan Ending* (1937) are fascinating. It was Virginia Woolf's Hogarth Press which published her first volume, *A Close Chaplet,* in 1926. Riding's integrity, her withdrawal from the world and her truth-telling suggest a modern Emily Dickinson. For her truth is "the muse that serves herself"; man's need to claim that his half truths are *the* truth leads to "Titanic dissipation." Let us read Laura Riding again, in an attempt to approach her abstract frontier of poetic truth. It is a world where there are no myths to deceive us.

The Short Order Cook in the Mountains · *Susan Schweik*

Lady, the fresh lake trout

you ask for
comes sealed
in plastic, its pink
eyes greased
with a film of Idaho
tap water.

I break its bag without remorse and paprika
its gills and curl its tail to tease you
with the illusion of fresh
speed, a violent rumba
of panic and heat.
I don't care if you do
pay more to choke on a local bone, Lady
Mark, Lady Menu, Lady Need.
I want you to know

they thaw from the deep freeze
in a sink. I stir them
with a spoon I call "Spawner."
Their tails are stubborn, stunned, feel
in the palm as passive and unreal
as sleeping in vaseline, as the give
of a glissade.

I stack the days like plates
to be scraped, like odds
against: nine to five. I call out
my short orders. Like you,
I get what I want. But friend,

friend, after the night shift
towards morning we'll wade out
into that dark infant chill
called Sacred Dancing
and feel the long and sharp
recede, recede
of glaciers in the small and twisting
bones of our spines—holding,
in each hand, hooks.

Basic Training · *Jane Shore*

Class dismissed! Half the activists pitched
tents in cornfields, half hitchhiked home.
National Guardsmen invaded the campus;
the State Police shot mace and tear gas
into the lobby of the freshman dorm.
Two canisters rolled down the elevator shaft,
paralyzing all 13 floors along its spine.
My students, Vietnam Vets against the War,
had a bazooka, stolen from the local arsenal,
trained on the Old State Capitol's gold dome
that cloistered their two political prisoners—
the President and a Dean.

Stationed on the steps of enemy headquarters,
the militant organizers reviewed the troops.
The poets staged a read-in.
Each group took turns hogging the bullhorn.
As at a revival meeting, the sweating audience
was born again during each activist's harangue.
Somebody figured out how to switch on
the electricity. Maneuvering across the platform's
DMZ, each speaker readjusted the microphone
to his individual height and pitch.
The poets ordered their priorities: they'd
"lay down their weapons, and stop writing."
The audience cheered. By nightfall,

the militant leader's speech impediment
made the word "political" sound like "poetical."
Wrenching the mike away from him, a poet,
my fellow grad student, a manic-depressive,
lately AWOL from the hospital's psych-ward,
tranquilized the fatigued listeners with his
sermon on the mount: "The east coast
and the west coast are two strips of bacon.
And the mid-west is one big flat fried egg."

High Holy Days · *Jane Shore*

It was hot. A size too large,
my wool winter suit scratched.
Indian summer flaring up through fall.
The shul's broken window
bled sunlight on the congregation; the Red Sea
of the center aisle parting the women from the men.
Mother next to daughter, father next to son,
flipped through prayerbooks in unison
trying to keep the place. Across the aisle,
my father wore a borrowed prayershawl.
A black yarmulke covered his baldspot.

The rabbi unlocked the ark
and slid the curtain open. Propped inside,
two scrolls of the Torah dressed like matching dolls,
each a king and a queen. Ribbons hung down
from their alabaster satin jackets,
each one wore two silver crowns.
I wondered, could the ancient kings
have been so small? So small,
and still have vanquished our enemies?
Didn't little David knock out a giant
with a rock?

The cantor's voice rose like smoke
over a sacrificial altar,
and lambs, we rose to echo the refrain.
Each time we sat down,
my mother rearranged her skirt.
Each time we stood up,
my head hurt from the heat, dizzy
from tripping over the alphabet's
black spikes and lyres, battalions
of stick figures marching to defend
the Second Temple of Jerusalem.

Rocking on their heels,
boats anchored in the harbor of devotion,
the elders davenned Kaddish,
mourning the dead, that, one by one,
they'd follow.
The man who owns the laundry down the street
still covers his right arm out of habit.
Like the indelible inkmarks
on my father's shirt collar,
five thousand years of washing
can't wash the numbers off our neighbor's arm.

Once I saw that whole arm disappear
into a tubful of soapy shirts,
rainbowed, buoyant as the pastel clouds
in *The Illustrated Children's Bible*,
where God's enormous hand reached down
and stopped a heathen army in its tracks.
But on the white-hot desert of the page
I was holding, it was noon,
the marching letters swam,
the spiked regiments wavered in the heat,
a red rain falling on their ranks.
I watched it fall one drop at a time.
I felt faint. I breathed out sharply—
my nose spattering blood across the page.

I watched it fall, and thought,
you are a Chosen One,
the child to lead your tribe.
I looked around the swaying room.
That the Messiah was overdue
was what they'd taught us in Hebrew School,
but who, here, would believe
this child sitting in their shul
could lead anyone, let alone herself,
to safety, to fresh air? Trying hard not to call
attention to myself, I tilted my head back
as my mother stanched the blood.

Why would God choose me to lead
this congregation of mostly strangers—
defend them against the broken windows,
the spray-painted writing on the walls?

As if God held me in His fist,
we stepped out into the dazed traffic
of another business day—
past shoppers, past school
in session as usual—
spat like Jonah from the whale
back into the Jew-hating world.

Doors Opening Here, and There ·
Marcia Southwick

A broken rainspout.

The dream about water rising up the stairs.
Mother and I trapped in a small rectangular room.
Her bones turning to plaster
when I touch them.

A melon rotting on the kitchen sill.

Doors opening here and there into rooms
where no one is permitted.

Mother pushing father away
without the use of physical force.
She looks at him as if from a great height,
the way one would look at stones on the ground
from the point of view of a roof.

All of this occurring over cups of coffee.

A few clouds scattered like minor complaints.

* * *

Mother's description of my brother's apartment:
no chairs, cardboard nailed over the windows,
and a wife who cries
when he returns from work and watches T.V.
without speaking.

Her possible description of me:
How one morning my son carried handfuls of ashes
out of the dead fire
and rubbed them into my hair as I slept,
stretched out, drunk, on the white couch.

Open windows. The wind disturbing the stillness
of the lamps and portraits.

The feeling of being lost among familiar objects,
of being unrecognized by the striped wallpaper
and dried flowers.

* * *

My husband in a closed room listening to Pachelbel.
In tears because his father, now dying,
used to close himself in a room and listen
to Pachelbel.

A crack in the wall that never shows itself.

My husband's father asleep in a chair
in the blue livingroom in California.
The wrong words that seem to seize him:
"How will you get there,
the four-lane hospital?"

The calm white of the almond trees.

The rain speaking in extinct syllables.

Connecticut. What mother said to father
about his change of career:
"I married a doctor, not a sculptor."
Father was measuring the distance
between my hairline and my chin.
For the bust.

What father said to me
on a ferry from Maine to Canada:
"Your mother's friends play golf.
I hate golf."

* * *

Noticed the apparent closeness of a couple
walking down the rainy street,
just beyond the neatly trimmed hedges.

Then realized the rain was responsible.

Not their emotions but the rain
causing them to huddle together
beneath the umbrella.

No comfort in knowing the trees have flowered
according to my belief that they would.

A few blackbirds jarring the ear with insults.

Fishes at Saint-Jean: Chagall, 1949 ·
Roberta Spear

I

Because the sea is also
in me, a sea so blue
that parrots fly through it
and horses and other women
who are true, I want to dive
and feel the ragged edges
of your canvas folding over me
like water.

On the ocean floor
the grass is swaying,
the horses are diminished
and delicate, and a mollusk
drifts between two lovers
fighting the urge
to rise. But up here,
the light freezes
the ivory walls of the museum.
The guard sleeps with his hands
in his pockets.
And the woman selling tickets
drowns in her cubicle,
the hard bubbles rising
from her lips toward the sun.
No one saw it sneaking in
through a diamond of glass,
etching its path of light.
As I follow, the seas part
and all the beautiful blind fish
are thrown at my feet.

If color
is the secret you share,
there are other things
I could tell you,
things that would please you
more than sapphires
or crushed tourmalines,
more than the indigo veins
of fish or birds,
the infinite drops of sea water,
more than the final blue note
of an accordion that carries us
through the warm night air.

II

Like an acrobat in a green suit,
the wave lifts, lets go and spins,
and then another follows.

The small stones clap softly
at the water's edge
where I press a mold for my body
and lie back, letting
the day's heat enter. They say
the agate of flesh inside me
will one day spin out,
floating beyond the children
catching foam in their arms,
beyond the last lacy swell
to a place where the water
barely moves and you are sculling
belly-up, like a great whale
filled with rooms of air
and darkness.

At the day's end, the sun
lifts its nets off the water
and the moon rises.
You swim in and find me
still staring out—the lights
on the barges and the new stars
becoming the same. Perhaps,
I will find my way back here
tonight while you are sleeping,
like other women who have left
their homes for these slashed shores.
And like another, I will make
a wreath of stones
for a small fire which, like the sea,
is the mother of all colors.

Though memories dissolve
in the waves of darkness, many nights
have been passed this way—
a woman waiting it out,
who can only guess how much
of herself she has given
to this world.

III

It's true.
My belly will soon be as round
as the dazed summer moon
or the lush little islands
off the coast.

You smile and tip
the scored carafe of cassis
into both our glasses.
Now, the crowds are filling
the cafes along the promenade,
angels wrapped in gauze
against the gentlest breeze.
Even flies dance on the light bulbs
and old women peek at themselves
in the gritty mirrors behind the bar.

You don't want others
looking at me the way they do—
men with eyes as quick as fish
or those saying nothing
as they melt into their own reflections
on the table next to us.
I like cassis,
the currant-red hills along the sea
where I dreamed mermaids live
in winter, knitting by fires
as red as this glass.

I can't hold it in any longer.
It is as round as the storm clouds
that sailed over as you swam
into shore. The patron
unrolls the awning to the curb
and a light rain collects
the softened faces at the edge
of our vision. We look for one
with a message,

the face of a gypsy child
who has your eyes
and plays a painted fiddle.
In his dish, coins
stamped with the names
of the old world we're in,
and one with the name
of the new world in me.

Days · *Elizabeth Spires*

Like jumping rope,
like old *New Yorkers* piling up,
or the inscrutable faces of dominoes lined in a row,
the days arrive, knocking insistently,
and you
on the other side of the door, not breathing or moving,
watching them through the keyhole.

Arm in arm, they goose-step down the boulevards—
so many of them!—
like actors out of work,
dressed in moth-eaten costumes and old band uniforms,
and always
the black armbands, a reminder of their constant decimation
(soon to be replaced with younger, more arrogant days
than the ones you have known).

Oh, you have suffered for them!
For their high-stepping ways!

Once you were dutiful.
Entertaining famous days of boredom
who languished
for weeks in peignoirs and smoking gowns,
calling out weakly, like invalids,
to be waited on.
And the forgotten days that took their revenge—
like drowned children under the pond
forever crying
in your sleep to please find them.

Some you ran away from—
they crouch in dark places, or hire hit men,
waiting for *the right time.*

Old debts accumulate. Losses
pile up. You think back, unwillingly, too nostalgic,
to days of poignancy and days of despair,
days of no letters,
                          and the hoped-for days of love,
mirage of tomorrow's tomorrow.

You who have only the present, never the future.

Ordinary Lives · *May Stevens*

My mother did not finish elementary school; my father finished a vocational high school. But art meant something to them somehow. My mother was married in a grey dress, accordion-pleated, fanning out over the shoulders like a shawl. She liked my being an artist.

My father painted and papered our house. I helped him slap the wallpaper paste on the back of the long strips that we carefully placed on the wall to match the pattern. I helped him cut the stencils to make a trim for the kitchen wall; he showed me how.

My father hated "garish" color. I bought a tweed suit at Peck and Peck in burnt orange. He called it "shit brindle." I bought him socks in the same color but he wouldn't wear them.

Rosa Bonheur's *Horse Fair* hung over our living room sofa—on the patterned wallpaper.

We also sang in my family. Not with good voices but we sang anyway—in the car on long trips or coming back at night: Irish songs, Scottish songs, "There's a long, long trail a-winding into the land of my dreams..." and hymns and carols.

My father really liked poetry. He cut it out or copied it in a scrapbook. He liked "Into the valley of death rode the six hundred . . . " and other things of an adventurous, moral nature. I was shocked when I found in his scrapbook: "I know there are no errors in the Great Eternal Plan / And that all things work together for the final good of man." For he was a pipe fitter living in a 4-room house with 2 children and a wife going mad.

He wanted me to be an artist, too.

Postcard · *Pamela Stewart*

Dusk, the sea is between colors
And our medallion star is ready to leave for China.
This is the brushstroke hour
You have already befriended.

I am here for the first time
Taking a rush of water into my mouth.
My ribs fold with a white salt weight.

Centuries ago, Mu Ch'i slipped his eye
From fog to indigo. A grain of sand
Dislodged from a monastery wall.

His six bitter orbs of fruit
Are still blindingly pure.
And everyday
His seventh, unpainted persimmon
Ripens across the sky.

The bell-blossom moon follows behind.

Here, in California, the day shakes once
And falls. The ocean pulls closer.
With luck, you say,
A sudden streak will flash toward the stars

As the flaming persimmon dips into salt.

In this way the eye will complete the day.
It will root in the heart.
My hands return from water, the water
Returns from China.

I would unstain my heart to carry it with me.

What Can You Do? · *Ruth Stone*

Mrs. Dubosky pulls a handful
of sharpened pencils out of her apron pocket.
They're for the grandchildren.
She picks envelopes out of wastepaper baskets
and soaks off the stamps.
The boys have a stamp collection.
Mrs. Dubosky is paying on a trailer.
She can't retire until she's paid off the seven thousand.
She's sixty-two.
Mrs. Dubosky says, "We'll see."
Her new daughter-in-law lives in the trailer.
Her old daughter-in-law has the house.
"What are you going to do?" Mrs. Dubosky says,
looking at me. "He's my only son.
He's come home. Want a kiss.
You know, those private things.
He's away all week pulling that semi to New Jersey.
And she says, 'Not now. I'm busy.'
Or, 'Leave me alone.'
He says, 'Ma, right then I knew.'
He made himself a bed upstairs.
He said, 'Let her go on, who cares?'
Then he asked her, 'How come Don is here
when I get home midnight? He's got a wife and kids.
What's he doing here all the time?' And she says,
'Are you accusing me?'
You know, I had my trailer on my son's land.
I had the hole under it for the flush toilet
and I had to move it to a trailer park.
That woman got everything."
Mrs. Dubosky wears other people's old tennis shoes.
Chemicals in the cleaning water eat right through them.
She's got a bad leg.
Her mother's legs were bad. They had to be amputated.

While her mother was in the hospital
her father's colostomy quit working and he got a blockage.
Her mother told her, "You burnt him. I know you did."
"Oh, no Ma."
"Yes, you did," she said. "I saw it in the paper."
"Marriage," says Mrs. Dubosky. "You know how it is.
I had just had the baby.
My husband was after me all the time.
You know, physical.
Oh, he slapped me but that's not what I mean.
My mother came over and she said,
'What's the matter with you?'
You know, the eye-bags was down on the cheeks.
I says, 'He's always after me,'
and she says, 'You're gonna come home.'
The judge said he'd never seen a case that bad.
You know what he called him? He said,
'You're nothing but a beast.' "
Mrs. Dubosky isn't sure. She says,
"What can you do?"
When she retires, she tells me,
she's going to get a dog. One of those nice little ones.
"When you rub them on the belly
they lie back limp," she says, "and just let you."

When the Furnace Goes On in a California Tract House · *Ruth Stone*

If the blower is on
you may experience otherness—
then the clear plastic saltshaker
with her wide bottom, sexy waist
and green plastic head,
her inner slope of free running crystals,
is visibly crumbling
in the sight of the frankly opaque pepper
who seems taller, even threatening,
though they are the same size,
in fact, a designed pair.
His contents are hotter.
"Yes," she sighs, "the pepper is strong.
How he asserts himself on the cream soup—"
Or, "What is an egg without his gesture?"
Little does she suspect in her ability to dissolve
without losing herself, that the very blood . . .
"It's degrading," she confides, "the way they pinch me."

Secondhand Coat · *Ruth Stone*

I feel
in her pockets; she wore nice cotton gloves,
kept a handkerchief box, washed her undies,
ate at the Holiday Inn, had a basement freezer,
belonged to a bridge club.
I think when I wake in the morning
that I have turned into her.
She hangs in the hall downstairs,
a shadow with pulled threads.
I slip her over my arms, skin of a matron.
Where are you? I say to myself, to the orphaned body,
and her coat says,
Get your purse, have you got your keys?

Poetry · *Ruth Stone*

I sit with my cup
to catch the crazy falling alphabet.
It crashes, it gravels down,
a fault in the hemispheres.
High rise L's, without windows —
buckling in slow motion;
Subway G's, Y's, twisted,
collapsing underground:
screams of passengers
buried in the terrible phonemes,
arms and legs paralyzed.
And no one, no one at all,
is sifting through the rubble.

On Ruth Stone

WHEN THE EDITORS of this special issue of *The Iowa Review* asked me if I knew of any "lost" women writers in contemporary America, I thought at once of the poet Ruth Stone. Ruth has published three superb collections *(In an Iridescent Time, Topography,* and *Cheap,* all Harcourt Brace), and her work has often been highly praised. Yet she is largely unknown outside a few towns in a few states where she has read and taught at one time or another.

I first met Ruth at Indiana University in 1973. We were both teaching creative writing classes and courses in modern poetry. But I had a regular tenure-track position while Ruth was on a visitorship, one of a series of temporary jobs that have kept her busing around the country from one campus to another during the last ten years. In her mid-sixties now, Ruth started teaching too late to establish herself in tenured comfort at any one school. By the time she was in her late fifties, that fall at Indiana, most department chairmen thought of her as a bad business deal, too near retirement to be worth an investment of tenure and all its attendant "perks." Besides, Ruth was too vivid, too shabby, too frank, too mysterious, too much—I have to say it!—too much a poet and thus too *strange* for tenure. Although, as Wendy Barker testifies, students flocked enthusiastically to her classes, she alarmed her colleagues and unnerved administrators. Looking sybilline, she would tell deans her visions of their secret wishes—and she would be right. Plainly, therefore, she was "wrong" for academia. Because of this "wrongness," indeed, she seems to me to have become, besides a woman I love and admire, a paradigm of the "lost" woman writer.

Ruth had always been a vivid and brilliant poet, but the lucidly articulated pain, the grievous clarity and the bitter music that now mark her work and that are, for me, associated with both her losses and her lostness, were born in 1960, when her husband died and she was left with three young children, no job, little money. At first she tried to raise her family in the old farmhouse on a Vermont mountain that was her only remaining asset, but the winters were deadly and besides she needed a salary, so there followed the exhausting round of visitorships I mentioned earlier. As Dorothy Gilbert points out, however, Ruth was "always writing" through all that confusion of travel and children, of bills and tickets. Yet she "disdains advantage," as Charlotte Painter wonderfully observes, and like so many of our mothers, she hesitates to put herself forward. So although, as Dorothy Gilbert also notes, she has an attic full of poems, she sent few of them away, failed to press her case with editors and publishers, did not (as it so often seems one must) play the game of "Po Biz." Every once in a while somebody one knows — somebody who seems always to have been safe, lucky, middle-class — slips through a gap in the net of business and friendship over which we all warily tread, and that is what happened to Ruth. By the time I met her in 1973, the small reputation she had begun to make in the early sixties had faded; when she wasn't "visiting" somewhere she was literally out in the cold, wintering alone on her mountain. From the point of view of the literary-academic Establishment, she had become a "lost" writer.

As I tell this story, I realize that it must seem increasingly hyperbolic, like a Victorian melodrama, so I hasten to note that it is not, finally, a tale of catastrophe. For Ruth *was* "always writing," even if she wasn't publishing — writing on buses, writing in sub-zero winters, writing in strange offices and rented rooms, never silenced. As the women's movement gains in power and popularity, and gains, often, through the attention given a few stars whose names we can all count on the fingers of one hand, we must remember Ruth and the others like her, women who make their art in obscurity and discomfort, as so many great artists always have. Indeed, we may well ask ourselves if it is not these "lost" women who constitute precisely the matrilineal literary tradition we feminist critics have been seeking for the last decade. For, preserving her poems in a New England attic while disdaining advantage, Ruth inevitably reminds us of the stubborn integrity of Emily Dickinson, who left *her* poems in neat unread packets in a New England bureau at least partly because she suspected that "Publication is the Auction of the mind of Man." Writing alone in the cold, Ruth evokes the powerful solitude of Emily Brontë, who elected to stay both literally and figuratively far from London's literary salons, and follow where her "own nature would be leading." Forgotten or ignored by academic critics, Ruth recalls the triumphant obscurity of her great near-contemporary H.D., whose major poems, until quite recently, were neither analyzed nor anthologized. If we are *feminist* critics, we must find and cherish these "lost" artists even while we honor those who live more publicly successful lives.

At the same time, however, we must also remember that Ruth and the other women writers she represents don't need us the way we need them. For in her isolation, Ruth preserves and enacts our vulnerability, our tenderness, our fear of heights. Still a sort of contemporary sybil, she is rarely sensible but almost always right. In obscurity, even in poverty, she is simultaneously grieving and joyful, anxious and exuberant, keeping continually at the heart of her work what Gerard Manley Hopkins, another "lost" writer, called "the dearest freshness." That is why, when we set the cozy geometry of our comforts—our lucky tenure, our little critical successes—against the terrible clarity of her vision, we must ask ourselves to reconsider our definitions of "lost" and "found." To herself, we must remember, Ruth has never been lost. If we have not yet found the meaning of her life and work, perhaps that is because it is we who are sometimes in danger of losing our way.

Sandra M. Gilbert

ONCE in a great while during graduate school you meet a guardian angel. They don't appear often. Ruth Stone is one: she tells the truth. She doesn't ask unimportant questions, she asks the big ones. And she reacts. Reacts to those truths so far down you're amazed she sees, knows.

She takes your poems as if accepting a valuable gift, holds the rough ditto copies as if they were made of Venetian glass, and reads your words as if they were holy. Hearing Ruth read her poems is amazing and wonderful. Hearing Ruth read your own work can change your life. Her daddy was a drummer; Ruth's sense of sound and rhythm is perfection. Listening to her read your clumsily revised third draft magically transports you to the country where your own poem might be finished, might someday grow to be as good as hers.

When you've felt your borders hedged by cynical, tired faculty, finding Ruth is finding yourself in new countries, countries of alpine meadows and high peaks, countries of black oceans seething with white whales, and finding ultimately that, because of Ruth, you can fly there anytime now, by yourself.

Wendy Barker

RUTH STONE lives in an eighteenth-century farmhouse near Brandon, Vermont. Just north of the house, across the road, is a long high spur of the Green Mountains; south of it, beyond the kitchen with its big black stove, the screened porch, and the backyard full of old fruit trees, is a distant view of the Adirondacks. In one second-story room of the house are chests of drawers, file cabinets, and high stacks of papers; they contain mostly poems that Ruth has written over the years but not typed up, poems she has typed up but not sent out, poems she has been wrestling with and mulling over for years and years, stuffed in among old bills and letters. Ruth is always writing. People stop by to see her—they are her three daughters, her former students, her friends—and she cooks dinner or entertains in front of the living room fireplace. People staying overnight may be put up in her own bedroom (the warmest), or in one of the tiny guestrooms. After they are in bed, she is working. Her pad is on her lap, her long auburn hair falls about her shoulders, and she looks intently out at something as if she saw her poems forming, hanging, in the air of the room. The poems are "a kind of physical rush coming through," she says; they have always felt that way to her. She lives in the farmhouse the year around, unless she has a teaching position or a poetry reading in some other part of the country. It can be forty below in the Brandon area in late winter, but she has often defied the climate.

Ruth has stayed with me in my apartment in Berkeley. When she comes we read each other our new work. She is the kind of literary friend who sees another's writing on its own terms, understands completely its intentions, and, if the work is at all successful, it takes on a new substance and vitality for its author after Ruth has seen it. Then it is real, it is born. On any visit, Ruth is still working. If we drive north to see friends who live right on the Pacific Coast, Ruth sits in the window looking out at the meadows and the windrows and the ocean, and again, one thinks she is seeing her poems materialize in the air. When we put her on the Greyhound bus on her return trip to Vermont (Ruth boycotts airplanes and can't afford a car) she seems to be in a sort of trance. We wave, we shout, but her eyes are closed this time, and she seems sealed in, not only by tinted glass and the stuffy bus atmosphere, but by that intensity, that determination, that will take her across California, Arizona, New Mexico, Texas, up into Tennessee and Virginia, on her seven-day journey home.

Dorothy Gilbert

326

RUTH STONE'S tough, specific, evocative poems stick in the mind, come back to you late at night. They seem to have arisen in that special place all poets try to batter a way into—the one where secret meaningful associations occur. Combine that Orphic voice with balladic cynicism, and you have Ruth's poetry. Any example seems too short:

> The quick brown poem jumped over the lazy woman.
> There it goes flapping like an orange with peeling wings.
> Like an old dried orange with hard peel wings.
> The thick brown poem jumped over the desperate woman.
> There you go my segments, my divided fruit, escaping.
> The thick woman jumped over the lousy poem. It's Brown,
>   she sighed.
> Watch it, the poem cried . . .

"Orange Poem, Praising Brown"
from *California Quarterly,* no. 16-17, Summer-Fall, 1980

Diana Ó Hehir

TO HEAR Ruth Stone read her poems in a group is a special experience in itself—and one especially true to poetry; the sound takes over the meaning and the hearers' sense of meaning. This is "reader response," hearer response, as it needs to be, established in the most direct relation possible. Every syllable matters. Listen!

Josephine Miles

I LOVE Ruth's work and consider her one of the major poets of her time. She has been sadly underestimated, yet there she is: clear, pure, fierce. What is distinguished and unique about her work, too, is what she writes about as well as how she writes it.

Tillie Olsen

I FIRST came upon Ruth Stone's work at the Radcliffe Institute where as a Fellow she won admirers among a small, dedicated group of colleagues. She wrote of what it was to be a woman in love, a wife, a mother, a widow, with a lyricism so naked, so completely womanly that we felt confident women everywhere would recognize it. That was more than fifteen years ago; the world did not immediately respond as we expected to that work, a reminder of the sad distance that may lie between the creative act and those for whom it was done.

Ruth Stone may not have been the first among us to understand that grief is a never-ending process, but she has showed us an unflinching willingness to return to the dark moments of her life as a creative source of an ever-deepening poetic expression. She has persevered under duress, even in poverty (as poets used to do), without benefit of the university tenure system that keeps most of our important poets in middle-class comfort. On those occasions when younger poets do meet with her in a teaching situation, they respond hungrily to those qualities she shares with the young, qualities others seek to rediscover in themselves and which she has apparently never lost, idealism and naiveté, freshness of response. There's something else special she shares with many young people — she disdains advantage, as Willa Cather put it, a perversity that nourishes her work and enhances its integrity and will at last find its reward.

Charlotte Painter

I REMEMBER encountering Ruth Stone for the first time at Sandra Gilbert's house in 1973. At a Thanksgiving dinner, over Elliot Gilbert's fine rendition of the family's heirloom recipe for spinach stuffing, my husband and 6-month-old baby and I met this disarmingly radiant woman in the mausoleum-like mansion the Gilberts were subletting. It had not been a simple year, moving to a small town from a big city with a little child. And, as wonderfully efficient at suckling and burping as young Molly was then, she had been difficult in other respects, as the dark smudges under her gray-green eyes testified. Or was it I who read pain in those smudges, motivated by my own discomfort at being her food source? The La Leche people, supportive though they were, had neglected to tell me about some of the by-products of nursing: nightmares about the baby crawling over my dead body in search of the source of sustenance, an unremitting low-grade fever, dehydration, bone-wearying exhaustion. Ruth looked at us in her shy, sly way, and said simply, about Molly, to Molly really, or maybe also to me, to my husband, "How amazing you are." We all cracked up.

What I value about Ruth Stone's poetry are the voices of a woman who has experienced herself as daughter, wife, mother, widow, understanding all the while how these roles define her without containing her. She has three daughters herself, and when I turned to her poetry, I learned from it about my own confusions. On the one hand, I overheard her telling her girls to try to speak when they are in need: "Don't confuse hunger with greed," she encouraged them in "Advice." On the other hand, she realized that their hazards were not hers, and hers would not be theirs. A poem like "I Have Three Daughters" implies that she understood even their impatience with her:

> I have three daughters
> Like greengage plums.
> They sat all day
> Sucking their thumbs.
> And more's the pity,
> They cried all day,
> Why doesn't our mother's brown hair
> Turn gray?

Here was a woman poet who wrote about mothers and daughters with the confidence of one who survived all the complexities and complicities of a relationship where the boundaries between selves become blurred, where each self threatens to digest the other or where it feels invaded by the other in the ache of knowing how the "I" is really part of "you."

Reading Ruth Stone's poetry reminds us that "Being a Woman" means "You can talk to yourself all you want to," for "You were the only one who ever heard / What you were saying." In the freedom of talking to herself, Ruth manages to explore the relationship between men, women, and children with lucidity and levity. There have got to be perfect readers for certain poems and sometimes I like to think of D. H. Lawrence reading Ruth's "Cocks and Mares": "Every man wants to be a stud," she begins, explaining that "He wants to bring forth God." The problem is that "He can't tell his cock / From a rooster's." Prancing up and down like a horse, he wonders what he is doing in the hen house, and the contrast between his stud-ied crowing and the wild mares in the night fields, "whistling through their nostrils," neither "fowl" nor "foul," is typical of Ruth's subversive wit.

Ruth's last volume of poetry, *Cheap,* contains a number of poems that point to the ways in which necessity mother her invention. But even in the face of poverty, the exuberance of her spirit refuses to spend itself. Some of her humor is an exasperated snort at inevitable failure: whispering to an unwanted older body that may be her own, the poet admonishes it to "Behave . . . / You have a wart on your cheek / And every one knows you drink" ("Periphery"). Sometimes it is the irony that grows out of her sense of commonality in the cutting room, the kitchen, with the silent, smooth head of an eggplant: "Which of us will it be?" ("Vegetables II"). No wonder she imagines her poetry as a necrophilic "habit," each poem a "joke," exhumed like a decaying corpse. At the same time, in some of her poems hilarity results from the pure and simple release of rage: " 'It's a good life, it's a good wife,' " says the self-satisfied husband in "The Song of Absinthe Granny"; his good wife's quiet response is unequivocal: "So I got the rifle out / To shoot him through the head." Happily he goes on smiling, watching as she and her children endure amidst the stubborn reversals and the rhythmic poundings that are her and Ruth Stone's passion. Like wary Absinthe Granny, Ruth Stone teaches us how to be chary with what's left. We can be sustained by this fine poet whose fantasies feed the heart, for even at their most ferocious, her visions of survival lend more substance to our loves than to our enmities.

Susan Gubar

How We Love Now · *Stephanie Strickland*

In bed you think of her
hollow cheek and strong jaw.
How difficult to graft them
to my apple face. Easier for eyes
than fingers. But your fingers
only go one place
urge me: you are anxious
to make us disappear on these sheets.
Her silence, her secrets; her complex
attention, how difficult to graft them
to me who want you
or not, in season. When I warm
along your length, when our heads touch
some whole circuit comes complete—
you could be a tree, I rock so high
on a tree-top. You are here for the tree
as I am here for her. And she
reminds you of your mother
when young, a flirt, hardheaded.
The image that compels you
when her long body swings by, you press
to my body, hot, rushing. I am surprised.
I feel her closer to me now
than I was ever able to bring her
before. I see how we are using her,
how she has used. And it all comes back,
what that was, being an embodiment, so close a match
to my lover's dream and he streaming toward me
from the sea of mine. Silver fever
lived out for three years, and rage
at what was not dream; leaving him. You there.
I blamed myself. If only
I weren't restless, I wouldn't have resisted
being exact, the matchless
match. How did we go on then?

This hot afternoon, years later,
when you bring her to my bed,
agitated, I'm remembering him
and what in all this time has stayed unsaid:
how more than once you saved my life,
and how many years it took
to say goodbye, to know I'd left;
how I've loved you and with whom.

Love That Gives Us Ourselves ·
Stephanie Strickland

— *Muriel Rukeyser, 1913-1980*

She said disowning
is the only treason. She said we pretend
coldness, or pretend
we are used to the world.
She said
all I touch has failed,
and the beginning was real
She said by imagining
the child can cope with loss,
be at home.
It is a work of images, difficult
and bare. Very slow. Like falling in love.
Desire shadows its fulfillment.
She said
now I speak only words I can believe:
no sly resonant pity.
Her short questions, the gravel
of her answers comes back to me again
and again, in waves:
turn with your whole life choosing.
Everything here is real, she said,
and of our joy. Her mother
didn't answer. Even past death
language incomplete
between them. Intense desire
scorches its fulfillment.
Muriel, the ashes
rise, the ashes are flying.

For My Aunt Florence Who When Praying Gives God Not Only Her Friends' Names but Also Their Addresses · *Nancy Sullivan*

Sure as the brakes on a Buick,
God is a mighty power.
Omnipotent, sure as there's light in the bulbs.
His wattage is wonderful.
But omniscience is a mackinaw we've buttoned him into.

(There must, surely there must somewhere
Be *someone* who knows *everything!*)

After the Fall, God rose as the fall guy.

Aunt Florence, knowing without knowing,
With a leatherette address book, both breviary
And Bible, directed God *exactly* giving house
Number, avenue or boulevard, sometimes even
The phone number: the Karl Sunderlunds on
4 Brave Drive in Minneapolis, Minnesota;
Alice Damark in Madison, Wisconsin —
Phone: (608) 238-8246;
Leo Spooner, 32 Farewell Street, Newport,
Rhode Island, Zip code 02840.
However else would he find them?
After all, the Sunderlunds were Lutherans and Alice a Jew.
She uttered this geography in a new litany
To lure him. She became his faithful navigator.

How did he keep us straight before he'd found her?
Let alone *find* us way out in Topeka, or up in the
Catskills, to say nothing of Brooklyn, Ethiopia,
Brazil, Scarsdale, London, the Bronx?

Let the mapmen honor you, Aunt Florence, lady of locales,
Tracer of those troubled by needs they'd not dreamed of.
And may the God in whose employ you labor
Find you always, especially when you've moved down
Into that last dirty apartment under the ground.

Pears · *Mary Swander*

Dipping each nail
in grease, she hammers
a porch around her house
so no one will see her
come or go, but I
stand here knocking,
the sun pouring
through the glass,
my back warm as the flame
in the stove she keeps
burning summer and
winter to drive
away evil. And no one
sees her slip through
the door, the walls
like sod, holding out
the heat, the rain,
and no one answers
my call as she slides
deeper into the far
room. She leaves
her shoes on the cellar
stairs and the mud-caked
soles dry into
their own faces,
dry into the shape
of the pears rotting
on the shelf. The light
fades into the wall,
into the cistern filling
with sand and stone.
The light fades
into the fence posts,
clothesline,

the heartwood of the pear
tree fallen down
behind the shed,
there to be chopped
for the stove inside,
there, where for days
I stand in her shoes
with an axe and do not
feel the rain, do not
hear the blossoms forming,
do not see them burn white
deep inside the walls
of their own stems.

My Grandmother's Hair · *Joan Swift*

She wanted to arrive in heaven with beautiful hair,
coppery glow, chestnut haloes of rectitude.
Milking the cows at dawn, she felt yesterday's
braids rocking against her cheeks, her head bent,
the pail giving back its metallic song.

So when they brought her home dead from the Blossburg hospital,
my mother brushed down from the cold scalp for hours.
Hair fanned out like a brown waterfall over the gray end of the coffin.

Lifting the head was hardest, to stroke each strand
and twine it in place.
She combed by kerosene lamplight.
When morning came and neighbors to the parlor door,
three circles shone on my grandmother's head.

Pink roses lay on the gray velvet,
each one letting a curl of pink ribbon down
with another rose knotted at the end. . . .

Kiss her goodbye, my mother said.

The stool was dark and embroidered.
When my lips touched the rigid cheek,
the finest of hairs, the little unmanageable wisps near the hairline,

brushed my face.

Father · *Joan Swift*

In the dining room painting of my childhood
the sheep are lost in a blizzard.
Against wild roses, they lean brown wool to brown wool
under the snow's diagonal.
The flakes gather in furrows on their coats
like a field where nothing is planted yet.
Their hooves disappear and all the soft parts
between their front and their back legs
are buried in weather.

Sheep can't say *cold* or *alone* or *save me*.
They can't say *where is the shepherd?*
A horse stamps in a barn somewhere not in the painting.
At the edges the sky is black and the center is blacker.
The sheep close their eyes against the wind.
For years they are closed.

Waiting for them to open in a bewilderment of spring
flowers, I drink snow milk   snow milk.

I wait forever.

Pneumonia · *Joan Swift*

The year of my mother's divorce
snow lay at the back door like a great hound.
The potatoes closed all their eyes in the root cellar.
I wore a patched coat to school, brown stockings.
I stepped in the bigger steps and carried
my hunger in wool hands.
But nothing was warm enough.
A draft blew in and out somewhere around my heart.

When it was time, they put my sickness
on a small cot near the pot-bellied stove.
Eight days I lay in fever,
one-hundred five, one-hundred six. . . .
Sunny, sunny, I said.
And my hands climbed all over the wallpaper
to gather the yellow day lilies,
the cut stems.

1933 · *Joan Swift*

The saw gleams in her hand like a cat's teeth,
dangerous light in the black cellar.
In her other hand, one leg of the oak table.

It is winter again and a cold house . . .
ten days since you came with any kind of kiss
for us or your arms swinging.

Now my mother begins the strange music.
She is holding the table like a cello or a baby.
She leans to the need with her difficult bow.

The legs go in through the furnace door.
The wild grain crackles.
Flames dance on the oval top in orange shoes.

It is not a table anymore, a place for the lamp,
three rings, and a gouge in the finish
where you threw the glass

and she sat crying. Only this heat,
a smell like nutmeg, smoke drawn up the chimney,
you drifting away.

Breaking a Voodoo · *Eve Triem*

young black woman knocks at my door
management doesn't answer   no blankets
Lana — 4 years — smiles   can i see your cats

exchanging life-stories over coffee
borrowed saucepan & cups   her need
is to tell: wild people follow me
never speaking   always following
from Chicago to Seattle   my father hates me

beauty hallucinated   a dreadful stamping
on flowers or the drowning of fireflies
enough money to stay one night in hotel
with small Lana   waiting for the sailor

she is too knowing to make a wax doll
riddled with pins or burn a candle to St. Jude
i tell her say NO   NO   NO to shadows
(she weeps into my hands)
the ship returns in tomorrow's light

Eve Triem: A Retrospective · *Carolyn Kizer*

What follows is a condensation of the introduction to a gathering of the poems of Eve Triem, a poet in her vigorous seventies, who presently lives in Seattle, where she is revered. I have written of her in hopes that, at last, she may become known to a wider audience.

TO READ the poems of Eve Triem is to discover her rare combination of naive delight in flowers, colors, art and gardens, along with her acute social perceptions, and her indignant response to injustice.   Eternally young herself, she has an immediate appeal to the young, who reject the notion that you can't be concerned equally with slums and humming-birds, as they reject the ancient shibboleths of the mind-body split or the body-spirit split.

From her first publication, the voice was clear, formed, Eve's own. In reading these poems of thirty-five, forty years ago, there is the same stab of pleasure one feels in reading early Pound, Graves, Kunitz, the best of Bogan:

> Your love is a parade of doves
> tamed to courtyard corn
> and marble bowls of water;
> and they tread softly their own shadows . . .
>
> If you left me now,
> startled by the noise of my heart . . .
>
> I would crush all summer
> like bergamot in my hands
> and go through the wrecked fields
> crying:
> "Have you seen a parade of doves
> brighter than scattered corn,
> and shining like water when they fly?"

or this:

> No longer a town blighting roses at noon; denying
> To trees their dryads, to Apollo his tripods . . .

Though we think bricks, and sheets on a line
And mill chimneys, are fixed forever to form,
The shape of things changes: there was meadow-flax,

Going in fable from thread to cloth, furious
For life each time; and every change was death —
But Death is a gate, and nothing is lost . . .

This Greek voice, this Sapphic voice has always been Eve's. In her sixties, she learned Greek. That fact alone proclaims Eve's uniqueness, the self-discipline that flows from her love of language and learning. In 1967 she gave us *Heliodora*, translations from the Greek. I value them as I value Mary Barnard's Sappho, or the poems of the rare H.D.:

> *Death's freshest loot
> 's a honey-bee* —
> poets sing of me
>   and Fate.

> I sang, too,
> collecting honey
> though my sunny
>   days were few.

> Hell's greedy prince
> likes sweet things most —
> my wingless ghost
>   laments.

> The Muses moan:
> Thy honey-store
> is tearful-dearer
>   than our own . . .

Here are not only exquisite poems, but a lesson in how to translate: the skilled use of compression, elision, compounds. All of Eve's abundant natural talent would not be enough to achieve these effects. It takes a world of craft, cunning and diligence as well.

Although Eve admires, and has been allied with poets who write in open forms, like Denise Levertov, and uses them herself, she is equally at home with forms. Her sonnets have an amazing ease and contemporaneity; and in her hands the neglected tetrameter line comes back into its own. For example, in "Flood":

> Through all windows and where a door was
> the river comes in. Whoever is
> overturned by the smell of marsh grass
> and heron cries, I like it, I like it!
> To help the river over chair and table,
> give it the best bed, and see in fireflies
> the lamps I paid for, is easy as milk. . . .

In "A Boy Downriver," she reveals another music in the 4-beat line:

> . . . The fun of being fish, clothes wet
> to the bone! Away from the shiny bait
> of honors in school (I, I am river)
> he lunges at berries, he breathes light,
>
> dazed into torment and joy throwing
> sticks at frogs, crushing the pungent snow-
> yarrow and shouting dirty words —
> a fertility rite his nerves know.
>
> Twilight. Hungry, young, afraid,
> he returns to a world he senses is mad —
> not really afraid but wishing for supper
> and the silent warm meadow of bed . . .

These last two quotes are from *The Process* (Poems 1960-75). And then, and then . . . we arrive at the group of poems Eve wrote to and about her husband, Paul, ninety-four years old, blind and helpless, but still, to Eve, every inch a man, lover, powerful adversary and friend. She waits at his bedside and holds his hand, and speaks to him as he dies. She buries him, she mourns him, she remembers him. The poetry rises to sublime heights. The intensity! Partly because their love still burns fiercely. Partly because Triem was a considerable man by anyone's standards. (See Denise Levertov's introduction to these poems, *Dark to Glow*, 1979.) Even now, in the midst of the squalor of hospitals and dying, Eve recalls and relives their passion:

> . . . He doesn't know me
> thinned by travelling
> his time and mine.
> Or remember our coupling
> that shook the thrones
> of stellar power.

The vocabulary calls up the aging hero, still a hero, part Don Quixote, part Odysseus, part Norman Thomas. . . .

> All of his banners
> shot down
> the last silk threads
> carried off
> by the ragpickers
>
> He tells the nurse
> sponging his weariness
> *so much left to do.* . . .

or this:

> Pillowed, a noble painted by Velasquez . . .
> I smooth
> clammy arms, hear the rattle in throat,
> wipe the death-dew from the brow of my lover. . . .

And Triem is gone. But Eve herself goes on, to constellations beyond tears, summons all the powers accumulated in her long life as a poet, looks—clear-eyed and steady—into the night and writes "For Paul":

I make no moan or outcry, just don't sleep.
The rain staining, etching the windowpane,
takes care of tears. Awake without hope
he will drink the morning with me, intone
a comment to my rhyme. What a lot of breath
went into the loving and now it's dying
we have to think of. The ghost on his path—
I refuse to believe what it is saying,

recalling the heron-river, books read aloud,
the nights we talked, sending the moon away.
The weedy places we rolled in and hid,
each to the other changing dark to glow.
You cannot lose me, said his ringing Yes
between the death-sweat and my forlorn kiss.

There will be more poems from her. Even as I say this, I know that in
the midst of that eternal Seattle rain Eve is bravely writing. I can see her
pure white hair, her gamine look, her lipstick, screaming red, and her
gap-tooth smile. May the Goddess bless her! and all you who read this,
who will go out and find her poems for yourselves.

from A Dictionary of Common Terms · *Alberta Turner*

Arch

Rainbow   Fountain
Bear the weight of Caesar and his triumphs
the weight of vision over the depths of error

Eyebrow   seedling   her feet
unmined remainder of a lode
vault

-bishop   -angel   -tempter   -fiend
Arch water without spilling
Arch the infinite over an apple
Overreach

Bliss

At mass   at meat
in a lusty husband's arms
of a child in her grace
Bliss on bliss

Felicity   ignorance
what the Pope has not got

A bliss of birds
a bliss of *yes*

Bliss   obsolete of *bless*

Die

In harness   in bed with your shoes on
at the stake   in your mother's lap

A calf   by witchcraft
A new child   by fondling

Lakes die   and barbarian nations
intricate vices   lard lamps   red trout
A good death   an utter death   die out

Franz, the World Is Abstract · *Chase Twichell*

They stroked me with white dust,
as though I should feel at home with dryness!
And in the fields around the house,
crickets produced a steady joy from friction.
I was a fish in the watery gleam,
dawn with its lake-light.
My window opened into the sky,
and I was consoled by the hugeness,
and the comfortable movements of the trees.

When I fell asleep,
I knew my world would leave me.
Sleep is full of comings and goings:
the queer, expressive faces of my parents,
the new thrill of rain.
Bending over the white crib,
my father says—and why so sadly?—
"Franz, the world is abstract,"
and I do not know what he means.

What they find lovely, meaningful, and sad,
is all I've ever known.
The surface of the lake distressed by wind
like thousands of pages riffled and turned,
or my mother on her haunches
in a heavy sweater, feeding the sweet,
thick fire with balsam twigs
on a cold morning when the year is ill.
The sumac's red spears.

Even now, as sleep consumes me
(for things happen without us in this world),
the pure, anachronistic flowers
of the hydrangea undo me, the bitter leaves.
My parents fret about the dead.
So many have died,
and we do not know where they are.
I thought they were fish in the river,
and close at hand, but I forget.

Starkweather House · *Chase Twichell*

How heavy the trees are with rain,
like trees from another century.

A pound of droplets weighs down
each branch of the lilac,

doubling the weight of its scent.
Above the wet meadow, the crows

float with surprising dignity,
or preen on the slate roof

which is speckled with lichens.
Whoever planted the white flowers

is dead now, with flowers on his grave.
And in the house, whoever wound the clocks

when they were new is dead,
though the clocks tick and chime

in the front hall, where pollen drops
onto the black table and is left there

because the yellow dust is pleasing
to those who are alive.

Someone who loved lilies
chose the paper on these walls,

silver and brown, as calming
as rain, or a glass of wine.

There is a breakdown in the cells
that improves everything,

makes men most delicious in their forties,
the plum when only a tension of the skin

holds in the juice. Did a man stand
in an upstairs room, looking out over

the leafy debris in the gutters
on a fallen evening like this?

Light curved among the slates
that reminded him of fish scales,

and his loneliness returned, a tender pain,
as he thought of the age of his parents.

The whole house smelled of cut flowers.
The crows shook out their ragged wings.

Running · *Leslie Ullman*

I

Lately my neighbor wheezes
pounding dough, her forearms
glazed with sweat and flour.
"At your age," my mother
writes, "I wanted babies.
I got pregnant
each time one of you
learned to walk."
I circle the block again
and again, until I run
outside my body.
This time last year
my husband stopped
speaking of the other woman
who slept poorly inside him.

She promised in another town
to give him up. All night she
tossed and tried to speak
until he spoke of his
father, who drank himself
into the cracked
well of his voice
and never touched bottom.
She made him wake sweating
and brooding in the close
room of his departure
while I ran past my neighbor's
lawn and plump loaves settling
in their heat
to an early shape of myself.

II

I've forgotten whose apartment
stretched like a tunnel,
shapeless and dark
the way my good dress hung
too large, a formal
body outside my body.
The other men drifted
alike behind their drinks
while he stood in one place
and spoke to me of *The Moviegoer*
which spoke, he said, to his very soul.

Sometimes I run in Louisiana,
where I've never been,
where the hero saw an egret gather
itself over swamp mist
and settle in a single oak
that rose to meet it.
Later he married his cousin
whose agile mind wandered,
glittering at the family table.
The dense mahogany.
The black butler
wheezed as he passed buttered beans.
She couldn't sleep, she
said, without pills.
Sometimes she slept for two days.
She promised she could
be like anyone, if he
would tell her each morning
how to pass that day.

That night, my skin
held me like liquid glass.
I wanted to slip
my hand beneath his elbow,
to dance,
to see the other women naked
inside their clothes.

III

Every morning I run
through pollen, late-summer
haze, or rain. My husband
is an illness I had
in another country.

The day he left
again and again he said
it wasn't my fault.
I circle the block, pump
and sweat until I run
outside my body.
My ribs ached.
He ran his hands
gently over them.

Inside my running
I write to him, breaking
the silence we keep
for his new wife:
I saw the sun disappear
into mist as it reached
the horizon. I saw an egret
airborne, circling all
this time.

The morning bus gathers
husbands and children
and leaves for a moment
a soft rope of exhaust.
I draw breath over breath
as the children

must breathe in their sleep.
My neighbor waves
from her doorway, watches
my easy stride. "Your waist,"
she says wistfully,
"fits the dress I wore as a bride."

Physics · *Jeanne Murray Walker*

The doors of the long semi-trailer truck
swing shut. A kid stands on the dock,
easing off his gloves, watching the tires roll,
hearing the engine grumble as it leaves
for one of those flat middle states,
dragging a hundred cardboard cartons labeled Grief.
Turning, he smears his red face with his shirt
and hoists another carton to the jaws
of another patient truck. His arms
are levers. His legs uncoil like springs.
In this gray town where houses are devoured
by ravenous black slate hills they cannot
help but cling to, grief is everywhere.
It rises out of chimneys, smelling like woodsmoke.
It airs its mug on new TV serials
and tackles his skinny brother
playing kickball in the vacant lot.
It settles in the blackened shack
that crazy William set on fire one night.
It crowds out asters like quack grass
and lifts its leg at the fire hydrant.
In prayer meeting grief scuffs its boots
on the pew it kneels by.
                              The kid
can't ship it out of town fast enough.
He swings his long legs over the dock during break.
They dangle weightless in a blaze of light.
He thinks about the only physics he has seen:
the love that bonds all elements
in their perpetual dance is grief.
He won't believe it, because he knows
how it might feel to sail over the rim of houses
into light. There nothing is held down
by the black fist of gravity.

Beyond the dock, beyond the roads, beyond
the tar paper roofs, beyond the stubble fields,
seething on the horizon, he sees
brilliant as a burst vein in his eye
a light that will not go away.
He blinks and blinks but it stays, as though
it were the lever to lift the city by.

Making the Painting · *Jeanne Murray Walker*

I

Like the criminal who waits across the street
for the nurse to snap the light on and undress
he sits before a Rembrandt, sketch pad on his knees.

She breaks from the umber shadow onto canvas,
the right plane of her face leaves dusk behind,
one earring dark, the other bright as a safety pin.

Straining her left shoulder forward, she gathers
amber light from his stare, her green gown
peeling away like ancient moss from new skin.

Skull neat as a cat's, her slender nose
cleared by the smell of turpentine, she craves him.
Their eyes lock into a beam between them.

Aroused to his feet, he stands peculiar for her.
His tee shirt's damp. His hands hang by his side,
ready for anything, veins blue as plums.

Then suddenly as though he'd found that Rembrandt
can be bettered, as though he'd taught the artist
how to see, he shuts his hands and strolls away.

II

I exit, trying to find some meaning in this.
Maybe I am the woman in the picture. It dawns
how the blurred room came clear for the first time

as he stood there. Light. I remember now
waiting through dark years for his blue stare.
All that time I couldn't guess what I was waiting for.

But it comes back. Before he packed his sketchbook
and wandered off, he brushed a fly
from my shoulder. His hand felt curious,

lingering by the secret curve of collarbone.
His voice breathed slang that might have made Eve step
from air. And I remember someone moaned.

But no. We are like drunks, mistaking our own tears for rain.
We see ourselves in everything. Whoever that boy was,
we crossed looks only once, and in an art museum.

His shirt is clean by now and Rembrandts hold their value.
Those two will get along together or apart
without the likes of us. Come. Let's not think of them again.

The Last Migration: Amherst, Mass., Winter 1981 · *Jeanne Murray Walker*

for Stephanie Kraft

The last shred of light falls on your wrist
like gauze. You lean at your hall window
to hear the hemlocks tossing in the wind
—old women, ankle deep in shadow
now, and wading deeper in. The dark ground
is glazed with ice. Winter's come early.
Hardly any sunlight bandages your hill's
steep cold.
        The birds that nest
in those old skirts should pack
their heads beneath their wings. Enough,
to dream about a burst of golden seeds
and summer in some place the sun finds
health. It's too late to fly south.

Your eyes watch them like lost hopes.
Everything must have some ending.
You recite their names: geese,
starlings, swallows, vesper sparrows,
and in this ceremony you are either accurate
or sorry. You are both.
        You get it right.
Truth is the thing you pull around your shoulders
like a shawl against the human chill. By incantation
like sunlight on the tongue, you name them.

As though they hear, they part the air
with beaks as dark as liver. Slow,
puffed out like foam, losing heat,
circling, they swoop, and almost stall. They rise.
Look. For all the weeks they need,
some knowledge inside their ribs will search
like lanterns the dark way they have to go.

Turning from the window, you pull
your sweater close. Through cold they drill
for those unlikely homes that you could name:
Peru, the Carolinas, Tennessee, Mexico.

Northern Liberties · *Jeanne Murray Walker*

This time I am going to tell the truth about what happened
the day we drove through your childhood by mistake.
As you were shifting into third, you said, "My God, it's Commerce Street,"
and there we were, idling in front of the yellow brick house
you lived in with your Jewish grandparents and your young, crazy parents,
the wrought iron gate you climbed still standing
underneath the giant lilac bush. The store where you bought caps
was advertising Jewish religious articles. Across the street
a Roman Catholic Cathedral with pink marble pillars and blue tile
loomed holy as a witch's sugar house, selling Novenas on Tuesdays at ten.
We turned the corner and drove around the block following an arthritic
                                                    trolly
past the long gone open market with beets lined up on trays
like the earth's skinned hearts. When we came back
to stare at the old house again, the sun had shifted between buildings
and shot us in the forehead. The lilac breathed fire.
I could see where you had fished for mackerel from the second storey
                                                    window,
where your pets lay buried, where you dug a hole to China with a
                                                    tablespoon,
where your Irish father leaned across his tart-tongued Jewish lover
with the improbably beauty of a tree turning in the fall.
In a minute the Rose of Sharon spread all over your back yard like applause
and the door to old Mr. Greenhagen's house slammed shut again.
You shifted into first. "Well, that's it," you said, looking at me.
And you pulled into traffic as though out of a dream.
I did not lay my finger on your wrist to stop you from going
anywhere you wanted even though it may be to the place
we both now know is China. Time has already stopped
so many things you want. I will say nothing that is not true.
When I looked back, I saw, beside the lilac bush which had turned
its green and natural self again, a boy running the streets of Northern
                                                    Liberties
into his feet, looking for you.

Necessity · *Jeanne Murray Walker*

Trees are minimal in winter
as the x-ray of a hand
showing bones, ghostly, white
but indisputable.
Every day these bones suck sustenance
from water, meat, and air
into long corridors
where they factor stories out.

Think of the stocking cap
that waits in the closet for a hand
to seize it. It may protect
as dearest warmth against expensive cold
but one day it will be delivered
to fire or garbage.

The bones say when.

Everything has brought them to this act,
birth, and food, and the chains
of swings in the playlot
which were so cold that children
told how skin would weld on contact
as it stuck with sweat
years later to other hands
it never trusted, but desired.

All our lives
skin comes and goes like weather
but bones are ghosts
which lurk beneath the skin
storing all our winters in their marrow.
They are like the fingers of snow-covered trees
whose shape we can't recall in summer,
the acts we won't believe in
till we feel ourselves
perform them.

For My Daughter's Twenty-First Birthday · *Jeanne Murray Walker*

I stroked her cheek with my finger
and she began to suck for dear life
like a fish in the last stages of suffocation above water.
When I poured my voice down to revive her
she grinned and graduated from college
Summa Cum Laude, schools of minnows parting before her.
"You are not a fish," I said to her.
"You are my daughter, and just born, too.
You should know your place.
At least we are going to start off right."
Like a woman whose hand has just been severed at the wrist
but who can still feel pain winking in the lost fingers,
I felt my stomach turn when she moved in her crib of seaweeds.
"Last month at this time," I said,
"you and my heart swam together like a pair of mackerel."
But she waved goodbye from a moving car,
hanging onto her straw hat with one hand,
light reflecting from the car window
as from an opened geode.
I wonder if she knows how I have stood for years
staring down through the fathoms between us
where her new body swims, paying out silver light.
It is as though I am still trying
to haul her up to me for food, for oxygen,
my finger in her mouth lodged like a hook.

Alice James · *Naomi Wolf*

*Her tragic health was the only practical
solution for the problem of life.*
—Henry James

I

I am a white rabbit in a hutch
fed by two giants:
their names are William and Henry.
Their great eyes peer at me
indulgently, through the wire.
They stuff me with bruised hearts
of lettuce, and chuckle
when I bite down on their fingers
with all my strength.

When I'm sick and my eyes are rhinestones
backed with tarnishing tin
they stroke the hot fur
on my fluttering belly.
But when I'm well they hold me
by my tender ears
and watch my paws drowning in the air.

When I go in the house
they all pretend I'm human,
trusting me with teacups and opinions.
They are proud as I preside
secure in my knowledge
that Professor Howe takes his with cream,
that I am well versed in macaroons.

"I will clothe myself in neutral tints, walk by still waters,
and possess my soul in silence."

The doctor insists that I'm fine
and his black bag clicks shut.
But I'm squirming with maggots like an old cheese.
They cling to his thick pink hands.

A rusty crow
has thrust its beak up my throat;
each wing wraps around a lung.
Its claws clutch my liver.
It beats sometimes, and caws,
but its voice is as weak
as mine.

II

I have no veins,
they are slim wise snakes.
Each of my toes is a snail
slick, tentative, blind.
The artery of my heart
is clotted with misshapen letters.
When I lie down at night
the beasts crawl
to the four corners of my bed
and when the word "greatness"
steps into me with its winged heel
my ribs constrict around it
like a snare.

"Dear Henry,
    I shall be arriving soon in Paris
to be an albatross round your neck."

They finally found that my breast held cancer
like a velvet-lined casket cradling a scarab.
I stroked it, crooning, "deliverer."
My nipple was the bud
on the apple of the Hesperides.
I slept well at last, happy,
listening to my cells' wild humming,
spreading the news.

A woman at the window · *Nellie Wong*

sees herself in a white silk linen blazer,
a black skirt with a slit, a cinnabar-red blouse,
and she sees herself through the plate glass
standing there with her hands thrust deep
into her pockets standing there watching the sun
sparkle in a thousand lights in pools of silver needles
as she wanders in search of memories
As usual the sun intrudes her darkness
her feelings of aloneness and privacy
and when the phone rings she dashes
to answer it, changes her mood from aloneness
to sounding office official sounding
like the secretary she is
though sometimes she forgets that she is a poet
and prefers to stand at the window, imagines
herself a mannequin in a shop window
posing with a vacuous stare with her hands extended
like hammers ready to crash through the plate glass
breaking loose from the wool and the silk
from the neon lights the store decorator
has knotted around her neck
If she crashes through the window she would
see blood dripping from her fingers
but she wouldn't lick them
she doesn't always like to taste red
but she knows the violence that is contained
inside her body as she feels trapped
like a silver fox desired for her skin
to be worn by a woman who passes her by
She knows instinctively that she is a woman
who wants to float in and out of other skins
a witch, a princess, a bag lady, a dim sum shop girl,

her mother dying of cancer, her grandmother who feeds
pigeons in the park, or a sewing factory woman
who plans to organize for higher wages,
for music and bright lights, for time to play
with her infant daughter
She doesn't understand her feelings of floating
water hyacinths or lilies
as a dragon imbued with powers
as wind that rages through her limbs
as a lion at the electric typewriter
as a voice of women and men of Asian America
She knows that she isn't alone or lonely
that the memories will find her standing
twenty-three floors above a city lake
that sunlight is her companion that the air
she breathes though filled with pollutants that she will
fight them with the swallowing of antihistamines
that she will fight them, a woman at the window
with her fingers that desire to become wings

Toward a 44th Birthday · *Nellie Wong*

Mornings and the eggshells crack, the eggshells scatter
to the wind. You carry them within you, the wind,
and lift your feet toward construction sites and know
that construction men eye women from the corners
of their eyes. Silence sniffs at you like a cat
and still you walk toward work, toward skyscrapers,
imagine the shattering of old plate glass. You forget
the Ko-Rec-Type, the carbon copies, the Xerox machines.
The time clock ticks, a medallion on the wall. You dream
of grinding coffee beans, relaxing in the hot sun of Egypt,
forget that the pyramids are a wonder of the world.
Is it another vacation you need, apple trees to sit
under, the longings of a girl searching for arms,
hands to link to her tiny fingers? You sigh, reading
of diamonds in millionaires' teeth, of maids tidying
beds for other maids, of a Luckys strikebreaker being struck
by a car. No, not a car, but a driver, a human being.
What life will you find in your roamings toward China,
toward Asian America in its kitchen crowded with dreams,
on its streets teeming with cracks, toward young men
being tried for killings at the Golden Dragon, toward
pioneer women of the 19th century, the pioneer women
who live within your bones and the voice of Sui Sin Far
nudges you awake. How far, how near will sisters talk?
Will art atrophy, or will it become the tools in our hands?

1978

371

Your Story · *Susan Wood*

We rose from the bed and sat at the table.
You were telling your story,
how your father would disappear for days
each morning with a tin pail full of cold meat
and thick bread to come home drunk
for a few hours' sleep and another bloodshot dawn.
Nights you lay so still
you scarcely breathed, wishing and wishing.
In family legend you had the Irish in you,
those high-horse looks at two, and charm,
the boy who's always "acting up."
You hid your young aunt's sandals in the icebox
while she was dressing for a date.
You laughed and wouldn't tell. She slapped your face.

Whole summers by the ocean escape you
and there's only the moment the cart is bolting,
leaving behind a blur of sand and sea,
the unfamiliar streets, the boardwalk. You were four
and proud to be minding your baby sister.
Your father had handed you two nickels
for the ride. On the far side of town
the driver stopped the pony,
made the children all get down, and drove on.
If your father had come just then to lead you home,
what would it matter? *All I remember is being lost,*
you said. And so do I. It's what we know
and can believe in, why the present wears the past,
each day knit to the next.
Or why this story is true as anything,

where the boy and girl are left in the forest.
I'd like to say it has a happy ending,
they find their way, love,
breadcrumbs the birds haven't eaten,
this table in the morning light.

Review of *Leaf's Boundary* by Sheila Zamora · *Sandra McPherson*

L'Epervier Press and W. D. Hoffstadt & Sons Press, 1980, 57 pages, $4.95 paperback.

WE OFTEN CANNOT judge the worth of a poet until after he or she has died. Sheila Zamora was the casualty of her husband's violence. When he shot her, she was thirty-one and a student in the Graduate Writing Program at Arizona State University. Her teachers and friends have gathered her fine poems into this collection. The book is far more than a gesture or a memorial; it is literature that lovers of the art should have. It is a strong and complete first book, fortunately, for this is the author's only chance to be read.

Zamora's work is remarkable for its delicacy. The book could be written in pencil and thread. There is gracefully worded attention to light, color, object, and line.

IF YOU OFFERED, THE THING I'D CHOOSE

would be you drawing water
through a nest of fingers,

as the fingers
of an ordinary gardener want

to carry a few clear drops
for the rosemary

scattering its pale blue specks
among stones.

Her tone is genuine and unaffected; the beauty she writes about is not precious. When she visits Indian houses on the outskirts of Mesa, she says, "Our accomplishment / is to lose our footing / in places where they danced for rain." She can take such common poetic actors as geraniums and butterflies and render fresh results with a complicated tone: "Fragile, in too much / light, they fall like butterflies / on leaf-wings // multi-colored and deeply blind."

It is because there is an urgency of purpose that these fragile scenes become powerful. The writer comes across as a woman of vulnerability and sensitivity, mother of two children, who is escaping a painful marriage and finding her spirit renewed by friendships with her teachers, fellow writing students, and artists. Some poems ("April" and "In Return") portray the husband who would kill her. But for the most part this is a book about saving love, platonic and otherwise. Her age lends maturity of purpose to the excitement of the new poet discovering what new thing words can do. She wrote about what most deeply concerned her and made those concerns beautiful perhaps as a kind of consolation. Her poems are written with the tenderness she was seeking in others.

Notes on Contributors

BARBARA ANDERSON was recently a Wallace Stegner Writing Fellow at Stanford University. A chapbook, *Ordinary Days*, is due out from Porch Press.

SARAH APPLETON writes that *Book of My Hunger, Book of the Earth* is "a series of poems and sentences given release by an understanding of the earth. It continues the pursuit of poetry through plant life and evolution begun in *The Plentitude We Cry For* (Doubleday, 1972) and *Ladder of the World's Joy* (Doubleday, 1976)." Last year she was poet-in-residence at Carlow College, and she is currently associated with Syracuse University in Strasbourg, France.

MARGARET ATWOOD's most recent collections of poetry are *Two-Headed Poems* (Oxford, 1978) and *True Stories* (Oxford, 1981). Her novel *Bodily Harm* was published by Simon & Schuster in 1981. She has won a Guggenheim Fellowship and is a Companion of the Order of Canada.

WENDY BARKER's poems have appeared in *Poetry, Poetry Now,* and other publications. She is completing a Ph.D. in American literature at U.C. Davis, writing about Emily Dickinson.

WENDY BATTIN's poems have appeared most recently in *Poetry Northwest* and *Seattle Review*. She is currently at the Provincetown Fine Arts Work Center.

BECKY BIRTHA's work has appeared in a number of feminist and lesbian-feminist publications. Her first book, a collection of short stories, is scheduled to be published by Frog in the Well in 1982.

ANNE BLACKFORD lives in Riegelsville, PA, and teaches in the Pennsylvania Poets in the Schools and at Douglass College, Rutgers.

MARTHA BOETHEL is a Texan, trying to learn to live and work in her native territory.

OLGA BROUMAS is living in upstate New York. *Beginning with O* was the Yale Younger Poets selection in 1977. Copper Canyon Press published a chapbook, *Soie Sauvage,* in 1979. A cassette of her recent work, *If I Yes,* is available from the Watershed Foundation.

CONSTANCE CARRIER's first collection of poems, *Middle Voice,* won the Lamont Award. She has also published *Angled Road,* and two translations of Roman poets, Propertius and Tibullus, and is currently at work on a project on witchcraft in Salem, 1692.

MICHELLE CLIFF is the author of *Claiming an Identity They Taught Me to Despise* (Persephone Press, 1980) and co-editor (with Adrienne Rich) of *Sinister Wisdom*.

JANE COOPER is at work on a third collection of poems, to be called *A Mission with the Night.* Her most recent publication was the chapbook *Threads: Rosa Luxemburg from Prison* (Flamingo Press). She teaches at Sarah Lawrence College.

MADELINE DeFREES is spending her Guggenheim Fellowship year on the Oregon coast. Her new book of poems, *Magpie on the Gallows,* will be out from Copper Canyon Press in 1982.

ALEXIS DeVEAUX is a poet, playwright, and novelist currently living in Brooklyn, NY. She is the author of *Spirits in the Street* (Doubleday), *Na-Ni* (Harper & Row), and *Don't Explain: A Song of Billie Holiday* (Harper & Row).

TOI DERRICOTTE's first book, *The Empress of the Death House*, was published by Lotus Press in 1978. Her work has appeared in many magazines, among them *Chrysalis* and *Conditions*. New work is in *Open Places*, *Woman Poet*, and *Home Girls: A Black Feminist Anthology*. Excerpts from her diary will appear in *Ariadne's Thread*, to be published in 1982 by Harper & Row.

SHIRLEY ELIASON is a professor of art at the University of Northern Iowa. She has previously been published in *Western Review*, *The Yale Review*, *The North American Review*, and the *College Art Journal*, and has exhibited prints, drawings, and paintings in numerous national and regional juried exhibitions.

LYNN EMANUEL teaches writing at the University of Pittsburgh. She received the Flora Strosse Award from *Prairie Schooner* and a Pennsylvania Council of the Arts Fellowship in 1981. Her work recently appeared in *The Georgia Review*.

KATHY ENGEL is a political activist and organizer. She has worked as an organizer for the Mobilization for Survival and was co-director of the Fund for Open Information and Accountability. She also has coordinated a series of anti-nuclear/peace benefit readings. She has recently been a fellow at the MacDowell Colony and is currently poetry editor for WIN magazine.

ABBIE HUSTON EVANS was born in 1881. *Collected Poems* (Pittsburgh, 1970) was her fourth book of poetry.

CAROLYN FORCHÉ's second book of poems, *The Country Between Us*, was the Lamont selection of the Academy of American Poets for 1981. The trade edition was published by Harper & Row; a fine edition will be published by the Copper Canyon Press.

KATHLEEN FRASER's most recent books are *Each Next* (The Figures Press, Berkeley), a collection of experimental prose and poem narratives, and *New Shoes* (Harper & Row), a collection of poems. She teaches in the graduate writing program at San Francisco State and has recently returned from a Guggenheim Fellowship year in Italy, where she worked on a new manuscript called *Leda. & Swan*.

TESS GALLAGHER has recently been working on a film, "The Night Belongs to the Police," with the film-maker J. J. Murphy, and has completed a book of short stories, *Other Women*. *Under Stars* (Graywolf) is her latest collection of poems.

JOAN GIBBS is a Black lesbian activist-writer, the author of one book of poetry, *Between a Rock and a Hard Place*, and co-compiler of *Top Ranking: A Collection of Essays on Racism and Classism in the Lesbian Community*. She is also co-editor of *Azalea: A Magazine by Third World Lesbians* and a member of Dykes Against Racism Everywhere (DARE), a New York City anti-racist lesbian group.

DOROTHY GILBERT lives in Berkeley, California, and has taught verse writing at U.C. Davis, Colorado College, and Fort Lewis College in Durango, CO. She writes poetry and fiction, and is currently translating a twelfth-century French Arthurian romance by Chrétien de Troyes.

SANDRA M. GILBERT's book of poems, *In the Fourth World*, was published by the University of Alabama Press in 1979. She has also co-authored (with Susan Gubar) *The Madwoman in the Attic: The Woman Writer and the 19th-Century Literary Imagination*.

ELLEN GILCHRIST is the author of a book of stories, *In the Land of Dreamy Dreams* (University of Arkansas Press), and a book of poems, *The Land Surveyor's Daughter* (Lost Roads Publishers). In 1979 she was the recipient of a fiction fellowship from the National Endowment for the Arts.

JORIE GRAHAM's *Hybrids of Plants and of Ghosts* is available from Princeton University Press. She teaches at Humboldt State University in California and will be a Bunting Fellow at Radcliffe in 1982-83.

JUDY GRAHN's poetry is collected in *The Work of a Common Woman* (St. Martin's). *The Queen of Wands* and a gay cultural history, *Another Mother Tongue: Stories from the Ancient Gay Traditions*, are forthcoming.

DEBORA GREGER is spending a year in England on an Ingram Merrill Foundation grant. Her first book of poems, *Cartography*, was published by Penumbra Press, and a larger collection, *Movable Islands*, was published by Princeton University Press.

LINDA GREGERSON has poems recent and forthcoming in *Poetry, New England Review*, and *Ohio Review*. Dragon Gate, Inc., will publish her first collection, *Fire in the Conservatory*, in the fall of 1982.

LOIS ELAINE GRIFFITH lives in New York. Her theater pieces have been produced by the New York Shakespeare Festival and El Puerto Rican Playwrites/Actors Workshop. She is seeking a publisher for a collection of poems, *Barbadian Fantasies*, and working on a collection of short stories, *Pull Back the Night*.

SUSAN GUBAR is the author of numerous critical essays. She has co-authored (with Sandra M. Gilbert) *The Madwoman in the Attic;* they have also co-edited *Shakespeare's Sisters*. She will teach at Tufts University in 1982-83.

H.D.'s major works are *Tribute to Freud, HERmione, Trilogy*, and *Helen in Egypt*, though there are many other wonderful poems, memoirs, novels, and short stories, both published and unpublished.

PAMELA WHITE HADAS is the author of *Designing Women* (1979) and *In Light of Genesis* (1981), recipient of the Witter Bynner Award of the American Academy of Arts and Letters (1980), Robert Frost Fellow at Bread Loaf Writers Conference (1979) and staff assistant there in 1980/81. She will be teaching at Middlebury College in spring 1982.

GWEN HEAD is editor and publisher of Dragon Gate, Inc. The University of Pittsburgh Press published her second collection of poems, *The Ten Thousandth Night*, in 1979. A chapbook from Chowder Review, *Hannah's Quilt*, will be out shortly.

JUDITH HEMSCHEMEYER is the 1981-82 Hodder Fellow (Princeton University) and is working on a complete translation of the poems of Anna Akhmatova. She has two collections of poems, *I Remember the Room Was Filled with Light* and *Very Close and Very Slow*, both published by Wesleyan.

AKUA LEZLI HOPE is a native New Yorker and a member of the steering committee of the Black Writers Union. Her work has appeared in *Ordinary Women, Keeping the Faith, Black Scholar*, and small press publications. She has a yet-to-be-published manuscript, *The Prize Is the Journey*, and seeks the evolution of a mythopoeic system which clarifies, educates, and inspires necessary change.

LAURA JENSEN was a recipient of an NEA Grant in 1980. She will have a new book, *Memory*, available from Dragon Gate, Inc., in spring 1982.

JUNE JORDAN's most recent books are *Passion: New Poems, 1977-80* and *Civil Wars: Political Essays, 1960-1980*. She is Professor of English at the State University of New York at Stony Brook.

SHIRLEY KAUFMAN lives in Jerusalem. She has published translations from Israeli poets as well as three volumes of her own poetry. The most recent collection is *From One Country to Another* (Pittsburgh).

JANE KENYON is working on a second collection of poems, tentatively called *Things*. The first collection, *From Room to Room*, was published by Alice James Books in 1978.

MAXINE HONG KINGSTON is the author of *The Woman Warrior* and *China Men*.

CAROLYN KIZER has written three books of poems, and a fourth, *Yin*, will emerge shortly. She lives in Berkeley with her husband, an architect and urban planner.

KENDRA KOPELKE received an M.A. from the Writing Seminars at The Johns Hopkins University, has published poems in a variety of journals, and is presently teaching in Baltimore.

MAXINE KUMIN is the current Consultant in Poetry to the Library of Congress. Her new and selected poems, titled *Our Ground Time Here Will Be Brief*, will be published by Viking/Penguin in 1982.

MARLENE LEAMON is an editor at Pacific Search Press. She has a small chapbook, *Each Stone Has a Voice* (Seal Press), and a book of poems forthcoming, *Woman in the Field* (Ahsahta Press). She has also published in *The Georgia Review*, *Poetry Northwest*, *Seattle Review*, among others.

JAN HELLER LEVI lives in Hastings-on-Hudson, New York, and is a graduate of Sarah Lawrence College. Her poems have appeared in *Pequod*. She is working on a manuscript of poems entitled *Baltimore*.

AUDRE LORDE will have two books published in 1982: *Chosen Poems Old and New* (Norton) and *Zami, A New Spelling of My Name* (Persephone Press). She describes *Zami* as "a biomythography."

CYNTHIA MACDONALD's third book of poems, *(W)holes*, was published in 1980 by Knopf. She lives in Houston where she teaches in and co-directs the University of Houston's Graduate Writing Program.

HEATHER McHUGH teaches in New York state and lives in north coastal Maine. Her two books of poems are *Dangers* and *A World of Difference*, both published by Houghton-Mifflin.

LYNNE McMAHON has just completed a booklength manuscript of poems entitled *White Gates*.

SANDRA McPHERSON teaches at the Oregon Writers Workshop in Portland. Ecco Press, publisher of her second and third collections, will soon reissue her first, *Elegies for the Hot Season*.

JANE MARCUS teaches at the University of Texas. The first volume of her *New Feminist Essays on Virginia Woolf* (Nebraska University Press) appeared in 1981, and Viking will soon publish her *The Young Rebecca West*. The second volume of Woolf essays will be out in 1982. She has introduced reprints of two suffrage novels, *The Convert* by Elizabeth Robins and *The Judge* by Rebecca West.

JOSEPHINE MILES's *Collected Poems 1928-83* is due out soon. She teaches at the University of California, Berkeley.

SARA MILES is a poet and editor of the anthology *Ordinary Women*. "Doing Time" is from her unpublished manuscript, *Native Dancer*.

VASSAR MILLER's *New and Selected Poems* is being published by Latitudes Press.

JUDITH MINTY is from Michigan and spends much of her time in the north woods there. Her first book, *Lake Songs and Other Fears*, was recipient of the United States Award of the International Poetry Forum. Her most recent book, also from Pittsburgh, is *In the Presence of the Mothers*.

JUDITH MOFFETT teaches at the University of Pennsylvania. Her book *Keeping Time* was published by Louisiana State University Press.

HONOR MOORE lives and works in New York City. She is the author of *Mourning Pictures*, a verse play published in *The New Women's Theatre: Ten Plays by Contemporary American Women*, which she edited. Her poetry chapbook, *Leaving and Coming Back*, is being published by Effie's Press.

ADALAIDE MORRIS teaches at The University of Iowa. She has published a book on the poetry of Wallace Stevens and essays on the poetry of Dickinson, H.D., and Rich.

LISEL MUELLER is the author of three volumes of poetry. The latest, *The Need to Hold Still*, won the 1981 American Book Award for poetry. She is also the translator of *Selected Later Poems of Marie Luise Kaschnitz*.

CAROL MUSKE's two collections of poems are *Camouflage* (Pittsburgh) and *Skylight* (Doubleday). She had a 1981 Guggenheim Fellowship and in spring 1982 taught at the Iowa Writers Workshop.

GERDA S. NORVIG teaches literature, moonlights occasionally as a poetry therapist, and has written a book on Blake to be published by the University of California Press. Her poems have appeared in *The Massachusetts Review, Response, Coast2Coast*, and most recently, *Voices Within the Ark: The Modern Jewish Poets*.

DIANA Ó HEHIR is working on a third collection of poetry, to be called *Second Chances*.

SHARON OLDS was given the San Francisco Poetry Center Award for 1981 for her first book, *Satan Says* (Pittsburgh, 1980). She was awarded a Guggenheim Fellowship for 1981 and an NEA Fellowship for 1982.

TILLIE OLSEN's books are *Tell Me A Riddle, Yonnondio: From the Thirties*, and *Silences*. No one has been more eloquent and generous in defending unrecognized women writers.

MERRILL OLIVER is a teaching assistant in English at the State University of New York at Binghamton.

CHARLOTTE PAINTER is a novelist *(Seeing Things)*, anthologist *(Revelations: Diaries of Women)*, and teacher at U.C. Davis and San Francisco State.

GRACE PALEY is a writer, teacher, and enemy of the government's war on poor countries, poor people, people of deep color, and all women.

LINDA PASTAN's newest book, *Waiting for My Life*, has been published recently by Norton.

PADMA PERERA has also written under the name of Padma Hejmadi. Author of *Dr. Salaam and Other Stories*, published in the United States, and *Coigns of Vantage*, published in her native India, she is now at work on *Sumi Spaces #3* and a book of fiction titled *Familiars*. She teaches at the University of Colorado, Boulder.

MARGE PIERCY's new novel is *Braided Lives* (Summit). Knopf is bringing out her selected poems, *Circles on the Water*, in 1982. She is just finishing a collection of her writings about poetry, called *Parti-Colored Blocks for a Quilt*, for the University of Michigan's Poets on Poetry Series.

MONICA RAYMOND is a retired college English teacher of thirty. She currently lives in Cambridge, MA, where she is at work finishing *Mersouri*, a novel in an unusual language. Her book of poems, *Sign Language*, was published by Whole Woman Press (Durham, N.C.) in 1980 and can be obtained from her at 570 Franklin Street, Cambridge 02139.

ADRIENNE RICH's newest book of poems, *A Wild Patience Has Taken Me This Far*, was published by Norton in 1981.

LEE SCHWARTZMAN is a student at the Lakeside School in Seattle. Her poems, drawings, and stories have appeared in the anthology *Miracle Finger* and in several issues of *Stone Soup*.

SUSAN SCHWEIK lives in a hayloft in Madison, CT, and is a graduate student in English at Yale University.

JANE SHORE's *Eye Level* (University of Massachusetts Press) won the Juniper Prize in 1977. She has received grants from the NEA and CAPS and currently teaches at Tufts University.

MARCIA SOUTHWICK's book, *The Night Won't Save Anyone*, was published by the University of Georgia Press in 1980, and in 1981, a chapbook of poems, *Connecticut: Eight Poems*, was published by Pym-Randall Press. Currently, she is a visiting lecturer at the Iowa Writers Workshop.

ROBERTA SPEAR's book, *Silks*, was published in 1980 by Holt, Rinehart & Winston, as part of the National Poetry Series. She was recently a visiting artist at Ohio University in Athens. She has new poems in *The New Yorker* and *Southern Poetry Review*.

ELIZABETH SPIRES's first book of poems, *Globe*, was published by Wesleyan University Press. She lives in Baltimore, MD.

MAY STEVENS is a painter who lives in New York City, and is a founding member of the collective which publishes *Heresies: A Feminist Publication on Art and Politics*. Her recently published artist's book is called *Ordinary, Extraordinary*.

PAMELA STEWART's second collection of poetry is *Cascades* (L'Epervier Press). She writes that she is tired of Arizona.

RUTH STONE is working on a manuscript to be called *Desperate Busses*. She hopes to be finished this year.

STEPHANIE STRICKLAND has had poems recently in *Ironwood, Conditions,* and *West Branch*. She works at Sarah Lawrence College as Women's Studies librarian. She received a New York State CAPS grant for 1981.

NANCY SULLIVAN, editor of the recently published *Treasury of American Short Stories* (Doubleday), teaches at Rhode Island College.

MARY SWANDER is author of *Succession* (University of Georgia Press).

JOAN SWIFT's *Parts of Speech* came out from Confluence Press in 1978. Her poems have appeared in *Field, Poetry Northwest, Chowder Review, Antioch Review, Montana Review, Antaeus,* and many others. A recent recipient of an NEA Fellowship, she plans to spend three months in Hawaii finishing her third collection of poetry.

EVE TRIEM's most recent book is *Dark to Glow*. She writes, "I have been published and prize-winning for forty-five years. Working on a new book of poems—now. Creativity is the fountain of youth."

ALBERTA TURNER is the author of *Need* (1971), *Learning to Count* (1974), *Lid and Spoon* (1977), editor of *50 Contemporary Poets* (1977), and *Poets Teaching* (1980). She is professor of English at Cleveland State University, director of the C.S.U. Poetry Center, and associate editor of *Field: Contemporary Poetry and Poetics*.

CHASE TWICHELL's first book, *Northern Spy*, was published by Pittsburgh in 1981.

LESLIE ULLMAN teaches in the creative writing program of the University of Texas, El Paso, and is also a faculty member of the Goddard MFA program at Vermont College. *Natural Histories* was the the 1978 choice of the Yale Younger Poets Series, and her poems have recently appeared in the *American Poetry Review*.

JEANNE MURRAY WALKER's first book, *Nailing Up the Home Sweet Home*, came out in 1980 from Cleveland State University Press.

NAOMI WOLF is a graduate student in English at Yale University. She will soon be traveling to Spain on a Robert E. Bates Fellowship to translate Ladino folk songs.

NELLIE WONG is a socialist feminist activist poet employed as a secretary. Her collection of poems, *Dreams in Harrison Railroad Park*, was published in 1977, 1978, and 1981 by Kelsey Street Press, Berkeley, CA. She has contributed work to many feminist, third world, and Asian-American journals and magazines.

SUSAN WOOD's book of poems, *Bazaar*, was published in 1981 by Holt, Rinehart, & Winston. She teaches at Rice University in Houston.